Grievance Arbitration

Emerging Issues in Employee Relations
John T. Dunlop and Arnold M. Zack, Editors

Grievance Arbitration
Issues on the Merits in Discipline, Discharge, and Contract Interpretation
Arnold M. Zack

The Management of Labor Unions
Strategic Planning in Historical Constraints
John T. Dunlop

Grievance Arbitration

Issues on the Merits in Discipline, Discharge, and Contract Interpretation

Arnold M. Zack
Harvard Trade Union Program

American Arbitration Association
New York, New York

Lexington Books
D.C. Heath and Company/Lexington, Massachusetts/Toronto

Library of Congress Cataloging-in-Publication Data

Zack, Arnold.
  Grievance arbitration.

  (Emerging issues in employee relations)
  Includes index.
  1. Grievance arbitration—United States.
I. Title. II. Series.
KF3424.Z33 1989   344.73′0189143   88–45306
ISBN 0–669–19458–1 (alk. paper) 347.304189143

Published simultaneously in Canada
Printed in the United States of America
International Standard Book Number: 0–669–19458–1
Library of Congress Catalog Card Number 88–45306

The paper used in this publication meets the minimum requirements of American National
Standard for Information Sciences—Permanence of Paper for Printed Library Materials, ANSI
Z39.48–1984. ∞™

88 89 90 91 92 8 7 6 5 4 3 2 1

Contents

Foreword

Arbitration, as a procedure for the resolution of certain classes of disputes, has come to enjoy widespread acceptability in the American community and a preferred status before the courts and administrative tribunals. It was not always so, as our institutions have experimented with alternate means of resolving various categories of conflict and disputes—litigation in the courts, resort to public agencies, or open warfare and other consequences of nonagreement. One of the great advantages of private arbitration is that the disputants can have a role in the choice of the arbitrator and shape the process, the time limits, the issues, and the standards to be applied.

In the past decade or two, the arbitration process has been expanded from labor-management questions under collective bargaining agreements and disputes over commercial transactions to a widening array of fields— landlord-tenant relations, domestic relations, business and environmentalists' conflicts, international disputes stipulated for resolution, and a variety of referrals from controversies in process of litigation. The silent partner of arbitration—the mediation process—has likewise been extending its role.

In the industrial relations arena arbitration is applied, as in the past, to some cases of dispute over the terms themselves of new or reopened collective agreements. There has even been a growing extension of arbitration to disputes of individual employees with a management even in the absence of union representation. Discharge or discipline cases have been referred to outside arbitrators under the terms of company personnel manuals or by consent in the face of growing litigation over the employment-at-will doctrine.

It is as a final step in the grievance procedure of contract administration that most arbitration takes place in the industrial relations scene. Here new issues are arising and new questions are posed in arbitration relating to such matters as drug and alcohol abuse, sexual harrassment, plant closure and relocations, fringe benefit packages, and forms of wage settlements. New groups of employees and new pressures on management also helped to generate new issues.

Arnold M. Zack, an experienced arbitrator and teacher, has designed a significant volume on grievance arbitration designed for the classroom and for the parties and their advocates. The concern is with the substance of the issues and an exposition of the way in which arbitrators generally approach, posit questions, and reach decisions on issues presented in a series of short cases organized by major topics that encompass the collective bargaining agreement. The accompanying text on each topic, and the questions for reflection and discussion, have the merit that the issues and decisions are also related to the state of the law regarding the duty of fair representation of a labor organization and the obligation of the management, employees and the union under current legislation as well as administrative and court decisions.

Prologue

Robert Coulson, President
American Arbitration Association

Arnold Zack is an experienced, professional labor arbitrator. He is also an educator, eager to share knowledge with fellow arbitrators and advocates.

This book will meet the needs of practitioners and scholars because it is based upon Zack's working experiences. It contains a mass of accumulated information about the nuts and bolts of labor arbitration.

Zack has an insatiable curiosity about labor relations. His book essentially tells advocates how to understand and win cases in labor arbitration.

There are differences among arbitrators. Not every arbitrator is an Arnold Zack. But, over the years, a pattern and practice have developed that make it possible for an experienced advocate to anticipate how most arbitrators will respond to the kinds of issues described in this book. What kinds of evidence will they find relevant and persuasive? How is it best to present particular issues? What questions are in the arbitrator's mind? This is a practical approach that will help parties plan a winning strategy.

The material is organized in a logical progression, from the adversaries' direct organizational concerns (management rights and union activities) to the issues most commonly encountered in grievance arbitration, such as discipline and discharge, wages, benefits, working conditions, time off, restructuring of the workforce, and job seniority. The final chapter discusses arbitral procedures.

Each subject is illustrated by a hypothetical case, followed by discussion and questions. This approach maintains the interest of the reader while at the same time allows a practitioner to dip into particular subjects of choice. For example, an advocate engaged in a subcontracting dispute can read a hypothetical subcontracting dispute focusing on relevant issues from the perspective of a particular case, an excellent educational approach. Many academic labor relations courses use hypothetical problems as a teaching tool. This book supports that method.

Grievance arbitration has flourished. During the past twenty years, it has migrated from the private sector into public employment. While working with the American Arbitration Association in the early 1960s, Zack played a leading role in fostering acceptance of grievance arbitration by public employers. He also played a creative role in pointing out that collective bargaining and grievance arbitration are techniques that can be used to resolve disputes where other organized groups are negotiating with institutions.

Arnold Zack has also lectured extensively in other countries, seeking to have grievance arbitration better known and accepted, augmenting worker rights and employer security by providing a fair and effective method for resolving the day-to-day disputes that arise in the work place. Now, grievance arbitration is essentially an American concept. As the global marketplace develops, I would hope that this democratic process, the product of good faith bargaining between labor and management, will be adopted around the world. When that happens, Arnold Zack deserves a special award.

This excellent book provides insights drawn from Zack's unique career as a peacemaker. I commend it to anyone who has an interest in understanding the role that arbitration plays in American-style collective bargaining.

Preface and Acknowledgments

Historically the collective bargaining process has been under constant pressures for change. But throughout its existence arbitration has been recognized as the dispute settlement mechanism of choice. Despite the pressures on collective bargaining, it has continued to survive and flourish. The 1980s has seen a continuing growth of arbitration into a multitude of new areas and fields that deserve examination.

First, outside of the traditional labor-management arena collective bargaining is now being used in commercial, accident, landlord/tenant, environmental, family, international, and other disputes. The American Arbitration Association has taken a leading role in adapting the forum to new and diverse fields including the use of arbitration techniques to resolve internal disputes within national and international organizations.

Second, in industry arbitration is gaining new adherents in innovative offshoots of the traditional labor management arbitration. Arbitration is gaining greater support through the development of management-administered arbitration systems, and its techniques are being adopted in the expanding arena of termination-at-will cases.

Third, perhaps the greatest expansion of arbitration is found in the traditional labor management arena. Collective bargaining is expanding into newly unionized sectors of the economy such as the public sector, the health care industry, the service industry, and organized sports.

Fourth, there are new problems arising within the traditional labor management arena. Court attitudes toward the duty of fair representation and toward drugs in the work place, problems of AIDs in the workplace, drug testing, contracting out of work, health care administration, work place discrimination against women and minorities, sexual harrassment, robotics, and alternative appeal remedies are some of the "new" variations on the old issues that have faced union and management teams over the past decades. Arbitration continues to be the preferred method of resolving these new issues.

Fifth, and perhaps of the greatest importance is the fact there is a constant influx of new union and management personnel coming to deal with this whole range of new problems. Some are in the management and personnel ranks of the enterprises adapting the traditional labor management concepts. Others are in the newly organized institutions on both the union and management side and who are now gaining familiarity with the problems and procedures they are coming to face. And in addition there is the constant flood of union and management replacements in the traditional collective bargaining arena eager to learn the most effective way of representing their side while resolving disputes and achieving harmonious labor management relations.

New and experienced arbitrators often benefit from examining the arbitration process from a different perspective.

This volume is intended to explore some of the new problems and to provide the tools union and management representatives need to process and resolve them. The problems set forth throughout this book are presented in a fashion that allows the three main participants—management, union, and neutral—to view a single fact situation and its ramifications from different perspectives. These different perspectives might provide the insights necessary to properly investigate and prepare their cases and resolve a dispute before invoking arbitration. For the arbitrators in particular the book will suggest related issues that must be considered in presentation and in the arbitrators decision making.

I have used a series of short, one-issue case studies of substantive issues frequently encountered in contract administration. The cases are real, the names are fictional. The objective has been to focus on a single issue from an actual case that might have involved a myriad of other issues, and focus on that issue, its preparation and presentation and some of the variations in facts that should be anticipated. The book suggests how most arbitrators would respond to the various issues in the hope that such a perspective will assist the participants in their preparation and concludes with a summary of the procedural aspects of arbitration.

A word of thanks is due to John T. Dunlop who initiated the idea of this volume and the series it launches, to Jim Litton and Carleton Snow for reviewing the manuscript, and to my wife Norma and children Jonathan and Rachel for tolerating my additional idiosyncracies during its preparation, and to my assistant Janet Devine in assuming the typing chores in addition to her other burdens.

1
Management Rights

Residual Rights

The "rights" of management are a matter of concern to both the employer and the union. Many disputes arise over the issue of whether such rights must be specified or whether they are inherent in the employer's authority to manage the enterprise. Prime examples of this conflict are found in the area of contracting out, determining staffing requirements, and scheduling. The subject underscores the problem of drawing the line between union and management authority. Prior to the institution of collective bargaining, employers have sole control over all aspects of the operation of their enterprise except, perhaps, as regulated by laws. They are free to hire, promote, lay off, discipline, and transfer employees without concern for seniority, without concern for just-cause standards, and without concern for established traditions or practices. With the organization of a union, with a representational union election, and with certification of the union as the exclusive bargaining agent of the employees, that unilateral power erodes. The union and the employer enter into negotiations to establish agreed-upon wages, hours, and working conditions, resulting in the parties' collective bargaining agreement, which binds both parties for the agreed-upon contract duration.

It is generally accepted that all the rights that the employer had the right to exercise with exclusivity prior to negotiations remain within its control, except for those negotiated away in the parties' collective bargaining agreement. Under this theory of residual rights, all authority not ceded to the union or to neutral determination under the parties' grievance and arbitration system is retained by the employer. Despite the theory of the employer's retaining such rights, it has been general practice for the parties to set forth certain management rights as a provision under the parties' collective bargaining agreement. The management's rights clause may be very general, or it may be quite specific. It may specify that the employer retains all rights except those specifically negotiated away in the particular provisions of the contract, or it may enumerate management's right to determine the operations of the plant, to hire, to fire, to discipline for just cause, and so on, with great specificity.

Arbitrators are frequently confronted with disputes over whether certain managerial rights have been negotiated away. Some arbitrators have ruled that those rights that are not covered by specific contract provisions are still retained by the employer. Other arbitrators have gone beyond such specificity to rule that employers have, in fact, negotiated away certain unspecified rights that are implied in their recognition of the union, in the seniority clause, in the wage provisions, and so on. For example, management has the inherent right to discipline and terminate employees. Regardless of whether collective bargaining agreements specify *just cause* as the basis for such discipline or termination, arbitrators universally apply that standard. Just cause becomes an essential element of the grievance and arbitration provisions. Arbitrators have ruled that by adhering to the precept of a mutually selected neutral to determine the propriety of a discipline or discharge, the standard of just cause is to be assumed. Thus, the managerial right to discipline or terminate must be interpreted in the light of that standard of equity, which thereby is read into the grievance and arbitration provision.

There are, however, certain managerial rights that are unaffected by contract language. Arbitrators will universally recognize the right of the employer to control the operations of the plant and to determine what is to be produced and how, the quantity of production, and the price of the product as exclusive managerial rights. Such rights are exercised outside the collective bargaining arrangement, which is generally interpreted to apply to the *impact* of such exclusively managerial authority on the members of the bargaining unit.

Arbitrators accordingly will grant to employers the exclusive authority to secure new machinery and equipment in order to maintain efficiency and competitiveness in industry. Yet the same arbitrators will consider the impact of such new equipment and machinery on the employees as a matter that properly is covered by the collective bargaining agreement.

CASE: THE SHRINKING TRASH CREW

For a number of years, the employer had maintained a crew of three trash collectors per truck. The last three collective bargaining agreements contained wage rates that were negotiated in the context of a three-person trash-collecting crew. After the negotiations of the parties' latest agreement, the employer purchased new trash trucks, which because of their design and more rapid trash-compaction features, enabled the employer to operate trucks with a crew of two, rather than requiring a three-person crew. The union filed a grievance protesting the reduction in crew size from three persons to two persons. The employer denied the grievance, and the case was appealed to arbitration.

The union argued that a reduction in crew size from three to two meant that each employee was required to handle one and one-half times as much trash as before, that this entailed more lifting and more work, and that the salary was negotiated initially under the prior three contracts on the basis of an expectation that there would be three people handling the trucks. The union asserted that the employer's reduction in crew size would result in the elimination of positions, in an erosion of the bargaining unit, and in the layoff of one-third of its personnel.

The employer took the position that it was responsible for the control of its operations, that this control vested in it the authority to determine the means and standards of production, and that it thus had the right to purchase more efficient equipment. It asserted that this right was a unique managerial authority that was excluded from the collective bargaining agreement and thus was not arbitrable. The employer further contended that the employees were working their regular shift hours, that the parties never negotiated for piecework or compensation based on the number of units of trash picked up or deposited in the machinery, and that the new equipment actually made the work easier because the new design of the trash trucks permitted the emptying of the barrels with much less physical effort.

In his decision, the arbitrator acknowledged that the employer had the right to control its operations, to improve the efficiency of those operations, and to secure the necessary equipment and machinery for its operations. The arbitrator further noted that although the employer had the right under the managerial-rights clause to purchase and introduce the new equipment, the union under the collective bargaining agreement had the right to enforce its contractual rights over the impact of the introduction of the new equipment on wages, hours, and working conditions. The arbitrator found nothing in the parties' collective bargaining agreement that granted the union the right to bar introduction of the new equipment or require negotiations over the introduction of such new equipment. Nor did he find any contractual guarantee of a three-person collection crew. The arbitrator noted that when the parties negotiated the wage rates for trash collectors, they did so in the context of certain work requirements then in effect, which had been in effect for the three prior agreements. The context of those negotiations was a three-person crew doing the trash removal. The arbitrator found that the introduction of two-person equipment did result in changes in the job requirements, a new condition ruled subject to negotiations between the parties. The issue of negotiations of the impact of the new equipment on the wage rates was remanded to the parties for further consideration.

Discussion Question 1: Would the result have been different if the parties had negotiated specific job classifications listing the work to be performed under each classification?
The negotiation of specific job descriptions would be viewed by most arbitrators as requiring that those job descriptions be continued unchanged during the life of the parties' agreement. The consequence would be to prohibit

any introduction of new equipment that might have altered the job description unless the changes were negotiated between the parties. Such negotiation would be tantamount to a right of the unions to veto any new equipment that might require a job performance different from that negotiated in the job description.

Other arbitrators would say that the management's rights clause, including the right to efficient operations of the enterprise and the right to introduce new equipment, would take precedence over any particular job description within the parties' agreement. However, this view would enable the employer to act contrary to the specific job description by introducing changes in the means or procedures of production, even if contrary to the specified job description. In deciding between the views, an arbitrator must weigh the language of the parties' agreement with great care, recognizing the need for the employer to maintain efficient operations in order to continue in business, while at the same time protecting the rights negotiated by the union in the parties' prior contract negotiations.

Discussion Question 2: What issues might the union have raised in the furtherance of the case?

The union might have placed greater emphasis on prior negotiations if it could show that the salary rate was based on volume of trash divided among the three-person crew. Of prime importance in a case such as this is evidence of the parties' negotiating history. Even though the contract language may not contain a specific reference to the issue, the parties in negotiating even the management's rights clause may have made certain assertions or demands that may reflect on their understanding at the time the contract was negotiated, assertions that might be pertinent to the issue in arbitration. Likewise, the negotiation of the prior wage rates for the trash-removal job may have contained references to the tasks that were performed or to the crew size as the basis for compensation. Additionally, the union might have provided comparable data, if available, to show how other communities had responded to the new equipment and to two-person crews by raising rates of compensation.

Work Contracted Out

The accepted contractual trade-off is that the company recognizes the union as the representative of employees for services to be performed pursuant to conditions agreed to in the collective bargaining agreement. The company controls the right to determine price and product and retains the right to manage the operation, including the right to fire, to direct the work force, and so on. Within that specific retention of recognized authority, the employer has the right to eliminate jobs if product demand falls off, the right to expand with the addition of new products, and the right to shrink operations by dropping such products.

But what about the company's right to remove work that is not eliminated but rather is moved elsewhere—out of the bargaining unit to another plant, to another employer, to a nonbargaining-unit employer? The issue can be anticipated during negotiations, with the parties debating the inclusion of language barring, restricting, or at least setting forth circumstances and conditions under which such subcontracting is to be handled. By agreeing to such language, they may be able to prescribe authorized contracting out of work and prevent protest over such action.

If the parties fail to negotiate such language, leaving the contract silent on the subcontracting issue, what standards are to be implied from the recognition clause? On the one hand, it may be a legitimate exercise of management's authority to control operations of the plant. On the other hand, a wholesale subcontracting of the entire operation to a nonunion contractor working at a lower rate would constitute an evasion, if not a direct violation, of the original commitment to have the work performed at the plant by the union's members at agreed-upon wages, hours, and working conditions.

To determine whether such contracting out is justified under a particular collective bargaining agreement, it is helpful to look at certain tests that have been employed by arbitrators in attempting to assess the bona fides of such contracting out.

1. Is there evidence of anti-union animus? Is the company's action undertaken to weaken or destroy the union, or is it a legitimate business decision?

2. Do the employees of the plant have the skills to perform the disputed work? Have they done it at the plant before? Have any employees done that work in jobs they held prior to coming to the plant? Is it feasible or too costly to train the employees to do the new work? Could new employees readily be hired who possess the requisite skills to do the new work? Are there employees on layoff who could be recalled to do it?

3. Is there time to do the work? Does the disputed task so disrupt routine operations that it can't be done during regular plant operations? Could it be done on another or a new shift? Could it be done by recalling laid-off employees or by having employees do it on overtime? Is there enough manpower available to get the work done by the specified deadline?

4. Is there a place to do the work? Is there enough equipment or sufficient tools, raw materials, or finished product space in the facility? Will the use of such space impede the performance of regular work? Can tem-

porary facilities or new facilities be erected or secured in which to do the work?

5. Is the work core work? Is the work to be contracted out ancillary to the main operations of the bargaining unit, or is it the core work of the bargaining unit? Has this work ever been done by the bargaining unit before? If its performance was stopped, why?

6. Is economy a determinant? Is the cheaper cost of doing the work outside sufficient to take it away from the bargaining unit? Is there any point at which cost saving justifies taking work from the bargaining unit? Should the union be permitted to renegotiate wages to permit the work to be done by the bargaining unit at the same or at lower cost?

7. Are there contract provisions that permit or bar the contracting out? Aside from specific language, are there other controlling provisions, such as the recognition clause, the recall provision, or wage rates?

CASE: THE SUBCONTRACTED WRAPPER

A large manufacturer of chocolate traditionally had produced and printed its own wrappers for its chocolate candy. Expansion of the business and new techniques in printing led the company to abandon its in-house printing operation in favor of having the candy wrappers printed by an outside printer.

The union filed a grievance protesting the contracting out of what had previously been bargaining-unit work, and the case was appealed to arbitration. The union argued that the printing of the candy wrappers always had been done by bargaining-unit personnel; that the collective bargaining agreement recognized the classifications of printing pressmen, printer's helper, press operator, and the like; that the parties had negotiated for those classifications based on the tasks that employees therein performed; and that the work thus was reserved for bargaining-unit personnel. It argued that the performance of the task by an outside printer would place the work in the hands of nonunion personnel and thus would be a device for eroding the bargaining unit. If allowed, it reasoned, it would be the first step in contracting out a series of company operations until no candy production would be continued under the parties' collective bargaining agreement, with the whole recognition clause having been totally vitiated.

The company argued that the printing work was ancillary to the production of chocolate and had been performed within the company facilities and by bargaining-unit personnel as long as the volume of work was within the production capabilities of its printing presses. It asserted that the new presses required were too expensive for the limited label-printing work needed in candy production; that there was no place within the company facility to locate such a large press; that the bargaining-unit personnel lacked the skills necessary to operate the new press; and that those who had been engaged in such occupations as printing pressman and press helper would have the right to exercise their preferences, under the collective bargaining agreement, to bump to available jobs elsewhere in the plant.

The arbitrator first determined whether there was a business need for the new printing equipment. He concluded that the current printing presses were old and in need of replacement or repair, that they were inadequate to meet the increased demand of expanding production within the plant, and that the label-printing requirements of production were best met on the new equipment proposed by the company. The arbitrator also determined that the purchase cost of such equipment would not be economically justified because the printing of the labels would not fully occupy the capability of the press and that there would be significant downtime if the company purchased the press. The arbitrator found that cost efficiency made it feasible to use the press only if it was used by the candy company part of the time and by other companies at other times. The arbitrator recognized that although the presses were to be operated by nonunion personnel, this was not the prime motivation of having the work done outside and that there was, therefore, no evidence of antiunion animus in the subcontracting effort.

The arbitrator concluded that the utilization of the outside press was a sound business judgment dictated by rational economic conclusions and that when coupled with (1) the lack of skill of bargaining-unit personnel to operate the new machine, (2) the absence of a place within the enterprise to locate the machine, and (3) the cost entailed in purchasing the machine, the employer's actions were justified. The arbitrator further noted that the potential displacement of the printing personnel was insufficient to preclude the company from introducing the presses as an exercise of sound managerial discretion and that those employees were protected under the parties' collective bargaining agreement just as they would be if the printing operation were done away with rather than contracted out.

Discussion Question 1: What if the work was subcontracted to a firm using identical equipment?
The arbitrator's decision was based primarily on the uniqueness of the new printing equipment, the size and cost thereof, and the increased sophistication of that equipment. If the company had proposed to replace aging equipment with an updated version of the same equipment, it is likely that the arbitrator would have considered that the new press was merely a replacement and not a technical improvement and that the parties had negotiated for bargaining-unit personnel to work successor equipment of the same type.

In the case of replaced equipment, it would be presumed that the skills for operating the older equipment would continue to apply to the new equipment and that the equipment would be placed in the same location as that which it replaced. If the subcontracted work was on equipment identical to what had previously been used in the plant, the arbitrator would assume that the bargaining-unit personnel could have produced it on the new printing press as they had on its predecessor.

Discussion Question 2: What information and arguments might the union have introduced to further its case?
The union could have examined the type of skills demanded on the new outside press and then developed a comparison of those skills with skills of bargaining-unit employees to show whether the skills were, the same. If skills were found to be different, the union might have produced evidence to show how much upgrading or training would have been necessary for employees to operate the new equipment. The union might have demonstrated that the same quality of production could have been achieved within the bargaining unit by the addition of accessory equipment on the present company-owned presses. The union also might have referred to the bargaining history to reveal the discussions during earlier negotiations about restrictions on contracting out. In addition, it could have detailed the substantial cost of doing the work outside and demonstrated potential savings by having the work done in-house.

Discussion Question 3: What points might have been developed by the company?
The company might have forestalled the grievance by having previously discussed the prospects for the new equipment. It could have discussed possible options with the union, including the temporary contracting out of some of the work while retaining other portions or the possible acquisition of new equipment in exchange for concessions from the bargaining-unit personnel. In anticipation of some of the union arguments, the company might have demonstrated its efforts to place the subcontracted work in the hands of unionized printing facilities, presented evidence of its effort to accommodate to the new printing demands within the bargaining unit, and presented the cost figures that demonstrated that it was more economical for the work to be performed outside. This showing of an initial effort to have the work done within the bargaining unit might have been viewed by the arbitrator as further evidence of a good-faith effort on the part of the employer and of absence of anti-union animus as motivation for contracting out the work.

Discussion Question 4: Would the same results have been achieved if the company had decided to have the work done by its own non-union personnel, perhaps in a different location?
It is unlikely that the arbitrator would have endorsed the work being taken from the bargaining unit and being given to nonbargaining-unit personnel

of the same employer unless there was some showing that there was no effort to undercut the bargaining unit in such reassignment. The arbitrator would likely have asked why, if the company was to have the work done by its own nonunion personnel, it could not have had it done by its own bargaining-unit personnel.

Discussion Question 5: Would the same results have been reached if the company had contracted out the production of its chocolate?

Even if the company was able to make a good argument for cost efficiency in having the work of chocolate manufacturing performed by nonbargaining-unit personnel, most arbitrators would say that the contracting out of the core work for which the collective bargaining agreement was initially negotiated would be a violation of the parties' agreement. This would be an erosion of the recognition clause and would run the risk of undercutting the basic rationale for recognition and negotiation of a collective bargaining agreement for employees engaged in chocolate manufacture.

Although the arbitrator might be sympathetic to the costs confronted by the employer in continuing to produce chocolate, in the bargaining-unit context the remedy for that problem would require discussion with the union about economizing procedures rather than the undertaking of a unilateral action to contract out such work in direct violation of the collective bargaining agreement and the recognition clause. This would be particularly true if the subcontracted work was to be performed by nonbargaining-unit personnel. Then the arbitrator might conclude that such subcontracting reflected an anti-union animus, and the subcontracting of such core work would be viewed with suspicion.

Levels of Staffing

The company's right to assign work to employees and to control the operation of its enterprise assumes the inherent right to establish jobs, to undertake new operations, to produce new products, to hire and train new staff, to handle new equipment, and to assign employees to those tasks arising in an expanding operation. The union endorses such expansion when done in conformity with the parties' agreement: expanded production means expanded employment, a larger union roster, and a more prosperous work force.

But expansion and prosperity are not guaranteed. It is an equally valid element of the employment picture for the employer to determine that reduction of personnel is required as a consequence of retrenchment in production, improved efficiency of operations, and introduction of new techniques, technology, or equipment. The anticipation of such reduction is a normal focus of the parties' negotiation and may be manifest in the laying off of employees on the basis of the contractual procedures. Expectations would be that within a period of time such work would reappear and employees would be called back to their regular employment.

The lay-off procedure may involve laying off junior employees, with others being granted the right to move, or bump, into their positions, or it may involve a mutual understanding to share remaining work among a larger group with reduced work hours. Generally, those who remain on lay-off for an extended period of time under negotiated conditions may relinquish their right to recall once the agreed-upon termination time is reached without recall.

The procedure for laying off employees under the parties' agreement generally anticipates a return to former levels of employment. However, other aspects of retrenchment may be invoked by an employer.

Eliminating Jobs

The cessation of certain operations, the elimination of tasks due to the introduction of new equipment and automated functions (including robotics), the off-site purchase of parts, and the contracting out of some company functions all result in the elimination of jobs. Most collective bargaining agreements do not guarantee the continuation of job titles for the life of the contract. Thus, when an employer determines that a position is to be eliminated, the problem of the incumbent's status arises. The lay-off procedures may be invoked, or the employer may assert that the skills of the replaced employees are unsuited to assignment elsewhere within the enterprise. The elimination of jobs is, in a sense, a logical corollary to the creation of new jobs and an expansion of the industry. It becomes a more cumbersome issue, however, because employees, once hired, acquire a vested interest in their jobs and logically undertake to protect against their elimination.

Combining Jobs

New technology, improved production techniques, and new equipment, rather than resulting in the elimination of a position, might reduce duties in a job so that they only occupy a portion of the workday. An employer, confronted with employees whose job requirements do not fill the normal workday, would naturally seek to utilize the time more effectively by assigning other tasks to replace those that have been eliminated. The employer will frequently combine jobs by taking two jobs that have less than full-time work requirements and making them into a single job. The consequence of such change, of course, may be to make one of the employees surplus. Such a prospect is generally anticipated by the parties' agreement and covered by the contract.

The management's rights question in such a situation concerns the assignment of the remaining tasks to the new job classification. There is no question of management's right to combine the jobs if there has not been any negotiated freeze on job reductions or guarantee of the preexisting classifications. However, should the job be assigned to the lower or to the higher paid of the two classifications? Has the arbitrator the authority to order negotiation of a new rate or create a new rate?

Particularly when impacting the number of employees seeking access to a reduced number of positions, the managerial right to retrench must be viewed in the context of the specific language negotiated to ameliorate the impact of such general job reduction. Many collective bargaining agreements provide for negotiation over job changes resulting from technological improvements or from product or process change. Arbitrators who may be unwilling to impede management in the exercise of its authority to introduce new equipment or processes may rely on the failure to adhere to negotiated procedural requirements to bar the employer from making a change to which it otherwise would be entitled.

CASE: A SHUTDOWN BY THE OLD MILL STREAM

The company's plant, an old facility located in a mill by a New England stream, had for seventy-five years been engaged in textile production. A crack in one of the walls of the building led the company to examine the facility and forced it to conclude that many millions of dollars of structural repair would be necessary. The amount of repair work would have cost substantially more than the profit accruing from the company's marginal operations at the facility. Accordingly, the company determined that it would terminate its operation at that facility.

The parties' collective bargaining agreement provided that the company advise the union of any *substantial change* in the nature of the operations that would impact the wages, hours, and working conditions of its employees. Such notification was required thirty days prior to the institution of such change. The union would have ten days in which to request negotiation over the resulting consequences.

In this case, the employer provided the requisite thirty days' notice of its intent to close the operation. The union filed a request to negotiate the consequences within the requisite ten days, but the employer declined to meet, asserting that the cessation of operations was not covered by the terms of the parties' agreement. The case went to arbitration.

At the arbitration hearing, the union argued that the termination of the operation was a substantial change in the conduct of the company's business, that it was within the intent of the parties' agreement to discuss such drastic changes prior to their implementation, that the union had the right to secure protection for its employees during that cessation of operations, and that the employer had no authority to proceed unilaterally with the cessation without prior discussions and negotiations with the union. It urged that the facility be reopened, and that discussions be undertaken.

The employer asserted that the intent of the negotiated language was to deal with changes in production techniques and changes in technology when such negotiation would lead to adjustments in compensation or job assignments after the changes were introduced. It argued that the cessation of operations was of such magnitude that there would be no operations continuing at the plant and that because there was language dealing with closure, there was no need to meet with the union to discuss the cessation of operations.

The employer also argued that the cessation of operations was strictly a managerial determination and that the cessation of operations was not a matter ceded by the employer as being subject to joint negotiations. In any event, the operation had closed and the equipment had been removed from the facility; the company argued that it would be pointless to consider a reopening.

The arbitrator examined the contract language and came to the conclusion that the intent of the parties was to negotiate the impact of any substantial change in the company's methods of production or structure, that there could be no more substantial change than the elimination of an entire operation, and that it was appropriate for the union to request such negotiation and to require the employer to respond to that request by negotiating the impact of the change on the bargaining-unit employees. The arbitrator argued that the fact that the parties had negotiated a lay-off procedure, which would have and did come into play once the plant was closed, did not deprive the union of the right to discuss that or any other changes or deprive it of the right to negotiate a variation of the lay-off procedure.

The arbitrator recognized that in this case, the company had closed the operation without fulfilling its obligation to negotiate with the union on the question of "impact." The closing, particularly since it involved the removal of equipment, precluded the reestablishment of the status quo as a remedy.

The arbitrator found, therefore, that although there had been a contract violation by the employer, the appropriate remedy was not to require the employer to reopen the plant, but rather to negotiate the impact of the plant closing, placing on the table for negotiation such costs as the company would have or did expend in the closing. The arbitrator retained jurisdiction over the case in the event the parties were unable to negotiate an **agreement** on the impact or cost thereof.

Discussion Question 1: What arguments might the union have used in its presentation?

The union could have examined its notes of the negotiations of the contract language to determine what the parties had said about substantial change or whether they had discussed plant closing. The union might have introduced evidence at the time of its requested negotiations, advising the employer of the risk it ran by closing the plant prior to such negotiations and placing the company on notice that it would challenge the closing. The union might also have collected data to establish that the lay-off provisions were inadequate to meet the new burdens of the plant closing and the economic dislocation of all employees.

Such economic data might constitute the basis for additional compensation to employees above and beyond what they would have received as a result of the lay-off procedures being invoked. The union also might have challenged the financial data on the cost of repairing the facility and perhaps have collected data on the impact of the change on the company's customers. When did they begin to purchase from competitors? Were their orders diverted to other plants owned by the same company? The union might even have undertaken to show that the closing was an excuse for siphoning work to other company facilities. The union could have sought reemployment in other company facilities as part of its requested remedy.

Discussion Question 2: What might the company have argued in its presentation?

The company could have emphasized the excessive costs of repairing or reopening the facility. It could have presented evidence that it had lost whatever customers it had and that it did not divert them to any other plants. It could have provided evidence of early discussions with the union concerning a plant closing, during which officials had asserted that the closing was beyond the scope of the disputed provision. The company might have introduced testimony to show that in closing the plant without negotiations, it acted in reliance on union officials' assurances that the case would not be pursued to arbitration. It also could have introduced negotiating history concerning the intent of the clause when originally negotiated, pointing out in particular that there was reference only to the continuation of the operation, rather than to plant closing, when such discussions originally took place.

Discussion Question 3: If the company had introduced evidence of discussions with union officials that the case was not going to proceed to arbitration, should the arbitrator have relied on such testimony?

Arbitrators are loathe to admit into evidence testimony of offers of settlement or off-the-record discussions that may not have been officially authorized. Arbitrators are particularly sensitive to the risk that a union officer may speak out of turn, thus committing his organization to a course of action that subsequently may be challenged in a duty-of-fair-representation suit. But if the union took the position that the employer had failed to protect the employees, the company had the right to submit evidence that there had been discussions with union representatives who had expressed their acquiescence in the company's closing of the facility.

Discussion Question 4: What if the evidence showed that the employer was utilizing the excuse of a plant closing for diversion of work to more profitable locations?

The issue before the arbitrator was whether or not the company had violated the parties' agreement by failing to enter into negotiations prior to the plant closing. If the arbitrator had found that the employer had acted within its rights in not negotiating with the union prior to the closing, then the fact that the work might have been diverted for economic or even anti-union animus might not come into play. But if the arbitrator had found that there was an obligation on the part of the employer to negotiate the closing with union, then the arbitrator presumably would have been more critical of an employer's effort to undercut the collective bargaining agreement. Such an effort might be established through evidence of the company's contracting that work out to nonunion shops. The arbitrator might have examined carefully the economics of the contracting-out arrangement if it assigned work to other operations of the same employer. Such an investigation might have led to the conclusion that reassignment of the work, rather than repair of the facility, was the employer's prime reason for closing the plant.

Discussion Question 5: Was the remedy in this case a make-whole solution?

The remedy that would have recreated the status quo would have been for the arbitrator to reopen the plant, reassign the equipment thereto, and hold the closing in abeyance while negotiations took place. Although intellectually neat, such a remedy ignores the fact that the company had presumably severed its contractual responsibilities with its purchasers and customers and could not, in fact, reestablish the status quo, particularly if the case came to arbitration six months or a year after the closing. In that context, the arbitrator was realistic in requiring negotiations with the goal of substituting some financial alternative for the reopening of the plant.

The problem with these negotiations occurring without the threat of the pending closing is that they would be less than realistic if the plant had already closed. In that respect, the arbitrator may have reached a solution to that lack of realistic deadline by retaining jurisdiction over the case. The difficulty with retention of jurisdiction in such a situation is that it forces the parties back to that same arbitrator, and in this context, it holds open for the employees the prospect of a financial gain, which the reality of the collective bargaining process and the impending closing might not have achieved.

Work/Shift Schedules And Job Transfers

One of the inherent rights of management is to schedule work. That right may be restricted by contract language negotiated between the parties. Such language may provide for a fixed workweek and for procedures allowing employees to exercise preferences in choice of shifts and in procedures for compensation in the event of changes in work schedules without adequate notice of such changes. The rationale for the scheduling of work being within management's perogative is based on the company's right to direct the work force and its right to improve the efficiency of its operation.

Among the problems that arise over scheduling of work is first, the temporary suspension of work. The company has the right to decide to cease operations on a temporary basis. Such a decision might be based on shortage of supplies, elimination of a particular market, excessive inventory, or changes in production or output. Although the parties may have negotiated what happens to employees under certain circumstances (that is, the impact of such suspension on employees), there is little question that the employer has the ultimate and unilateral authority to determine when there should be temporary suspensions of work.

A second area of conflict is in the area of scheduling overtime. The employer may seek to eliminate overtime work for any given period or even permanently. On the other hand, the employer may require mandatory overtime of employees, whereas, previous practice had permitted voluntary overtime and had not demanded the attendance of employees on an overtime basis.

A third area of dispute arises in the changing of shifts. Employers have the right to assign work, including to determine the shifts during which the work is to be performed. The employer has the right in its direction of the work force and its operation of the plant to determine whether there shall be only one shift. Similarly, if there is to be more than one shift, the employer should have the right to determine the assignments of employees to those shifts. The restriction on that right occurs as a consequence of negotiations. Unions anticipating multi-shift operations generally make it a point to establish controls over that unilateral right of the employer to assign employees. They press for contract language that establishes a rational, foreseeable method of deciding which employees are to be selected for various shifts. The simplest method is for the union to secure language making shift designation a consequence of employee seniority. That goal is often diluted by the need for a diversity of skills on each shift. The employer may retain the right to determine which classifications of employees are to be assigned to different shifts, with the seniority principle brought into effect in designating which of the qualified employees within a classification would be assigned to a particular shift.

The fourth area of dispute in scheduling problems arises as a consequence of negotiated restrictions on the employer's assumed right to direct the work force in the area of scheduling. Even though there may be collective bargaining restrictions on the managerial authority to schedule and assign work, and even though the parties negotiated restrictions on that unilateral right, situations may occur in which the employer may be required to invoke its entrepreneurial authority to change the work schedule because of unforeseen emergencies.

Most collective bargaining agreements that set forth restrictions on management's right to schedule recognize that the employer may have to depart from those negotiated standards during emergencies. The question that comes to arbitration is what constitutes an emergency. The parties usually negotiate language to forestall such disputes by seeking to define an emergency as an unforeseeable circumstance, an act of God, a condition beyond the control of the employer, or a situation that could not reasonably have been foreseen. In such emergency situations, the employer is likely to be relieved of its contractual obligations and perhaps even of the contractually negotiated report-in pay for those who do report to work when work is cancelled because of an emergency.

A fifth area of dispute is in scheduling the assignment and transfer of employees. The concept of management's right to direct the work force strongly implies that it has the authority to assign employees to particular tasks, and once having assigned them, to transfer them to other tasks. Absent any restrictions on that right negotiated by the union, that inherent right of assignment and transfer would prevail. Yet this is another arena in which the unions undertake to negotiate restrictions on such moves, particularly in the area of transfers.

Employees, once in a position, and assigned to certain tasks, hours, and responsibilities, rely on the union to codify their tenure through contract language that restricts the employer's rights to further transfer incumbents or to replace incumbents with transferred employees. Contract language restricting transfers focuses on the duration and frequency of such transfers and seeks to introduce seniority as a controlling factor in the making of such transfers. These restrictions generally do not bar such transfers, but rather serve as an effort by the union to regulate what would otherwise be a unilateral management authority to transfer.

A sixth area that might also be considered in the area of scheduling is in the employer's right to promote and demote employees. The employer's right of assignment grants it the right promote employees to provide certain job tasks within the employee's ability. The unilateral right to promote is frequently restricted by negotiated language through which the union seeks to protect against arbitrary employer action in promotions, making certain that employees have full knowledge of promotional opportunities. The union's negotiated language calls for the posting of promotional opportunities for fixed periods at fixed locations and for prescribed procedures for employees to submit bids for promotions as well as for procedures for the selection by the employer.

In establishing the standard for employee selection for promotion, the employer seeks to rely on employee skill, ability, and qualifications while the union seeks to have seniority as the sole, or at least the primary factor for promotion. The resultant language negotiated between the parties may reduce the areas of conflict by establishing procedures and standards, with unresolved conflicts being arbitrated

A somewhat different standard applies in the case of employees who are on the way down, rather than on the way up. Once having been promoted to a position, an employee naturally seeks to preserve that position. However, the employer may determine that the employee lacks the required qualifications. Inherent managerial authority to direct the work force would indicate that the employer should have the right to demote an employee unfit for a position.

The employer is faced with two methods of resolving that problem. One method is to discipline the employee for poor workmanship and inability to meet the requirements of the position. The expectation of the discipline procedure is that an employee will be encouraged into better work performance, and it assumes the employee's competence to respond. If the employee is incapable of meeting the requirements of the higher position, then the result of the disciplinary ruling may well be termination.

The alternate method is to demote the employee to a position consistent with that employee's qualifications and ability. Such demotion should not be regarded as a disciplinary action. Rather, it is an effort to place the employee in a position where the worker is capable of performing the tasks and avoiding discipline for poor performance.

Frequently arbitrators are confronted with the question of whether a demotion is, in fact, a disciplinary action. Many arbitrators view demotion as a permanent penalty and conclude that if demotion is to be a disciplinary action to correct misbehavior, an employee should be remanded after a period of time to his earlier position and provided an opportunity to demonstrate benefit from the temporary demotion.

CASE: AN-ACT-OF-GOD SHUTDOWN

The company had been having difficulty with its electrical power and had been advised by an electrician that it needed to replace certain equipment to avoid future power outages. On the day in question, a severe electrical storm buffeted the area around the plant. As a consequence of the storm, the company lost its power at 5:00 A.M. two hours prior to the shift's normal starting time. The company contacted the local radio and television stations, which announced at 6:00 A.M., that the plant was not in operation that day and that employees should not come to work.

One employee, William Post, lived in a rural area 20 miles from the plant. He left his house fifteen minutes earlier than his usual departure time because of the bad weather and road conditions. He was on the road when the 6:00 A.M. announcement was made, but because he had no radio in his car, he did not hear it. He arrived at the plant at 6:45 A.M. and was told that the plant was not in operation that day because of the storm. He went home. The next work day Post filed a grievance for call-in pay as provided for under a clause in the parties' agreement. The clause reads, "If an employee reports to work, he shall be granted a minimum of four hours' pay except if there is shutdown due to unforeseen emergency or acts of God." The grievance was denied, and the case was appealed to arbitration.

At the hearing, the union argued that the grievant had every right to expect that his normal work hours would be available to him on the day in question; that he left his home early to make certain that he would be at work on time because of the storm; that he was under no contractual obligation to have a radio in his car, let alone to listen to it to learn whether the plant was in operation that day; and that he was entitled to compensation for reporting to work. The union argued further that a storm was not an excuse for failure to provide employees with an opportunity to do their normally scheduled work; that the company had been placed on alert that its electrical system was inadequate and at risk for future breakdowns; that it did nothing to correct that deficiency; and that an electrical outage was indeed a foreseeable event, not an emergency or an act of God that might otherwise relieve the employer of its call-in pay obligation.

The company took the position that there was an emergency power outage, that the emergency was not foreseeable, that it was unrelated to earlier suggestions for improvements in its electrical operation, that the company made every diligent effort to advise employees of the unavailability of work, that most employees learned of and responded to the advisory not to report to work, and that it could not be held responsible for the grievant's failure to hear the message or to telephone to ascertain whether work was available on the day in question. It argued that to grant the employee call-in pay in this situation would place a premium on employees' ignoring notices of emergency closings and would subject the employer to unnecessary and deliberate payments when any reasonable person would have realized that work was not available or would have telephoned to ascertain whether work was available. Accordingly, the employer urged the grievance be denied.

The arbitrator divided her ruling into two parts. The first determined whether or not there was a legitimate emergency to justify the closing of the plant; if so, the second part determined whether or not the employee was entitled to compensation for having reported to work on the day in question.

On the first point, the arbitrator found that the company's failure to respond to the earlier electrical warnings was not the proximate cause of the power outage on the day in question; the storm was the cause. The arbitrator determined that the storm was a condition beyond the employer's control and could not reasonably have been foreseen or forestalled. It was an act of God, relieving the employer of responsibility for operating the shift and for paying reporting pay to employees who appeared.

On the issue of the employee's entitlement to compensation on the day in question, the arbitrator held that because an act of God justified the failure of the plant to open that day, the employer was relieved of any responsibility to those employees who either were not notified of the closing or who for other reasons were not aware of it. The arbitrator ruled that although Post had acted in good faith and had made an extra effort to arrive at work on time, any right to call-in pay was based on the contractual provision.

Because the employer was legitimately out of operation on the day in question due to an act of God, the act-of-God clause relieved it of its obligation to provide reporting pay even to those who legitimately and honestly reported to work expecting work to be available. Accordingly, the arbitrator denied the grievance.

Discussion Question 1: What presentation might the union have made?
To establish a direct link between the warning and the breakdown of the system, the union might have sought the testimony of the electrician who had first examined the company's electrical system. That information might have been secured from the electrician or from documentary evidence in company files provided to the union on request. The union might have examined what transpired in other plants that day to determine whether other companies were shut down or whether they were similarly affected by the electrical blackout. If the evidence showed that other companies were not affected by the blackout and that the blackout was unique to the plant rather

than systemic, then the union's argument that the power outage has been a foreseeable breakdown and not an act of God would have been strengthened.

The union also might have provided evidence of the number of employees who reported to work to show that the employer had not provided adequate notice of the plant closing. Thus, the reliance on the act-of-God clause was merely a device to avoid meeting contractual obligations to provide report-in pay.

Discussion Question 2: What position might the employer have taken?
The employer might have provided evidence of what transpired in other plants if its investigation had shown that most other plants in the area likewise had been shut down by the storm. The employer also could have provided evidence from the electrical contractor to show that the breakdown of the electrical system was not due to its earlier electrical problems and that it was, therefore, a legitimate act of God. The employer might have produced evidence to show that most employees were aware of the closing and that only a few came to work, providing that its procedure for shutdown notification was correct.

Discussion Question 3: To what extent should arbitrator have inquired about the relationship between the earlier electrical malfunctions and the shutdown?
As the arbitrator ruled, the initial task was to determine whether the power outage was an act of God or a foreseeable event. The arbitrator would have looked for evidence to show a connection between the earlier warning and the power outage, with the burden of proof on the union.

That burden might have been met by showing that the earlier electrical failure was in the same part of the system that broke down on the night in question. The arbitrator probably would not have solicited such evidence, nor would the arbitrator have relied solely on an assertion that the earlier breakdown was the cause of the outage. Any assertion would have to be supported by testimony or expert witnesses and could be rebutted by the employer's showing that a different part of the electrical facility was in jeopardy on the night of the closing. However, most arbitrators would rely on the company to point out that unsubstantiated assertion would require evidence from the union to raise the assertion to proof.

Discussion Question 4: Would not an electrical storm per se be an act of God, justifying closing?
The arbitrator is governed by the language of the parties' agreement, and if the contract clause in dispute was not limited to an act of God to excuse an emergency closing but defined an emergency as a condition beyond the control of the employer or which might not reasonably have been foreseen, then

the arbitrator would have had to look into the question of whether or not the earlier warning placed the employer on notice of the need for repair. The employer in that case would have had to bear the risk of not having responded to that warning by making the necessary electrical repairs prior to the shutdown. If the employer had been warned of the risk of further breakdown, the later breakdown might not have qualified as an emergency.

Discussion Question 5: Is not Post an innocent victim of the company's shutdown?
There is no question that Post acted in good faith and undertook an additional effort by leaving early in order to report to work on time, but good faith does not create a contractual right if the employer has the right to determine when the plant will be open or shut. The parties negotiate restrictions on that right, and those restrictions apply to the grievant as well as to the arbitrator. Thus, if the arbitrator found that the employer had not acted improperly or in violation of the contract in shutting down the plant and that the employer was by contract language relieved of the responsibility for paying report-in pay, then there would be no grounds for Post, even as an innocent victim of the shutdown, to receive compensation. The contract's report-in pay clause was held not controlling in the light of the act-of-God shutdown.

The Agreement as a Treaty

The prevailing theory of retained rights holds that management retains those rights that are not ceded by it in the parties' collective bargaining agreement. The collective bargaining agreement is the document whereby the union and management, in most cases, have set forth the rights of the employees, the rights of the union, and the specified rights of the management.

A collective bargaining agreement generally covers wages, hours, and working conditions and is, in effect, a treaty between union and management. The grievance and arbitration clause arises from a recognition by the parties that the treaty may not anticipate the entire range of the parties' conduct during the life of the agreement. They therefore negotiated a procedure for the employee or the union to register challenges to the employer's action, with the understanding that the dispute, if unresolved by the parties and their representatives at the early stages of the grievance procedure, may be appealed to the contractually negotiated arbitration clause and resolved by an arbitrator of their mutual choice.

Such disputes between the parties, whether resolved by the representative at the lower stages of the grievance procedure or resolved by the arbitrator at the arbitration step, are based on differing interpretations of what is permitted or prohibited by the terms of the agreement. Thus, the contract language becomes a crucial element in determining the result of any dispute between the parties.

It is assumed that the parties who negotiate the contract have specific interpretations and viewpoints in mind at the time of the negotiations and agreements and that both parties share that understanding when they agree on the contract language. The words are sometimes clear, as in "Notice of a promotional opening shall be posted for five working days." At other times, however, the language may not be so precise. If the parties agree on the following language, "The vacancies shall be posted for five days," there arises the question of whether the contract language means five working days or five calendar days.

The parties may have a joint recollection that they intended the words to mean either calendar or working days, but they may not have such joint understanding. A dispute about intent may be resolved by testimony concerning what was said by participants at the negotiating sessions. A dispute also may be resolved by reference to participants' notes taken during the contract negotiations; references may have been made to either working days or calendar days.

Evidence of intent may be expressed a third way, by past practice. Although the parties may have no evidence about what transpired during negotiation of the word *days*, the practice of the facility may be to post such notices for five workdays, even though the employer asserts that the posting need only have been for five calendar days. If the union is able to show that such prior notices were indeed posted for five workdays or had dates of removal reflecting a five-workday posting, then the arbitrator may find that the contract language was intended to conform to a preexisting practice of posting for five workdays or that it has been interpreted by the parties under the agreement as requiring a five-workday posting.

Evidence of the parties' intent also may be concluded from signed agreements, amendments, or letters of understanding agreed to by the parties after the date of the main collective bargaining agreement. For example, the company may have written to the union in the settlement of a grievance that it was their intent thereafter to post such vacancies for five workdays, rather than to adhere to the prior practice of posting such notices for five calendar days. Or the ancillary agreement may be a letter from one party to the other. For example, the union business agent may have written to the company personnel director as follows: "In accordance with our understanding reached at the meeting yesterday, hereinafter such posted notices will be listed on the bulletin board for only five calendar days."

A fifth standard for interpreting the intent of the parties arises from prior arbitrations concerning the same issue between the same parties. One of the parties may introduce into evidence at an arbitration hearing an award rendered in an earlier case under the current agreement, in which the arbitrator found that *days* meant either calendar or working days. If that arbitration involved the posting of vacancies, most arbitrators would feel that that issue had already been litigated and would endorse the previous arbitrator's award unless the second arbitrator found the award arbitrary, capricious, or unreasonable.

If the interpretation of *days* as being either working or calendar days was made in connection with another contract provision, such as days of vacation entitlement, the arbitrator might either endorse that award as controlling the parties' intent in all uses of *days* or might use that award as persuasive evidence of what the parties' intent was throughout the agreement. Evidence of how the word was used elsewhere in the agreement may provide further evidence of intent. If *workdays* was used throughout the agreement except in the posting provision, the arbitrator may conclude that it was an oversight or indeed that a different use of the term was intended.

Finally, the arbitrator may rely on legal standards as articulated in statute or by court decision in interpreting contract language. Thus, in the public sector if a statute required promotions to fill vacancies be posted for five workdays, most arbitrators would conclude that the contract language was negotiated in the context of the prevailing statutory standard. Absent any evidence of intent to contradict that statutory standard, the contract use of *days* must be read in light of that statutory precondition.

Parole Evidence

In determining what the parties agreed to in their "treaty," arbitrators look to the contract wording and the evidence of how the parties have interpreted or lived with that wording. But arbitrators also look to what the parties intended when they negotiated the words. Sometimes the parties negotiate provisions excluding evidence of practice or incorporate that practice into the contract. Arbitrators frequently are confronted with an objection by one of the parties to the introduction of extraneous testimony about what was meant by the use of a term. Such an objection is based on the theory that the contract language speaks for itself and that the arbitrator must confine the ruling to the actual language of the agreement. The legal doctrine of *parole evidence* calls for the introduction of ancillary evidence concerning the meaning of words only when such meaning is not clear on the face of the parties' agreement. Although the word *days* is subject to varying interpretations of whether workdays or calendar days were intended, a dispute still might arise if the contract specified workdays and the Saturday in question was a regularly unscheduled day on which certain employees were called in for emergency overtime. One of the parties might argue that the term *workday* is clear and applies to days on which work is actually performed;

this precludes any evidence that Saturday was unscheduled and never contemplated as a workday.

The agreements between union and management are generally based on a preexisting relationship and based on an expectation of continuity in that relationship. Therefore, they are considerably different from contracts generally found in a commercial arrangement, in which there is no such continuity of dealings. Arbitrators seek to interpret and apply the words of the agreement as the parties themselves used them, not only throughout the life of their relationship but also during their negotiations. The written word as found in the contract may be only a shorthand way of expressing a long understood meaning that is quite different. In the light of that unusual "marriage" relationship, arbitrators are more likely to receive ancillary evidence of intent under any exceptions to parole evidence, rather than adhere strictly to the mere words found in the contract unless the parties have agreed to bar such reference to past practice, outside agreements or understandings or negotiate a zipper clause.

Zipper Clause

The parties frequently negotiate a clause that specifies that "this agreement contains a full understanding of the parties and can not be varied by any extraneous evidence of understandings, past practice, etc." Although arbitrators are bound by such *zipper clauses,* as they are by any other language agreed to by the parties, such clauses generally are not viewed as a barrier to an arbitrator's effort to understand the parties' intent in the meaning of the agreed-upon words.

Arbitrators recognize such zipper clauses as excluding from consideration past practice and other arrangements made between the parties but not reflected in the agreement. Nonetheless, arbitrators must have evidence of the parties' understanding of the contract language in order to issue a decision based on that language, even with the presence of a zipper clause. A zipper clause thus would exclude outside agreements but not preclude evidence about what the agreement was intended to mean.

Maintenance-of-Standards Clause

At the other extreme from the zipper clause are the *maintenance-of-standards clause*. The parties frequently negotiate language that says that all conditions, benefits, and terms of employment previously in effect shall not be altered by the current agreement. That wide, broad language opens the record to evidence that may indeed vary specific understanding of the contract language. Arbitrators may view prior conditions as being continued despite the fact that they may be at variance with subsequently negotiated contract terms. However, most arbitrators would hold that later specific contract language would prevail over the more general prior practice in the event of contradiction between the two.

2
Union Activities

The collective bargaining agreement is, as noted earlier, a treaty between management and the designated collective bargaining representative of the employees. Negotiation of that contract involves mutual recognition of the rights of each party. There is recognition of management's inherent rights as well as of those rights of the employer specified in the management's rights clause and elsewhere in the contract. The union, too, negotiates recognition by management of its rights, particularly the rights of recognition, representation of union members, entitlement to time to be devoted to union activities, and preferences to be accorded to union officers.

Union Representation and Discipline

The Union's Right to Be Present at Discipline

The parties' agreement to establish a grievance and arbitration system constitutes recognition of the need for a systematized procedure for ascertaining the facts of any dispute, of the benefit of having the parties' higher-level representatives with greater authority at each step review the issue, and of the desirability of a judicial determination by a mutual designee to resolve disputes if necessary. Agreement creating the preliminary steps of the appeal procedure constitutes recognition by both parties of the benefits of attempting to resolve conflicts before they escalate to arbitration. Yet despite this recognition of mutuality and equality in the process, the very nature of the employer-employee relationship, with the employer having the authority to impose discipline on the employee and the employee reacting through a grievance, creates a disparate situation in that the union has not participated in the triggering exercise of managerial authority.

In many cases, there may be no factual dispute about what transpired at the time the employer took its action, but in other situations, there may be factual conflict (1) over what transpired and/or (2) over whether the discipline was appropriate. Many employers recognize the potential of challenge to their version of events and therefore have observers present during the imposition of discipline. The observers can later serve as witnesses if there is any dispute about what was said. The employee generally lacks a counterpart witness in such events and may indeed lack the experience or skill to parry the employer's initial imposition of discipline. For this reason, many unions have negotiated contract language that requires the employer to contact the union prior to any disciplinary session. The presence of a union witness in such a situation may help to avoid subsequent disputes about what was said, as well as to dispel disputes over whether the session involved a disciplinary action or an admonition. Such a contractual requirement of union presence at any disciplinary session by definition may reduce any confrontation to less than discipline if the union official is not present. Also, the presence of a union representative may help the employer to avoid subsequent appeal through the grievance and arbitration system if the union witness accepts the propriety of the discipline and the way it was imposed. The official may be effective in persuading the grievant to heed the warnings rather than resort to the grievance procedure to protest what might have been a valid disciplinary action.

The requirement of having a union representative present during disciplinary action may impose certain procedural burdens. The employer must delay imposing discipline until a union representative is secured, and this may involve bringing someone from another department or even from another shift. Although this may avoid impulsive disciplinary actions, it is disruptive in terms of the time delay involved. The requirement also may stimulate more arguments between the union's representative and the supervisor than would occur if the exchange were merely between the supervisor and the employee. Finally, a contractual requirement of having a union representative present may itself engender disputes about whether a disciplinary action or an admonition was involved.

Aside from any contractual requirements for the presence of a union representative during disciplinary action, the employee has certain independent rights outside the contract under the National Labor Relations Act of 1935 as amended (NLRA). The U.S. Supreme Court, in the case of *NLRB v. J. Weingarten, Inc.*, 95 S. Ct. 959 (1975), has held that the individual employee had a right to refuse to participate in an interview without a union representative if the employee reasonably could have believed it would have resulted in the imposition of disciplinary action. Unless the contract so provides, the employer is not required to advise the employer of this so-called Weingarten right.

CASE: THE TILTED DECAL

The supervisor noticed that the decals on the tail assembly of the aircraft were not straight. As the aircraft was being wheeled out of the factory to the hangar, he called over Jason DeLong and said, "Jason, I've warned you four times about putting the numbers on straight. You even got a two-day suspension. Now you've messed them up again. I've got to give you a five-day discipline. There is no shop steward around and the plane's leaving, so just sign this form that says I've told you about the tilted decals." The shop steward was on lunch break at the other end of the factory. DeLong signed the form and filed a grievance protesting the supervisor's action. The case was appealed to arbitration.

An article of the parties' agreement provided that "any available shop steward shall be called to witness the imposition of any disciplinary action." At the hearing, the union argued that the imposition of discipline was flawed; that the employer made no effort to find the shop steward, who was out to lunch; that the grievant's signature on the form was secured under duress; and that the disciplinary action should be held to be invalid.

The employer argued that the discipline was appropriate; that the aircraft was on the way out of the facility; that there was no time to wait for the shop steward to return from lunch to witness the event; and that, in any event, DeLong had acknowledged the accuracy of the company's version of the facts when he signed the note. The employer urged the grievance be denied.

The arbitrator found that the article provided for the calling of "any available shop steward," that the shop steward was on lunch break at the time of the incident, and that the aircraft was leaving the facility. The arbitrator focused on the term *available*, holding that there was a shop steward in the factory, albeit at a substantial distance away and on lunch break; that the employer was obligated to advise the shop steward of the pending discipline, including the imminent departure of the aircraft; and that any waiver of the right of the shop steward to be present had to come from the shop steward's declining to be present, rather than from the employee or the foreman deciding not to contact the steward. The arbitrator ruled that the employer violated the parties' agreement in imposing the discipline without first, at least, attempting to secure the presence of the steward; that the grievant's signature on the form contradicted the spirit and intent of the parties' agreement in providing for a steward to act on the employee's behalf at the time of discipline; and that the disciplinary suspension was overruled.

Discussion Question 1: What evidence could the union have provided?
The union could have provided information about the distance to the lunchroom, the time of the incident in relation to the steward's lunch break, and the amount of time it would have taken the steward to come to the scene, as well as information about telephone accessibility or about consistency of the supervisor's or employer's securing of shop stewards under similar situations. it could have shown the availability of the aircraft at its next location for inspection of the alleged defect or the feasibility of taking a photograph of the aircraft to be used as subsequent evidence.

Discussion Question 2: What could the employer have shown?
In addition to favorable evidence of past practice on the issues involved, the employer could have shown that the departure of the aircraft from the factory removed it from its jurisdiction or that DeLong explicitly declined to have a shop steward present. In addition, it might have secured witnesses to the exchange, particularly to contradict any union claim of the supervisor pressuring DeLong into signing.

Discussion Question 3: Would the result have been different if DeLong had been a former shop steward?
If DeLong had been a former shop steward, the arbitrator might have held him responsible for not securing the current shop steward. The arbitrator might have attributed to him the right to waive access to the shop steward because the purpose of the article, to assert a right on behalf of an inarticulate, unsophisticated employee, was fulfilled in that DeLong had held the position of shop steward.

Discussion Question 4: Would the union have the right to file a grievance if the grievant had declined to do so?
Although the right to dispute the discipline might be ruled as being unique to the grievant, the union, as the party to the agreement, also was entitled to be present at the disciplinary action and would have a right to file a grievance over the employer's denial of that right. To hold that the union was precluded from this would create a precedent that might be construed against the union's future right to file a grievance over deprivation of its, rather than the grievant's rights. If the union had prevailed in its assertion that the discipline was ineffective without a shop steward being present, the requested remedy of vitiating the discipline might still be achieved even if DeLong himself had not disputed it.

The Union Representative as Grievant

The visibility of the shop steward or other union official during the exercise of that individual's union responsibility may involve union officials themselves as the subject of discipline while exercising their union roles. The union shop steward called in during the imposition of discipline upon another employee, either pursuant to the contract or upon the employee's invocation of Weingarten rights, is there for the specific purpose of defending the employee against the discipline being imposed.

That defense need not be and usually is not a passive observance of events and exchanges between supervisors and employees. The problem arises when the union official's advocacy role is responded to by the imposition of discipline for insubordination. The shop steward or union officer certainly has a right to protest the actions of the supervisor against the grievant, but inherent in that right to defend and argue on behalf of the grievant is a responsibility as a union official to abide by the collective bargaining agreement and the prohibition against subordination. Many arbitrators hold that a shop steward or union official has a higher duty to conform to reasonable practices than does the often uninformed rank-and-file union member.

Arbitrators have ruled that holding a union position itself does not render an employee immune from discipline and that such union officials are still subject to discipline for their actions as employees. They may get some protection from the fact that they are union officials if it can be shown that the disciplinary action was based on their union status, with the real goal of the penalty being an anti-union animus reflecting the employer's dislike of the union officers or revenge for their prior exercise of their union role.

CASE: THE DOUBLE PUNCH-IN

The supervisor, Fred Simmons, accused the employee, Lowell Malcolm, of having punched in the time card of Walter Delaney at the same time he punched in his own. Malcolm was called into Simmons's office. He requested the presence of Marvin Joslow, his shop steward, to accompany him to the meeting. Joslow had not known of the incident until the grievant had told him about it.

When they arrived at the supervisor's office, Simmons related what he had heard had happened. Malcolm denied any wrongdoing. Joslow stated that the discipline was unjustified and that he himself had seen Delaney punch in his own time card that morning. The discipline nonetheless was imposed on Malcolm, and a few days later, a letter of warning was issued to the shop steward for giving false testimony at the meeting. A grievance concerning the letter of warning was filed, and the matter was appealed to arbitration.

At the hearing, the employer argued that the shop steward had lied at the supervisor's meeting, that there had been two witnesses who had seen the grievant punch in two time cards, and that the shop steward's rights as a representative did not excuse his behavior. Thus, the imposition of Joslow's discipline was for just cause, according to the employer.

The union asserted that the shop steward was engaged in his representational duties at the time of the meeting, that he had a responsibility to protect the grievant against unfair discipline, that his actions as shop steward made him immune from discipline, and that the imposition of discipline against him was not for just cause. It urged the grievance be sustained.

The arbitrator held that the shop steward did have certain protections and immunity against discipline for actions in carrying out his responsibilities. The arbitrator recognized that despite instances in which the representative role of the shop steward might result in conflict with management, outspoken conflict on the part of the steward was not of itself grounds for disciplinary action. Such activity, even if provocative, was seen as a legitimate exercise of the shop steward's role in protecting the employee.

However, the arbitrator continued that intensity of support for the grievant's position did not excuse providing false testimony. The shop steward's role, the arbitrator concluded, was one in which the objective was to ascertain truth as a means of resolving conflict, rather than to mislead the employer and cover for or condone improper behavior, and thus was not protected activity. The arbitrator ruled that the imposition of discipline on the shop steward was justified.

Discussion Question 1: What position might the union have pursued?
The union might have solicited the testimony of Delaney to show that he had signed in on his own, if such had been the case. It also might have researched comparable cases of shop-steward discipline to discern whether the employer had been consistent in its imposition of penalties for false statements.

Discussion Question 2: What position might the employer have taken?
The employer might have produced the testimony of the supervisor who had witnessed the double punch-in. It might have provided witnesses to testify about prior instances in which the shop steward had engaged in lying or providing false testimony.

Discussion Question 3: What if instead of offering false testimony, the shop steward had said to the supervisor, "If you impose this discipline on Malcolm, you'd better watch out for yourself. I know where you live."?
Most arbitrators would conclude that such a statement was threatening language, that it went beyond the zealousness permitted in the representational role, and that it exceeded the immunity conferred upon union officers in their representational role. As such, an arbitrator undoubtedly would conclude that the warning or threat was an abuse of discretion by the union officer and, therefore, outside any immunity grant. Thus it properly would be subject to discipline.

Leaves of Absence for Union Work

There are two situations in which union representatives are released from their employee responsibilities to attend to union work. One is for absences of some duration and are negotiated leaves of absence for employees to take time off for union business. Sometimes the work involves a leave for attendance at union meetings and functions for up to several days. At other times there may be a leave for extended programs of union training for one or two weeks. Yet at other times, the leave of absence may be for extended periods while the individual fills a union position, such as business agent or union president, entailing work away at the union's headquarters.

Although the parties may have negotiated language to provide employees with the opportunity for leaves of absence for attending to union responsibilities, the language generally does not leave to the union total discretion concerning when such leaves of absence will be provided. The contractual stipulation is that such leave is to be for union business, and the union may be required to offer proof, before the grant of leave is made by the employer, that the leave is for the purpose covered by the agreement. Contract language also will determine whether such leaves are to be with or without pay, with or without the continuing accretion of seniority, and whether other benefits (such as vacation or holiday entitlement or overtime access rights) will be protected during such periods of leave.

The second situation in which time away from normal employee functions is granted is the time taken by union officials for processing union grievances or for other union business during the normal workday. A common example of such leave would be time off by a shop steward for processing or investigating grievances. Generally, the parties negotiate language that assures the shop steward time for the processing of grievances. But even if such language is not negotiated, the right to process or investigate grievances on company time and pay is a benefit that many arbitrators might interpret as implicit in the agreement's recognition clause and in furtherance of the goal to resolve disputes at the earliest steps. Rapid investigation of grievances is a necessary attribute of the union's role in protecting employee rights, because prompt investigation and interviewing of witnesses is frequently crucial to the union's ability to adequately represent employees.

The right to process and investigate grievances, however, is not a right without limitations. It does not give shop stewards the right to neglect their work responsibilities, to disrupt the workplace, or to distract other employees from their responsibilities for extended periods of time in the furtherance of union duties. The shop steward's right to interview grievants and witnesses generally is considered to be subject to permission of the supervisor, with the understanding that such permission will not be withheld arbitrarily. Thus when a shop steward seeks to interview a witness during the middle of a machine run in which that witness is an integral member of the team, the supervisor is not acting arbitrarily or capriciously when he or she defers that interview until the machine run is completed. Likewise, the shop steward generally is not expected to have free access to the plant without asking for permission to interview certain employees. In this manner, the time and location of the interview is not excessively disruptive to the work operation. In such cases, the permission of the supervisor generally is sought and, likewise, presumably is granted in good faith.

CASE: THE LONG INTERVIEW

David Ivory was a shop steward who had been investigating a series of disciplinary cases involving several employees in his work area. He followed the practice of asking the supervisors for permission to interview the witnesses, but when the times of such interviews increased from fifteen to thirty minutes, the supervisor appeared to grow increasingly irritated with the amount of time the grievant spent in such interviews.

On the day in question, Ivory asked the supervisor for a chance to return to further interview three employees on the other side of the department. The supervisor responded, "You've had enough time interviewing the witnesses. You may do it on your own time if you need any more interviews with those employees, but they have to go on with their work and your request is denied." Ivory filed a grievance objecting to the refusal of the employer, and the case was appealed to arbitration.

The union argued that the shop steward was involved in the legitimate exercise of his responsibilities, that the employees he was seeking to interview were crucial witnesses to the events in dispute, that he had the right to interview them at work rather than outside of work, and that the promptness in interviewing was essential to the proper preparation of the case. It urged that the grievance be sustained.

The employer argued that the supervisor had been lenient in permitting Ivory to meet with whatever witnesses he wished; that Ivory had gone beyond the rule of reason by making the interviews longer and longer; and that the three individuals in question had, in fact, been interviewed earlier. Any further information that Ivory might have wished to secure could be attained after work, the employer asserted. A rapid interview had been provided, and the amount of time Ivory was requesting was excessive and interfered with his work as well as that of the three employees. It concluded that the suggestion that they be interviewed off the job was appropriate and that the grievance should be denied.

The arbitrator was faced with the issue of determining whether the interviews were a legitimate exercise of Ivory's investigatory responsibilities or whether they were an abuse of that discretion. The arbitrator concluded on the basis of the evidence presented by the witnesses that the case was, in fact, a complicated dispute; that the need to return to the witnesses arose because of the statements made by other witnesses to Ivory during the lunch period; and that the follow-up with the three witnesses in the afternoon constituted a legitimate exercise of the shop steward's right of access to witnesses during the workday. Accordingly, the arbitrator sustained the grievance.

Discussion Question 1: What arguments might the company have raised?
The company might have provided evidence of the frequency or duration of interviews on the basis of prior experience with other shop stewards. It might have provided evidence of Ivory's prior excesses, if such were the case, in time spent with the witnesses or even evidence of Ivory having been disciplined for wasting time on the job or for talking to employees in his non-union capacity.

Discussion Question 2: What arguments might the union have raised?
The union might have sought to introduce testimony showing that the grievant's supervisor had displayed prior animus toward the grievants, the union, or Ivory; that the supervisor had in the past imposed restrictions on any solicitation of witnesses' views; and that Ivory in the past had appealed to higher-level supervisors for permission to interview witnesses; or that the supervisor's refusal was based on the fact that the grievance under investigation was directed at him and in which he had a personal stake. The union also might have introduced evidence that Ivory had been reasonable in his prior requests to interview witnesses; that he had not used all the time allocated to him in the past for such interviews; or that the amount of time that Ivory spent interviewing witnesses was, indeed, less than was allowed to other shop stewards.

Discussion Question 3: How could the participants have avoided this escalating into a grievance?
Once either one of the parties sensed animosity or a potential escalation of hostility, it would have been prudent to have postponed their discussion for a few minutes until the participants calmed down. Then, when the grievant was told that he could not meet with the witnesses, he could have asked to meet with the supervisor to point out why the additional time was necessary, citing, perhaps, that information that needed confirmation had been discovered during the lunch period. He also could have pointed out that these witnesses would be unavailable after work. Ivory could have gone on record saying that he wished to register a protest or to have the matter resolved by a higher authority. It would have been possible for Ivory to have discussed with management the need for meeting with the witnesses without revealing any confidential matters or without even revealing the content of the grievance, but instead pointing out the uniqueness of the situation and the need for an exception to the general practice of single interviews.

The supervisor likewise could have sought to diffuse the conflict by pointing out the pressures in the workplace requiring the witnesses to proceed with work without interruption. He could have sought to arrange an interview somewhat later when work pressures were reduced or even to ask Ivory why there were such pressures for an immediate meeting.

Both participants had a role to play in diffusing the situation. As in any kind of dispute, an overture expressing a desire to try to work out potential conflicts without permitting them to escalate would usually result in a more cooperative stance. At the very minimum, such discussions would provide a record of reasonableness in trying to diffuse an issue at the earliest possible steps, in the event the dispute would escalate.

Discussion Question 4: What controls may the employer exercise over employees taking extended leaves of time for union activity?
If a collective bargaining agreement provided for a fixed period of leave for union activity for someone holding union office, the position of the employer in granting such would be dependent on the contract language. If the contract specified that "the union shall have the right to designate the time and individual to take the leave for union activity," the employer's discretion would be far less than if the contract gave the employer the right to determine the length of time for such leave, if it set forth a maximum time for such leave, or if it included a prerequisite that such leave not interfere with the operations of the employer's enterprise.

In a case where the union had the right to have an employee placed on a half-time schedule for union activity, the employer might refuse to be reasonable if the nature of the work performed by that individual was such that it could not be carried out on a half-time basis. This might occur if the employee had unique skills or was one of a team of employees for which no part-time replacements were available. The general rule is that employees who are released for such union activity are, in fact, continued on the payroll as employees. They thus may be subject to other contract provisions, and perhaps even to the rules of just cause, for discipline imposed for actions undertaken while on union leave that are viewed by the employer as an abuse of that leave. An employee who is on a leave of absence for union business and who engineers or participates in a wildcat strike against the employer may accordingly be disciplined for an abuse of that leave discretion. An employee who is released for attendance at a union collective bargaining course might have some of that leave time denied if it is found that the employee had gone on a vacation instead of attending the course.

Union Rights and Responsibilities

Union officers, particularly shop stewards, are in a unique role at the workplace. They possess rights as employees, as well as additional rights as union officials. They have responsibilities as employees coupled with responsibilities as union officials. Their positions in this respect involve a careful balancing of rights and responsibilities.

The union official possesses the same rights as any other member of the bargaining unit unless contractually recognized to have additional rights arising from his union office. As an employee, the union official retains the right to file a grievance and have that grievance appealed to the arbitration step if the parties are unable to resolve it.

As a union official, the employee has an added set of rights arising from the authority to represent the employees in the collective bargaining relationship. That right brings with it, as a function of this representational role, the opportunity for communication with representatives of management. The shop steward has a right beyond that of the individual employee to seek to persuade the supervisor to the union's point of view. In many cases, that effort results in animated exchanges and provocative language. The employer, through the supervisor, is expected to be cognizant of that representational role and to apply a less authoritative standard in dealing with the union's representative.

Arbitrators tend to permit a higher level of vocal confrontation as a facet of that representational responsibility, while at the same time protecting the supervisor from any excesses of behavior from the union representative. One of the reasons that union stewards are permitted greater leeway in arguing and confronting supervision is that the imposition of discipline on union stewards in the exercise of their responsibilities would result in a chilling factor, deterring them as employees from the assertion of their rights as enforcers of the collective bargaining agreement. Thus, in the language of arbitrator Eli Rock, *Singer Fidelity, Inc*, 42 LA 746, 749 (1963),

> Obviously, the right of a steward to do his job properly must be strictly protected, without fear of retaliation of any kind for the performance of that proper role. Mere militancy or zealousness can never justify punishment; nor can a steward be limited to the language or behavior of the parlor. As the union points out, the steward is certainly entitled to be wrong in the issues he presses or fights over, on behalf of his constituents. (F. Elkouri and E.A. Elkouri, *How Arbitration Works* [Washington, D.C.: BNA, 1985], 186)

The supervisor may be required to tolerate an escalated level of communication but certainly is not required to submit to abuse or to physical attack, as such behavior exceeds the expected role of the parties in implementing the collective bargaining agreement or in seeking to resolve disputes thereunder. The union representative likewise is properly cautioned to be articulate in representation but to avoid excesses that could be labeled as offensive or abusive exercises of the representational role.

Union and management share responsibility for adhering to the terms of the parties' collective bargaining agreement and for utilizing the dispute-settlement process of the grievance and arbitration system. Accordingly, a shop steward who believes he or she is being denied the right to investigate a grievance or to interview witnesses has recourse to the filing of a grievance over such alleged deprivation of union rights. Similarly, a shop steward who has been subject to discipline for insubordination when trying to placate or resolve a dispute has recourse to the filing of a grievance as a means of rectifying the situation and as a means of clarifying the relationship between union representative and employer. In both cases, the shop steward who is denied what he or she believes to be contractual rights has the responsibility to comply with the supervisor's order to return to work. The precept of "obey now and grieve later" is equally applicable to shop steward, union officer, and rank-and-file employee.

Tranquility in the workplace can be maintained only by all parties conforming to the rules. Indeed, it is argued that the shop steward or union officer should have a higher sense of responsibility than the rank-and-file employee when it comes to knowing the rules and the extent to which an employee may challenge a supervisor. Holding a union office does not make an employee immune from discipline. Employers, to the contrary, may impose discipline on that shop steward or union officer particularly because of the higher degree of responsibility needed to set an example for other employees.

CASE: THE OVERLOADED HAMPER

John Clark, shop steward, observed a fellow employee having difficulty pushing a hamper of heavy parts. He pointed out to the employee that the cart was overloaded and was told by the employee that his supervisor had told him to carry a full load. Clark took the employee over to a supervisor and complained that the cart was overloaded and thus a safety hazard. The supervisor told Clark that the matter was not his responsibility and that if the employee himself wished to complain he could do so. The employee remained silent, but Clark reasserted the unsafe condition. The supervisor ordered Clark to return to his job, saying that he had fulfilled his responsibility in reporting the alleged overloading and that his jurisdiction over the case was ended.

Clark refused to return to work. Instead, he went to the general foreman and told him, "I complained to the supervisor about the overloaded hamper, but he refuses to do anything about it. Would you order him to have the hamper overload taken off so that it is reduced to a normal size?" The general foreman replied, "Go back to work. You were told by your supervisor to report to work. Go do so." Clark again refused, saying the hamper was too heavy to push, that the employee's doctor had warned him against such heavy loads, and that he would not return to work until the excess load was removed from the cart. The supervisor warned of suspension if Clark did not go back to work. The general foreman said to Clark, "You are suspended for the remainder of the shift. Please clock out and go to the labor relations office." Clark filed a grievance that thereafter was appealed to arbitration.

At the arbitration hearing, the union argued that Clark had a right to complain; that it was his responsibility to alert management to dangerous health and safety conditions; and that because the supervisor ignored the complaint, he was within his right in policing unsafe loads by reporting the dangerous condition to the general foreman. It argued that Clark was engaged in the legitimate exercise of his shop steward's role and had a right to appeal to the general foreman. The general foreman's order that he punch out was improper, an abuse of discretion, and a violation of Clark's rights as a shop steward. The union argued that there was no just cause for the imposition of discipline and that the grievance should be sustained.

The company took the position that the employee may have had the right to bring the supervisor's attention to what Clark believed to be an unsafe condition, but that his responsibility ended at that notification. It argued that Clark was disruptive; that he refused to take no for an answer; that he had no right to go beyond the order of a supervisor to the general foreman; that he was given a specific order by the supervisor to return to work, which he ignored; that he continued to harass management; and that it was within the discretion of the general foreman to order him to return to work or face the consequences. When Clark declined to do so, he was properly subject to discipline, according to the company.

At the arbitration hearing, the arbitrator held that the shop steward was within his proper authority in calling the attention of the supervisor to the overloaded hamper as a potentially unsafe condition. At that point, management was made aware of the condition, and Clark had fulfilled his responsibilities. When the supervisor declined to reduce the overloaded hamper, the issue became one that could have been pursued by the employee involved through his refusal to push the hamper on the grounds that there was imminent danger to his own health and safety. That was a right of protest that was privileged to the employee concerned and that would have justified the employee's refusal to carry out the order. The shop steward's responsibility at that point was to advise the employee of his right to decline to push the overloaded hamper or to utilize the grievance procedure on the employee's behalf as the means of protesting the supervisor's failure to act on the alleged unsafe condition.

There is no question that the supervisor was alert to Clark's complaint, nor is there any question that the supervisor gave Clark an order to return to work. Clark was bound to conform to that order. Although he was the shop steward, his responsibility ran to representing the employee in protesting the unsafe condition, but once that responsibility had been implemented, Clark was obligated to conform to the order of the supervisor, which was to return to work. If Clark felt that that order was improper, his recourse was through the grievance procedure, either in the form of a protest over the supervisor's permitting and condoning an unsafe act or in protest of the supervisor's refusal to permit Clark to explain the unsafe condition.

In neither event was Clark justified in going beyond the supervisor, the legitimate representative of managerial authority, to the higher level of general foreman to seek a countermand of the supervisor's order. The arbitrator held that Clark acted improperly in appealing to the higher level supervisor and that he compounded the wrong by refusing to adhere to the second order, this time by the general foreman, to return to work. Clark unquestionably had the right to protest the allegedly unsafe condition on behalf of the employee. He also had the right to be heard by the supervisor on that allegation. This apparently occurred. Once it occurred, Clark had fulfilled his shop-steward function. Management was aware of his protest. Its failure to grant his request did not give him any authority to bypass the grievance procedure by declining to file a grievance. His action in appealing to a higher level of management was beyond his legitimate role as a shop steward. When he refused the order to return to work, appealed to the supervisor, and refused the second order to return to work, he was acting *ultra vires*, or beyond his authority as shop steward and in his role as an employee. At that point, having exceeded his responsibility, he was properly subject to discipline as an employee for failing to adhere to a direct order to return to work. Under the circumstances, there was just cause for the imposition of discipline. The grievance was denied.

Discussion Question 1: What arguments might the union have raised in its case?

The union might have introduced evidence to show animus on the part of the supervisor and general foreman. It might have introduced testimony by witnesses to the scene who could corroborate Clark's testimony that the supervisors disregarded his complaint. It might even have produced witnesses who had worked nearby to testify that Clark had not been disruptive and that there had been no interruption in their work by the exchange. The union also might have introduced evidence of a past practice by Clark or other employees of talking to various higher levels of management without having been subject to discipline. That would have shown condonation of such conduct. On the issue of imminent danger to the employee's health and safety, the union could have produced a doctor's certificate or other evidence of medical treatment for the employee's back to show that Clark was alert to the seriousness of the employees' health problem and was acting in his behalf.

Discussion Question 2: What might the company have done in its processing of the case?
The company might have produced testimony of witnesses concerning Clark's hostility and his disruption of work in the area or evidence that the supervisor had explained that the load was not overloaded. It might have produced as a witness the supervisor who allegedly had ordered the overloading if that supervisor was to testify that the overloading was voluntary, that he was unaware of it, or that there had been a past practice by the employee of loading the hamper to that level. The employer also might have introduced evidence of prior hostility on the part of the shop steward or the grievant in dealings with either the supervisor or the general foreman. The company might have challenged the union's medical evidence or produced its own to show that there was no immediate risk to health and safety and that the employee could have done the work. Testimony of supervisors who had seen the employee push heavier loads would have bolstered the case.

Discussion Question 3: Would the results have been different if the shop steward himself had been the person pushing the hamper?
If Clark had been the person pushing the hamper, he would have had the right as an employee to refuse to push the hamper on the grounds that the action was a danger to his health and safety. In support of that argument, it would have been helpful for the union to supply evidence of what was a safe load or of injury to other employees by their having been required to push a similarly loaded hamper. If, in this alternative scenario, the supervisor had said, "Continue to push the hamper or you're going to be disciplined," Clark would have been within his rights, as would any employee, in declining to push the hamper if there was a valid claim of imminent risk to health and safety.

The ultimate resolution of the question of whether the hamper was in an unsafe condition would have been resolved through the grievance and arbitration system. If Clark had declined to push the hamper, had been told to do so, and had been disciplined for declining to do so, the issue before the arbitrator would have been to determine if there were reasonable grounds for believing there had been a health and safety violation. If the arbitrator so found, then the discipline for failing to move the hamper would have been overruled, and the employee would have been compensated for earnings lost.

Discussion Question 4: What if Clark had told the employee not to push the hamper even though there was no question of it being overloaded?
The responsibility of the shop steward is to assure that there is conformity to the collective bargaining agreement by both management and employees.

Although the steward might have had the right as a fellow employee to give another employee advice, a different situation would arise if the employee declined to push a safe hamper, a supervisor told him to do so, and the shop steward intervened and told him not to do so. Union representatives have a responsibility to assure that there is adherence to reasonable rules within the plant. A shop steward should therefore not order or encourage disregard for or disobedience of a legitimate management order.

The shop steward has a positive responsibility to assure that fellow employees take the appropriate remedy for protest by using the grievance and arbitration system. Any efforts to encourage employees to disregard orders is properly subject to discipline. It is not a protected activity anticipated by collective bargaining for a shop steward to order an insubordinate act. Accordingly, the shop steward would properly have been subject to discipline for ordering or encouraging an employee to disobey a management order.

The Union's Role under External Law: Duty of Fair Representation

The union has an obligation as the collective bargaining representative of the employees to represent them in processing complaints against the employer. It has a duty to represent such employees fairly, and it runs the risk of being sued by the union for failure to exercise and implement a *duty of fair representation* on behalf of the bargaining-unit employees it represents. That authority is, in turn, based on the expectation that the union will act properly in processing claims on behalf of employees. But that obligation is restricted to processing complaints alleging violation of the collective bargaining agreement.

A different question arises when an employee seeks to enforce a right granted by statute, such as the National Labor Relations Act (1935), the Equal Employment Opportunity Act (1972), the Occupational Safety and Health Act (1970), or other statutes that protect individuals whether or not they are employees of a company that is organized by a union. Such individuals have the right to process such appeals through administrative and judicial appeals procedures culminating in court proceedings, but that right is an individual right. It is not a right that arises by virtue of the parties' collective bargaining agreement and, therefore, does not impose any obligation upon the union to process the claim on the employee's behalf.

The problem of representation occurs when a claim arises that may be not only an alleged violation of the collective agreement, but also a violation of statute. Thus, the case of a black employee who is denied promotion to a position for which he claims himself qualified could be processed through the collective bargaining agreement as a violation of the promotion clause.

In addition, it could be processed under the agreement as a violation of a provision against discriminatory treatment on the basis of race. It might also be processed as a suit under Title VII of the Civil Rights Act (1964). Each appeal is, in fact, quite distinct, but in practice there has tended to be an overlap in such processing. In some cases, there has been dual processing of the case, although usually with initial processing through the grievance and arbitration step. In the enforcement of statutes, the National Labor Relations Board (NLRB) has taken a position of deferral to arbitrators' awards if the arbitrators considered the issues that would be relevant to statutory violation of the NLRA.

The NLRB, if a case is initiated with it rather than through arbitration, has followed the practice of deferring such cases to arbitration, reserving the right to review the consistency of the arbitrator's award with their statutory enforcement obligations. In the case of alleged violations of the Civil Rights Act, the U.S. Supreme Court in the famous case of *Alexander v. Gardner-Denver*, 94 S. Ct. 1011 (1974), has held that courts will give great weight to the decision of the arbitrator dealing with the same issue if certain procedural requirements are met.

There has been a willingness on the part of judges to concede jurisdiction to arbitration or to ratify arbitration awards when the issue involved is the same as is being raised in the statutory proceeding. This prospect places on the union the responsibility for processing the case through the grievance and arbitration system in the proper manner.

In processing such cases through the grievance and arbitration system, the union must adhere to certain procedural requirements to assure that there is a due-process compliance. In the Gardner-Denver decision, in foot note 21 the Supreme Court noted that it adopted no standards concerning the weight to be accorded to an arbitral decision because that weight depended on the facts and circumstances of each case. It did, however, state that relevant factors:

> include the existence of provisions in the collective bargaining agreement that conform substantially with Title VII, the degree of procedural fairness in the arbitral forum, adequacy of the record with respect to the issue of discrimination, and the special competence of the particular arbitrators. When an arbitral determination gives full consideration to an employee's Title VII rights, a court may properly accord it great weight. This is especially true where the issue is solely one of fact specifically addressed by the parties and decided by the arbitrator on the basis of an adequate record. But courts should ever be mindful that Congress in enacting Title VII thought it necessary to provide a judicial forum for the ultimate resolution of discriminatory employment claims. It is the duty of courts to assure the full availability of this forum. (*Alexander v. Gardner* Denver 94 S. Ct. 1011 [1974])

CASE: THE TARDY GASKETS

Ellen Margolis, a five-year employee, was a parts expediter with responsibility for emergency delivery of tools and parts to various parts of the factory. On the day in question, she was told to deliver quickly six gaskets to the final assembly area because a team of four needed the gaskets to continue their assembly work. Margolis secured the gaskets at 10:58 A.M. but then took her 11:00 A.M. break, arriving at the final assembly area at 11:15 A.M. The team was sitting awaiting her arrival. The crew discovered she had brought only five gaskets, so she had to return for a sixth, further delaying the operation.

The foreman terminated her. Her record consisted of a written warning, a three-day suspension, and a ten-day suspension. She filed a grievance protesting the action, although her local president told her the discipline was justified. She also filed an unfair labor charge with the NLRB, alleging that the discipline was imposed because of her role in trying to organize a rival union and that the union was in conspiracy with the company to build up a disciplinary record to support her termination.

At the arbitration hearing, the employer argued that the grievant's discipline was justified; that her routine responsibility was quick delivery of parts; that she had been told that this delivery was particularly rushed because of the idle crew; that she improperly took her break before, rather than after, the delivery; and that her delivery of an inadequate number of gaskets resulted in a one-hour delay in the final assembly operation. The employer further argued that the termination penalty was appropriate in light of her record of union-tested discipline; that there was no evidence to support the charge of anti-union animus; and that, in any event, such an issue belonged before that NLRB and could not properly be submitted to the arbitrator.

The union argued that Margolis acted within her contractual rights in taking her break period; that the constant pressure of her job to provide immediate delivery would otherwise deprive her of any break periods; that the final assembly team could have made its request earlier or even after the break period; and that since the failure to deliver the sixth gasket was a matter of innocent oversight, she should not have been subjected to any discipline. It argued further that the disciplinary penalty was unjustified and masked a deliberate effort by the company to remove Margolis as a troublemaker. It asserted that the termination constituted a violation of the NLRA and that because the NLRB case had been deferred to arbitration, the arbitrator must address that issue.

The arbitrator took the position that the grievant was aware of the particular pressure for delivery of the six gaskets; that she was obligated to either deliver them before her break, to postpone her break, to find someone else to deliver them, or at least to inform her supervisor or the team supervisor that she was opting to take her break. Even if the break time was fixed, the arbitrator continued, she was obligated to inform the supervisor of the impending fifteen-minute delay so that arrangements could be made for substitute delivery or a delayed break period. On the issue of the missing gasket, the arbitrator held that securing and delivering specified numbers of parts was an essential element of Margolis's job, that she had been disciplined for inadequate performance in the past, and that discipline also was appropriate for the added delay in securing the sixth gasket. The arbitrator found that in light of the grievant's record, the termination penalty was justified and that there was no evidence of anti-union animus in the company's action.

Discussion Question 1: What should the union have presented?
The union may have been in an awkward position if it approved of the termination and then also was charged with an unfair labor practice. Since the union could hardly have been expected to pursue persuasively the grievant's charge of a union and management conspiracy to remove her, one solution would have been to permit the grievant to secure her own counsel, with the union bearing the cost of the outside advocate.

The union, in presenting its own case, could have provided evidence of the general awareness of the 11:00 A.M. break, of the grievant's own consistent taking of that break and of the knowledge or acquiescence of her supervisor in her habitually taking that break. It also could have provided evidence that the missing gasket was not her fault. Concerning the penalty, the union could have distinguished Margolis's prior infractions as being unrelated to this problem and could have presented evidence of prior cases of progressive discipline that had been more lenient. For example, it could have cited cases in which an employee had been given a fifteen- or thirty-day suspension or cases of employees being reinstated without back pay. To increase the chances of a favorable outcome, the union could have admitted the grievant's wrongdoing on the day in question, arguing instead that the penalty was excessive. That argument coupled with a requested remedy of reinstatement without back pay might have been more appealing to the arbitrator.

Discussion Question 2: What position might the employer have taken?
The employer might have introduced evidence of breaks being deferred in cases of emergency deliveries, evidence that employees had been told to make such deliveries instantly, evidence of prior discipline for comparable delays involving the grievant or other employees, and evidence of the cost of the delay in this instance and in other cases involving the imposition of discipline. Evidence of the grievant's prior infractions, constituting effective warning that repetition could bring removal, also could have been presented.

Concerning the issue of the unfair labor charge, the employer could have offered evidence of other employees' being treated similarly for like offenses. It also could have provided evidence of complete access and exercise of legal and contractual rights on the part of the grievant and other rivals, evidence of its hands-off attitude in union representation issues, and evidence that the union had effectively advocated the grievance on Margolis's behalf.

Discussion Question 3: What is the appropriate role for an arbitrator in dealing with the NLRB charges?

The jurisdiction of the arbitrator is limited to the enforcement of the parties' agreement. The arbitrator has no authority to bind the NLRB, although the traditional role of the NLRB is to defer to the finding of the arbitrator when the underlying unfair-labor charge is dealt with in the arbitrator's decision. Although the arbitrator acts within the strictures of his or her authority by confining the scope of decision to the just cause concepts under the contract, ignoring the unfair-labor charges runs the risk that the NLRA challenge will remain unresolved, perpetuating further litigation. Therefore, in an effort to bring closure to the dispute, most arbitrators who find that the disciplinary penalty is justified will add that such a finding supports the conclusion that there was no anti-union animus in the employer's action. Such a holding is likely to bring closure to the disputes in both fora.

A different result occurs if the arbitrator finds that the removal was not justified. If the employee is reinstated with full seniority and back pay on the contractual just cause issue, that may obviate the need to pursue the NLRA charge. But if there is reinstatement with some disciplinary penalty, the external NLRA issues still may contain an incentive for pursuing remedies thereunder. Arbitrators differ on the question of whether they should address the unfair-labor charge in such instances. Some do on the grounds that the issue has been deferred to them. Others decline on the grounds that their jurisdiction is limited to the parties' agreement or on the grounds that they lack the expertise to resolve NLRB issues. In such cases, the NLRB proceedings will continue independent of the arbitrator's ruling.

A particularly difficult problem arises with NLRA issues when only one or neither of the parties is represented by advocates conversant with the NLRA or with NLRB and court rulings. Some arbitrators will, in such cases, expand their traditional contractual role to assure full processing of the unfair-labor charges by a more active inquiry or legal research. But most arbitrators are reluctant to serve as advocate for a party that is unrepresented by expert legal counsel.

Discussion Question 4: If the union asked for reinstatement without back pay, would it restrict the arbitrator's choice of remedies?

If the parties in the submission grant the arbitrator jurisdiction over the remedy, the arbitrator is free to impose the remedy deemed most suitable to the case. But if the union at the hearing merely requests reinstatement while the grievance form seeks reinstatement with full back pay, the arbitrator is more likely to consider the unions' request as the maximum relief sought. To grant a greater remedy would not only usurp the union's role as the grievant's spokesman, it also would risk mandating a remedy that was not within the range of the submission as articulated by the union in its arguments.

A different situation may exist when the union is charged with an animus against the grievant and the grievant's anti-incumbent group. In such a situation, the arbitrator might endeavor to ascertain if the reduced-remedy request would be acceptable to the grievant or whether, if granted, it would be the prelude to NLRB litigation. A private meeting with the advocates is probably the most effective way of ascertaining the answer. The union advocate can then make representations on behalf of the grievant concerning what remedy is acceptable. Most arbitrators, unless requested by the advocates, would be loathe to discuss the issue with the grievant herself, if only because of the raised expectations it might engender.

Superseniority in Layoff, Vacation, and Holiday Choice

The purpose of the collective bargaining agreement is to provide bargaining-unit members with a contract securing them with certain rights that they otherwise would not enjoy. In order to protect the employees in the assertion of their rights, it is the role of the union to assign or to elect shop stewards and officers who are on call to represent an employee in the event he or she believes these rights have been encroached upon.

Those employees designated as shop steward and union officers carry with them the seniority rights of any employee. Thus, their seniority may determine whether or not they gain access to a more desirable shift or to whether they will be affected by a transfer or a layoff. Were their representational capacity dependent on the vagaries of their seniority as mere employees, in the event of a layoff or transfer they could be affected, thus depriving employees left behind of union representation. It is to protect those remaining employees against unfair employer action and to assure continuity of union representation that the parties negotiate special arrangements protecting union officials from transfers and layoffs that otherwise would affect them as rank-and-file members. The union membership as a whole has the right to designate their representatives. It would be a deprivation of union rights to limit representational authority to those most senior who may also be least competent to serve as union representative.

These provisions for so-called superseniority are often subject to challenge as a form of favoritism extended to union officers, rather than being recognized as a device for assuring continued protection of all members under the collective bargaining agreement. The purpose of such representation is continuity of union representation. There is not likely to be any challenges to this purpose, although there have been challenges under the NLRA of superseniority clauses that go beyond mere continuity of protection (such as when superseniority constitutes favoritism with financial or seniority benefit to union officers). The NLRB has gone so far as to deny superseniority to those union officials who do not serve in a shop-steward-type representational role.

The concept of superseniority for representational purposes is well ingrained in collective bargaining, and it assures shop stewards and other representational officers that they will be held available for the remaining employees in the event there is a need for filing a grievance or for representation in dealings with the supervisor. Thus, an employee serving as a shop steward is to be protected against layoff so that the remaining employees will have representation. Such provisions are usually matters of explicit negotiation, which assures that the rank-and-file employees approve of the preferential treatment.

The prevalence of superseniority clauses for representational purposes demonstrates the extent to which the rank-and-file membership supports agreements containing provisions for preferential treatment for union officers. Were such provisions not negotiated, the employer might be tempted to contrive union officers' removal through the creation of layoff situations.

CASE: THE COMPETING SHOP STEWARDS

Rachel Brown was president of the union of biochemical laboratory assistants. The laboratory suffered a cutback in work, forcing the layoff of 25 percent of its personnel. Justin O'Brien was the shop steward. Article 3 of the parties' agreement provided that "in the event of a layoff, a union representative shall be retained at work to serve as shop steward for remaining employees."

Brown, who was senior to O'Brien, informed the company that she would assume the position of shop steward. O'Brien, the regular shop steward who would be laid off were he not serving as shop steward, filed a grievance, which was denied and appealed to arbitration.

At the arbitration hearing, O'Brien had his own counsel, who argued that O'Brien was the regular shop steward and that the agreement called for retention of the shop steward. He further argued that O'Brien had more experience in the position than Brown, the newly elected president, and that as the intent of the contract language was to provide the most competent representation to the remaining employees, his grievance should be sustained.

The company argued that the article did not require the continuation of the previous shop steward, that selection of the shop steward was the internal responsibility of the union, and that it accepted the assurances of Brown that she was the proper person to serve as shop steward. In any event, the company would prefer Brown, as her seniority entitled her to remain on the job, obviating their having to retain O'Brien while laying off someone senior to him.

The arbitrator denied the grievance despite recognizing O'Brien's greater experience as shop steward and his desire to insulate himself from layoff. The arbitrator endorsed the designation of shop steward as an internal union matter, noting that the negotiated language endorsed retaining a person "to serve as" shop steward, rather than requiring the incumbent shop steward be retained. The arbitrator further held that the company acted properly in laying off O'Brien, as the superseniority clause did not require it to retain a junior shop steward when there was a senior union official still at work who could serve effectively in the shop-steward role.

Discussion Question 1: What could the union have argued?

O'Brien could have introduced evidence about how union representation had been handled in prior layoffs, including evidence of negotiating history to show that the parties' intent was to retain the experienced shop steward, if such was the case. O'Brien's representative also could have tried to introduce evidence of internal union politics or animosity working against him, although if objected to, such testimony probably would have been excluded.

Discussion Question 2: What could the employer have presented?

The employer likewise could have presented favorable evidence concerning past practice and negotiating history. The employer also could have offered testimony on the union's procedure for designating shop stewards to show that its procedure in this case was consistent with its own rules and the parties' agreement.

Discussion Question 3: Should the company have called Rachel Brown as one of its witnesses?

Although there is no contractual or legal bar to the employer's calling union members or officers as witnesses, the accepted practice is that management usually will not call one union member to testify against another. The consequences of such an act would be to sow animosity among employees who have to work together and to create disruption within the work force. Most managements would refrain from calling Brown, relying instead on the testimony of other witnesses, perhaps including hearsay. When the testimony of a union member is involved, arbitrators tend to be more liberal in allowing hearsay as the lesser evil to management's calling union members as witnesses.

Pay For Time on Union Business

The parties' mutual goal is prompt resolution of disputes at the earliest possible stage. This dictates that there be a speedy investigation and discussion of a grievance once the incident giving rise to it has occurred. Additionally, the parties' collective bargaining agreement provides a maximum time limit during which grievances initially may be processed. It is, therefore, to the mutual interest of both parties to have these grievances investigated promptly in the hope that communications between the shop steward and the foreman may, indeed, preclude the need to file a grievance or that if filed, the grievance can be resolved amicably and promptly.

Because of the disparate areas in which employees may live, it usually is expected that the union would have the opportunity to investigate the grievance and to interview the grievant and witnesses while they are at work. Shop stewards responsible for such interviews generally conduct them on company time. This raises the question of whether or not employees serving as shop stewards are to be paid for the time they spend while interviewing witnesses during the work shift and on company premises. The general practice is that shop stewards are paid for such time. This may be a matter of negotiation between the parties, providing for a fixed time period during which union business can be conducted on company time, providing a maximum number of shop stewards or union officers to do such work, or in larger installations allowing the union official charged with the grievance investigation to be paid on a full-time basis, even though not performing productive work for the employer.

Even though the parties may not have negotiated specifically for compensation to be paid to shop stewards during the investigation of grievances, the prevailing practice is for such payment to be made. The rationale for payments is that every shop steward, although a representative of the union, is providing a service to the employer by investigating protests, claims, and problems before they escalate into formal conflicts. In this respect, the shop steward is viewed as an aid to the employer in the parties' joint effort to reduce disputes. It is, in addition, to the benefit of all concerned that the union be given the opportunity for prompt investigation of complaints while the matters are still fresh in the minds of witnesses. One can imagine the work that would not be performed and the disputes that would not be resolved if the shop stewards were not paid for their union work and had to perform it on their own time. The practice of paying shop stewards for the time spent handling protests is, therefore, a minimal financial investment compared with the benefits the parties reap from rapid and experienced processing of potentially explosive issues.

The expectation of compensation for shop stewards is based on the prospects of reasonable time being spent in union activity. Employers may properly be concerned when shop stewards, in the perception of the employers, abuse their entitlement and use such investigations as a ruse for avoiding their normal work performance.

A somewhat similar issue arises in the area of investigating and researching company records. While it is generally accepted that shop stewards and union officers will have the right to examine company records in the preparation of their grievances or their arbitration cases, employers are, of course, loathe to provide compensation for a shop steward engaging in a fishing expedition. In instances where a shop steward is deprived of the opportunity to conduct research of company records claimed to be necessary for the presentation of the case, such denial of access may be disputed and the matter subsequently brought to an arbitrator for resolution.

The same standard for employers' paying shop stewards investigating grievances may apply to compensation for time spent by union officials while attending joint labor and management appeal steps in the grievance procedure and while attending arbitration hearings. In many establishments, either by contract or past practice, arrangements are made as well to compensate employees who are called as witnesses to testify at arbitration hearings.

CASE: THE UNPAID WITNESS

Jason Koornick was a shop steward who found it necessary to interview several witnesses for a grievance that had been filed recently. The investigation of the incident and the interrogation of the witnesses consumed two hours of his time. At that point, the supervisor told Koornick that he would have to return to work because the time he had taken was excessive.

Koornick told the supervisor that he needed an extra half hour to collate his notes and to write up the grievance. The supervisor said that it was impossible to give him additional time and that he had to return to work immediately. Koornick did so, and at home later that evening he spent approximately one hour writing up the grievance and collecting and organizing his notes. He filed a grievance requesting one hour's pay on an overtime basis for the time spent after his normal workday. The employer denied the grievance, and the case was appealed to arbitration.

At the arbitration hearing, the employer argued that it needed the employee to be at work as part of a team; that it had exercised forbearance in allowing him two hours of time, paid for by the employer, while he conducted the investigation; and that the interrogation was completed within that time. Thus, it had no obligation to pay Koornick for any work he did outside the plant, particularly when it was not authorized by the employer.

The union argued that the case in dispute was complicated; that the witnesses were detailed in their presentation and interviewing them took a longer time than anticipated; and that if the witnesses had not taken so long in reciting their stories, Koornick would have had time to write up the grievance prior to being ordered to return work. However, since he was unable to complete the entire preparation of the grievance during the time allotted to him and since he felt it important to obey his supervisor and file a grievance later, he acted properly in taking the incomplete grievance home to finish.

The union also argued that such work was of mutual benefit to both parties, that it was an integral part of Koornick's responsibility, that it should have been done on company premises and company time, and that failure to complete it at the plant was due entirely to the employer's conduct in barring his doing any more on the grievance while at the workplace. Accordingly, Koornick acted properly in completing the work at home and in requesting the employer to compensate him for that work, the union stated. It concluded that because the work was performed after Koornick's normal shift, he was entitled to compensation at the overtime rate.

The arbitrator held that although it was to the parties' mutual advantage to investigate and attempt to resolve the disputes quickly, the union's entitlement to investigate and inquire of witnesses was not unlimited. The union may not without authorization and permission from the employer consume an excessive amount of time conducting such investigations.

The evidence indicated that the grievant spent two hours conducting his investigation, that he had concluded his inquiry of the employees, and that the order to return to his job had not interferred with his effort to investigate and interrogate the witnesses. The arbitrator asserted that the issue, therefore, was not whether the grievant was given ample time at work to do the investigation, but whether he was entitled to compensation for work that need not have been done on company premises and easily could have been done on the employer's own time. The arbitrator concluded that the work performed by Koornick in digesting and summarizing the testimony of the witnesses and writing up the grievance was clerical work, which the employer was under no obligation to pay for. The arbitrator concluded that such at-home writing of notes and documentation (which could not be clocked by the employer) after such an extended period of investigation was work beyond that which the employer was obligated to compensate. Therefore, the grievance was denied.

Discussion Question 1: What evidence might the union have provided to support its position?
The union might have introduced evidence of prior tolerance of longer periods of investigation. It might have introduced evidence of shop stewards

having been paid by the employer for doing clerical work while on the premises, and it might have sought out evidence, if available, of the employer's paying employees while doing union work outside company time and premises. It might have tried to establish an analogy between time spent by union witnesses at arbitration hearings (if they were paid for such appearances) and the time spent on the case by the grievant outside the premises and off company time.

The union also might have introduced evidence to show that the complexity of the case justified all the time that had been spent on the investigation, as well as evidence of how the time spent by the grievant at home was disruptive to his normal family obligations and routine.

Discussion Question 2: What arguments might the company have raised?
The company could have argued that it had a practice of limiting the amount of time spent in such investigations. It might have shown that the supervisor had, indeed, been very lenient in the amount of time granted the grievant in this case, time far beyond the amount usually spent. It could have argued that the failure of the grievant to wrap up his investigation earlier had been disruptive of production, particularly in the light of the grievant's role as a member of a team, which had to wait for the conclusion of his inquiry. The company could have cited examples of other investigations conducted by union officials on their own time, either on or off company premises, that had not been compensated by the employer. It could have sought to show that the amount of time spent by the grievant in his home preparation in fact had been *de minimus,* a minimal amount of time, rather than the hour that the grievant claimed.

Discussion Question 3: If the arbitrator had held that the work was properly compensable, would there have been justification for the payment of overtime for such work?
Most arbitrators who would provide for compensation for such additional preparation time at home probably would not grant compensation at an overtime rate. The rationale for overtime pay is that it is work assigned by the employer and work that the employer in advance recognizes is to be compensated at the higher rate. In this case, the company presumably had no knowledge that additional preparation work was to be performed at home and certainly had no knowledge in advance of the amount of time this preparation would entail, let alone any committment to compensate that time at an overtime rate.

The union might have argued that this was merely a continuation of the employee's normal workday. Most arbitrators, however, would decline to grant compensation at the overtime rate on the grounds that it was unmonitored time of the employee's own creation. The work perhaps could have been performed either that day at work, with better allocation of available time, or the next day at work. Most arbitrators would deny such self-help effort at securing overtime or compensation.

The Union's Authority to Bind Employees

Most collective bargaining agreements distinguish the right of the individual employee to file a grievance over a matter affecting wages, hours, or working conditions from disputes or grievances filed on behalf of the union and alleging that the employer has in some way violated the union's rights. In the latter cases, the union has the right to resolve the dispute in the manner it sees fit. But in a forum with individual rights at stake, it generally is recognized that the grievance is personal to the employee who filed it. The employee has a stake therein, and most unions would respect the right of the employee to take part in a final determination about whether a grievance is to be further processed, resolved, compromised, or withdrawn.

Indeed, with the increasing prevalence of lawsuits against unions by individual union members on the grounds of failure to represent them fairly, unions are increasingly cognizant of the risks they run by agreeing to a resolution of a dispute without the participation of the employee. They also are cognizant of the risks in accepting a compromise if the employee who filed the grievance is not agreeable to such resolution.

A gray area arises in cases with multiple grievants. In such instances, the union may persuade employees that the grievance has become a union grievance rather than a grievance filed by a group of individuals. Thus, it may seek to establish a standard by which that grievance might be settled, either on the basis of it being the union's responsibility or on the basis of an acceptable arrangement being made among all the grievants.

A different situation, however, occurs in the case of grievances appealed to the arbitration level. While a grievance short of arbitration and still under the jurisdiction of the parties themselves may be viewed as proprietary to the grievant involved, most collective bargaining agreements proclaim that it is the union, rather the grievant, that has the right to determine whether a case will be appealed to the final step of arbitration. There are some collective bargaining agreements, indeed, that grant to the individual employee the right to determine whether a case will be appealed to arbitration, but such authority being delegated to individual employees is rare compared with the prevailing theory that the union owns the grievance when it is appealed to the arbitration step. In such cases, the appeal to arbitration is a matter to be determined by the union, rather than by the employee. The union also must therefore be presumed to have the authority to resolve the dispute when it comes to that level of appeal.

In such cases when the case has been appealed to arbitration and is resolved by the parties after the appeal to arbitration has been undertaken by the union, the prevailing view is that the union has authority to resolve that dispute either by withdrawal or compromise. If the parties' collective bargaining agreement is clear in granting the union the authority to appeal such cases to arbitration, the right to resolve them flows from that grant of authority, and most unions would be considered to be free of liability on the basis of a duty to fair representation.

The Union Bulletin Board

One of the recognized vehicles for permitting and facilitating communication among union members is the use of bulletin-board space, made available on company premises and for posting notices, bulletins, and communciations among union members. The parties may negotiate the conditions of the use of such bulletin boards, which are, after all, affixed to the walls of the company building itself.

The parties often negotiate on the size of notices, on the duration of time they may be posted, and more importantly, on the nature of the items to be posted. Generally, the objective is to enable the union to post notices that are of interest to its members and that are consistent with its role as collective bargaining representative, yet at the same time are not defamatory and do not constitute harrassment or embarrassment of the employer or lead to disruption in the workplace. In some contracts, the employer retains the right to approve of items to be posted on the bulletin board. In other cases, the union secures control over what is to be posted. The cases that come to arbitration are frequently those in which the standard of propriety of the notice posted is challenged by the employer, leading to the filing of the grievance.

After reviewing the case law on the subject, Frank Elkouri and Edna A. Elkouri reached the following conclusion:

> Thus, the cases noted above indicate that notices for posting on union bulletin boards (1) may not stray in subject from the reasonable concept of what constitutes union business at the particular plant, (2) May not be of such a nature as to have a detrimental effect upon employee morale, or of such nature as to inflame employees against each other or against the employer, (3) May not contain elements which defame the employer or are patently detrimental or disloyal to him, and (4) May not be rejected if the notices clearly are matters of "union business" even though they approach being inflamatory or adverse to the company's interest. (*How Arbitration Works* [Washington, D.C.: BNA, 1985] 801)

3
Discipline and Discharge

Most of the cases that come to arbitration arise from challenges to the employer's imposition of discipline or discharge. It is understood by both parties that employers have the right to expect certain standards of conduct from employees, that employees will know those standards, and that discipline will be imposed for failure to adhere to those standards.

Prior to the advent of collective bargaining, the employer was free to discipline or discharge employees for whatever reasons the company saw fit as long as the action did not violate the law. Employees had no recourse against such actions, even if they were arbitrary or capricious. With collective bargaining agreements, however, the employer and union in 95 percent of contracts agreed to grievance and arbitration procedures as means for permitting the continued operation of the enterprise while the parties sought to resolve their disputes. The agreements recognized that if the disputes were not resolved, there would be access to a mutually selected neutral party to resolve them. The procedure was particularly important in the area of discipline and discharge. Although the parties usually did not negotiate specific standards concerning what would or would not be subject to discipline or what penalties would apply, they came to accept the standard of just cause as the determinant of the appropriateness of disciplinary action.

The standard of just cause has become the universal rule for measuring the propriety of discipline and the disciplinary penalty. In the final analysis, the determination of what is just cause resides with the arbitrator if the parties are unable to resolve their disputes. The arbitrator is guided in turn by the standards followed by the parties in a particular enterprise. Thus, what may be just cause in one facility may not be just cause in another. If an employer is very strict about tardiness, an employee who is eight minutes late will expect to be disciplined; in another plant where the employer is less stringent, discipline may not be imposed until ten minutes after shift start. Thus, the arbitrator's ruling on what is just cause will differ in each instance.

Despite the uncertainty of quantifying just cause, it has come to be the recognized benchmark for maintaining discipline within an enterprise. Arbitrators rely on the concept as a means of determining equity and due process both in procedural aspects concerning disciplinary rules and in the substantive areas of disciplinary infractions.

Disciplinary Rules

Notification of Rules

The establishment of disciplinary rules not only assures employees of fair treatment when they have done wrong, it also enhances the credibility of the employers disciplinary program and in that way serves as a deterrent to others who come to recognize the legitimacy of the employer's rights. Among the elements of such a program are notification of the rules, uniformity in their application, relevance to the operation, escalated penalties, a commitment to corrective discipline, adherence to the announced procedures, and timeliness of imposition of discipline. Notifying employees of the employer's standards is crucial if disciplinary rules are to be effective. This notification may be accomplished in any one of several ways. The rules may be negotiated between the parties and set forth as part of their collective bargaining agreement, although such a procedure is rare. Far more common is for the employer to develop a set of company rules or a personnel manual, perhaps with a range of penalties for violations thereof, and then make the rules available to employees, either by providing them in printed form at the time of hire or by posting them prominently on a company bulletin board. Employees are held responsible for having read such posted notices. Sometimes the rules are conveyed to the employee orally at the time of hire or during meetings thereafter. Changes in or additions to the rules must be similarly brought to the employee's attention if the employer is to rely on these rules in imposing discipline. Verification that the employee has received the written rules by having the employee sign that he or she has received them is a convenient means of protecting against an employee's later denial of knowledge of a rule or of a penalty for its violation.

Regardless of whether specific conduct is proscribed in posted rules, there are certain employee actions that reasonable sense dictates are wrong and thus are properly subject to discipline. Among these are fighting on the job, particularly fighting with a supervisor, theft of property, selling drugs on company property, working on hazardous tasks under the influence of drugs or alcohol, and insubordination.

Uniformity of Application

Uniformity of application of discipline is an essential element in establishing and maintaining a disciplinary system. Employees must be made aware that certain conduct is prohibited and that discipline will result if there is a violation of those rules. To penalize one employee for an infraction, such as sleeping on the job, while permitting another employee to go undisciplined for the same offense brings into question the sincerity of the employer's disciplinary program and raises legitimate questions of favoritism, inconsistency, and prejudice. If management is to instill employee faith in the disciplinary code, the employee must be satisfied that all employees are equally subject to discipline for committing the same offense. While the degree of penalty may vary depending on the record, experience, and seniority of the employee, a disciplinary program dictates that a particular infraction will result in some level of discipline whenever it occurs. An employee with a previously clear record thus may be given only a warning for smoking in a restricted area, while an employee who has committed that same offense several times with escalating penalties because of a failure to correct behavior may be terminated for the offense. Nonetheless, it is important that every employee know that smoking in a restricted area will result in some level of discipline.

Although this adherence to uniformity in the application of disciplinary penalties is important to advise employees of the risk they run by violating the rules, it is perhaps more important when a challenge to the discipline is filed on appeal to arbitration. If an arbitrator is persuaded that the employer has been less than consistent in imposing discipline for a particular offense, the arbitrator may well exonerate the grievant, with resulting reinstatement with full back pay. Arbitrators have exonerated employees when a company rule against a certain wrongdoing has been inequitably applied or when violations thereof have been condoned and tolerated. A grievant who followed an example of another employee who had not been disciplined for the same behavior may be excused for a violation and relieved of the imposition of any disciplinary penalty if the employee had grounds to believe that his or her conduct would be tolerated and not be subject to discipline.

Relevance to Operations

The expectancy that the employer will establish rules governing discipline and discharge is based on the employer's right to maintain a tranquil and efficient workplace. Company rules are established in order to deter inappropriate behavior and to permit the employer to efficiently manage its work force. But the employer's authority over the employee is generally considered to be limited to times of the employee's presence at the workplace and during contracted hours of work. Thus, while an employer would have the authority to discipline an employee for engaging in a fight with a fellow employee during company time and on company premises, that right to discipline may not extend to when that employee is not at work or on company premises and when the altercation is unrelated to his or her role as employee.

Are employees totally free of discipline by employers for all behavior on their own time or off company premises? The general standard is that employers may impose discipline for off-duty or off-premises conduct if it has an impact on the employment relationship or performance. Thus, a fight with a supervisor outside work hours and off the premises may be sufficiently related to work operation as to justify the imposition of discipline. If the dispute arose from the work relationship or if the altercation was expected to have a subsequent impact on the employee's return to work, then discipline would be appropriate. Such would be the case if the employee effectively attacked the supervisor so as to interfere with the latter's ability to supervise that individual without fear of bodily harm on the employee's return to work.

An employee is prohibited under company rules from drinking on the job. Of course, that employee is free to drink off the job on his or her own time. However, if the employee consumes alcohol prior to coming to work and that consumption results in his or her being under the influence of alcohol while at work, the employee is properly subject to discipline for that off-duty conduct because it violates the company rule against being under the influence of alcohol while at work.

One area in which the interrelationship between on-duty and off-duty conduct has become increasingly important and sensitive is in the area of drugs other than alcohol. Employees are entitled to their private lives, and employers have no right to interfere provided there is no impact on the employment relationship. The introduction of drug testing is an area that encroaches on both personal and employment lives. An employer is entitled to assure itself that employees who are operating motorized vehicles or dangerous equipment are free of the influence of any drugs that might impair their safety, their reaction time, or their job performance. Thus, a test of drugs or alcohol may be appropriate for all vehicle drivers if done on a uniform basis or if done when there is a reasonable grounds for concluding that an employee is under the influence of drugs.

Appropriate Escalation of Discipline

The effectiveness of the disciplinary program or set of rules is dependent on an employee's awareness of the risk of failing to respond to the early levels of discipline. An employee must be made aware that if behavior is not corrected, there is a risk of escalated penalty until the employee who fails to reform his or her conduct is adjudged to be incorrigible and therefore is terminated.

The levels of discipline should be known in advance so that employees are alert to the risks of further rule violation and so that all employees are cognizant of the risks of becoming involved in any rule violations. That standard of anticipated stiffer penalties works only as long as it is applied consistently. Thus, to give an employee a three-day suspension for a second infraction and a written warning for a third infraction of the same type vitiates the benefit of escalated penalties as a deterrent for future infractions and leads the employee into a false belief that he or she may have escaped more severe penalties. It sets an undesirable precedent for other employees who may come to rely on a written warning for a third infraction after a disciplinary layoff for a second infraction. For an employer to impose a series of written warnings in place of escalating discipline leads employees to anticipate that yet another infraction will result in yet another written warning without the fear of a more severe penalty and the compensation loss that would come from a disciplinary suspension.

One of the most effective aspects of progressive discipline is the prospect of heavier discipline arising from repeated infractions. The ever-greater penalty for failure to reform conduct is one of the strengths of the progressive discipline system. An employee who is issued an oral warning or a written warning has merely a piece of paper in his record to contend with, but the awareness that the third infraction may lead to a loss of income and that a fourth infraction may lead to yet heavier losses of income by suspensions of longer duration and finally termination make escalated penalties a most effective tool. When the employee's pocketbook is hurt, there is a greater urgency to reform, not only to reduce the income loss, but also to forestall termination with the company.

Corrective Discipline

A corollary to the escalation of penalties is the concept of progressive, corrective discipline. The intent of the disciplinary program is to correct behavior at the lowest levels of the process before the heavier penalties are reached. To impose a heavy penalty, such as a two-week suspension or even termination, for a first offense would be to deprive the employee of the opportunity to correct wrongdoing while potentially depriving the employer of the opportunity to retain in its employ an employee who has reformed. Nonetheless, there are certain infractions for which corrective discipline has been determined to be inappropriate. Those are offenses that never can be tolerated in an enterprise, such as theft, assaulting one's supervisor, smoking in a dynamite factory, and the like. To impose a penalty of less than termination for such "capital offense" would be to grant all employees the right to commit the same offense at least once. For such egregious misconduct, arbitrators have generally held that the employer is entitled to impose discharge for the first infraction. Such capital offenses should be clearly posted and made known to the employees or be so obvious that an employee would be aware of the result of violating such a basic tenet of the employment relationship. It is true that employees who are terminated for such first offenses are denied the opportunity for corrective discipline, but the standard of termination, while punitive, is also a recognition that such behavior cannot be tolerated at the workplace.

Procedural Conformity

In setting forth rules for employee conduct, the employer frequently also sets forth the procedures it will follow in imposing such discipline. The parties may also negotiate rules governing the filing and appeal of grievances that may arise from following such disciplinary penalties. For the employer to have credibility in the imposition of discipline under its disciplinary program, it must conform to the rules and procedures it set forth. A failure to adhere to those procedural standards may be grounds for reversal of the employer's action if a case is appealed to the grievance and arbitration system. Some arbitrators will say that failure to adhere to the procedural requirements vitiates the entire discipline. Others will hold that a procedural failing may affect only the degree of penalty to be imposed for the infraction. Yet other arbitrators may find that the procedural failing is insignificant in contrast to the extent of the violation and may disregard such procedural irregularities. But the general rule followed by arbitrators is that if the employer or the parties have committed themselves to abide by certain procedural requirements, conformity to those procedures is a prerequisite for the imposition of discipline. The failure to provide requisite hearings, for instance, may be viewed as sufficiently detrimental to employees because it denies them the crucial opportunity to present their versions of what transpired. Such a version, if recited, might have precluded the imposition of discipline. In such an event, an arbitrator may rescind the termination and remand the case back for reprocessing with the requisite hearing being held. Employers who fail to abide by their own procedures or by the contractual negotiating procedures do so at their own peril. Arbitrators are bound by the contract language, just as the employer seeks to have employees bind themselves to the disciplinary code of the employer. Arbitrators are similarly bound by the parties' negotiated procedures and may therefore feel bound by the procedures set forth by the employer under the company rules. To hold otherwise might constitute a denial of industrial due process.

Timeliness of Discipline

If an employer expects employees to conform to its rules and to anticipate discipline for the violation of those rules, it must impose discipline sufficiently soon after the incident to impress upon the employee the nature of the wrongdoing and to protect against the disciplinary decision being viewed in the light of, or influenced by, subsequent events. Prompt imposition of discipline also provides employees with reasonable opportunity to collect relevant data or testimony of eyewitnesses necessary to challenge such discipline through the grievance procedure. To impose a discipline weeks or months after an infraction would constitute an abuse of the employer's authority because it effectively would deny the employee, but not the employer, the opportunity to collect timely evidence of the impropriety of the employer's action. Likewise, to permit the employer to accumulate a number of infractions before imposing a discipline would deprive the employee of the opportunity to benefit from corrective discipline by undertaking prompt reformation of unacceptable behavior. The withholding of discipline for an extended period after a wrongdoing also conveys to the employee and to others that such wrongdoing is tolerated and condoned by the employer, an impression not in the employer's best interest.

Disciplinary Infractions

Participation in a Job Action

The parties' agreement to create and utilize a grievance and arbitration system represents a trade-off. The union foregoes wildcat strikes or work stoppages during the life of the contract, agreeing instead to submit to the grievance and arbitration system any conflict over the interpretation or application of the agreement. The management, for its part, also agrees to conform to the grievance and arbitration procedure and to forego its unilateral authority to make final decisions regarding the supervision of its work force in favor of submitting to, abiding by, and implementing the decisions of its arbitrators. With such a joint commitment, it follows that any efforts to bypass the agreed-upon procedure through self-help would be viewed as in violation of the agreement.

CASE: A PERSONAL JOB ACTION

Robert Jason had worked for the enterprise for fourteen years and had a good work record except for his attendance problem. In the past two years, he had been issued a letter of warning, a suspension, and a seven-day suspension. When he returned from this last suspension, Jason was given a letter stating that if he was ever out again, he would have to bring a medical certificate explaining the reason for the absence. This infuriated Jason, who felt he had served his disciplinary sentence and should not be penalized beyond that by being required to see a physician every time he was absent. In a calm manner, he told his supervisor that he resented the added penalty;

then he continued his work delivering hampers of completed product to the shipping room.

About two hours into the shift, the foreman of the shipping room noticed that Jason was not keeping up with the deliveries and was bringing hampers only half filled. The foreman asked Jason what had happened, and Jason responded that it was nothing personal against the foreman, but he felt the requirement of the medical note was unfair and that he would continue to deliver half-filled hampers as a personal protest until the letter demanding medical certification was withdrawn. The foreman responded that he needed more product and warned Jason that he ran the risk of discipline for poor workmanship and insubordination if he did not resume immediately the delivery of full hampers.

Jason continued with his protest. The foreman reported the matter to the labor relations office. Jason was issued a letter of removal for insubordination. He filed a grievance, and the case was appealed to arbitration.

The employer argued that the letter requiring medical substantiation was to protect Jason from further discipline for unexcused absence; that Jason had acted improperly in deliberately holding back deliveries; that he was warned that doing so risked discipline for insubordination; and that when the grievant continued his protest, it justified the imposition of disciplinary action. The employer asserted that adherence to the dictates of progressive discipline called for an escalated penalty beyond those already issued to the grievant and that in the light of his prior record, removal was appropriate and for just cause.

The union argued that Jason already had served the one-week suspension, thinking it the full penalty for his earlier absenteeism, and that the imposition of the written certification requirement constituted a further disciplinary action for which there was no cause. It asserted that although Jason should have fulfilled all his work responsibilities, his failure to do so was a logical response to an unwarranted additional penalty. It urged the removal be rescinded and that the grievance be sustained.

The arbitrator ruled that the letter of notification to provide medical certification for absences could not be viewed as a separate discipline or as an additional penalty, but rather was a part of and arose directly out of Jason's completion of his seven-day suspension. The letter was merely information about what the employer had the right to do and was provided to the grievant to help him avoid any further discipline.

The main issue of the case, according to the arbitrator, was the grievant's effort to exert pressure on the management to rescind its directive. Jason clearly had a dispute with the employer. The proper forum for resolving such disputes was not through self-help, but rather through the grievance procedure. The parties negotiated it precisely to avoid the pressures of one party's exercising unwarranted pressure upon the other party in order to

bring about a change in that relationship. Whether the self-help be a concerted effort by the union through a wildcat strike on behalf of all employees
or a single effort by one employee to restrict his output so that management
would respond by rescinding the disputed letter, the action was a violation
of the essence of the parties' agreement to the grievance and arbitration
system.

The arbitrator held that the grievant acted in violation of his obligations
as an employee to invoke the grievance system and that he was insubordinate. However, in light of his long service, of the prior disciplinary penalties
being confined to attendance, and of the issue being a miscomprehension of
employee responsibilities, the arbitrator ruled the discipline should be con-
verted to a two-week suspension, with the grievant being made whole for
earnings lost.

*Discussion Question 1: What could the union have done to strengthen its
case?*
The union could have shown that prior self-help had been tolerated and not
penalized or that the grievant was unaware of his right to invoke the grievance procedure for such an after-discipline warning. It could have provided
witnesses to rebut the supervisor's testimony of a warning of discipline for
not resuming full work.

*Discussion Question 2: What could the employer have done to strengthen
its case?*
The employer could have produced evidence that Jason was familiar with
the grievance procedure or witnesses to statements that he was aware of the
consequences of his actions. It also could have provided evidence of such a
medical certificate requirement being a routine requirement on return from
disciplinary layoff or evidence that the grievant knew the need to provide
medical evidence at the time the discipline was imposed.

*Discussion Question 3: What if the entire work force had refused to work
because of this issue?*
The employer could have brought suit against the union if it was at fault for
violating the parties' agreement, but absent proof of union endorsement of
the action, the employer would have had just cause for disciplining those
employees who engaged in the job action. If an arbitrator had held the
withholding of services improper, the issue in each case then would have
focused on whether the employee had, in fact, participated in that withholding of services. Many collective bargaining agreements contain provisions
restricting the arbitrators' authority to determining whether or not an individual took part in such work stoppage, but such agreements may prohibit

the arbitrator from reviewing the propriety of any penalty imposed for such action.

Discussion Question 4: What if Jason had been the leader of a general slowdown? Should he have been penalized more heavily?
Most arbitrators would hold that a union representative has a unique responsibility to abide by the grievance and arbitration procedures and to encourage referral of disputes to that channel, discouraging slowdowns or other self-help. If Jason had been a union official encouraging such action, he probably would have been subject to a greater penalty. The theory behind that difference is the recognition that a union official has a particular duty to abide by the terms and procedures of the contract. A leader of a job action who was not a union officer would not have such a strong burden, although he or she as instigator of the action would face a heavier penalty than the followers.

Discussion Question 5: In a group action, must all participants be penalized equally?
Aside from heavier discipline imposed on union officials or the leaders of job actions, arbitrators may vary the penalties imposed on participants depending on their degree of culpability and on the employer's ability to prove involvement. Thus, during a sick-out, a person who established proof of illness that would have kept him or her from work that day might be protected from discipline, as might an employee who could not be identified as having participated in a picket line. Once discipline is levied, it must be equitably imposed, consistent with the offense and the employee's disciplinary record.

Absenteeism

Probably the most troublesome area of discipline is absenteeism. There must be an equitable balance between the employee's right to remain away from work when legitimately ill and the employer's need for reliable attendance to assure the smooth operation of the enterprise.

Employers recognize that the inevitability of illness will necessitate employees being absent from work on occasion. When the absences are infrequent and within the range that an employer deems to be normal, there is no question about the propriety of the claim of illness or about the need for verification of its legitimacy. But when the frequency or duration of the absences exceeds what the employer assumes to be normal, efforts are undertaken to control and reduce such absenteeism, particularly if it comes to be viewed as a widespread problem affecting several employees. In this latter context, management resorts to attendance rules, to absence verification, to discipline for excesses, and to more formalized programs to bring attendance to acceptable norms. The attendance cases that come to arbitration are usually issues of (1) whether a particular absence was legitimate, (2) whether the employee followed the proper procedure for advising of absenteeism or verifying its bona fides, (3) whether despite legitimacy, the absence drags on too long, or is too frequent, (4) the propriety of the penalty imposed for absenteeism, and (5) the weight to be accorded to a program of no fault attendance control containing prescribed penalties for infractions.

Legitimacy of Absence. Management recognizes that employees may on occasion be absent for illness. As long as the absences aren't excessive the employer may accept the employee's word that he or she was ill. But when absences become a problem the employer may seek documentation to verify their legitimacy.

CASE: THE FRIDAY ABSENCE SYNDROME

Aaron Passell had a disciplinary record of a letter of warning, a three-day suspension, and a five-day suspension, all for being absent on a series of Mondays and Fridays. On Friday, June 25, he telephoned his supervisor one hour prior to his 7:00 A.M. shift to say that he was ill with a cold and would not be coming to work. His supervisor reminded him of his record and warned him that if he didn't come to work, it could result in a ten-day suspension. Passell did not report for work during his shift. He came to work on Monday and told his supervisors that he had been sick in bed all weekend but had not gone to a physician and that he now felt much better. He was issued a ten-day disciplinary suspension. Passell filed a grievance and appealed to arbitration.

At the arbitration hearing, the grievant's wife testified that he had been in bed all day Friday, Saturday, and Sunday; that he had had a 103-degree temperature; that he had taken aspirin all weekend; that they had canceled plans for a Saturday evening party at their home; and that he forced himself to return to work on Monday even though he still felt weak. The union argued that Passell was sick in bed all weekend, that his wife's testimony supported that claim, that he had not been told when he called on Friday that he needed a medical certificate, that a visit to a doctor would have required him to leave his sickbed at considerable financial cost, and that the coincidence of this last illness occurring on a Friday was insufficient to establish that it was a fraud.

The employer argued that Passell had a history of Friday and Monday absences, that he had been warned of the consequences of staying out yet another Friday, that his wife's statements were not proof of the legitimacy of his illness, and that he should have secured medical certification of his illness to prove he was sick. It urged the penalty be upheld.

The arbitrator ruled that the burden was on the employer to establish that there was just cause for the imposition of any discipline for the absence on June 25 and, if that was proven, that there was just cause for the imposition of a ten-day suspension for that infraction. On the issue of the legitimacy of the absence, the arbitrator held that the testimony of Passell and his wife was persuasive that the grievant was ill; that he had been given no instructions to secure medical verification of illness for that absence; that a cold did not normally necessitate a medical visit; and that although the grievant's record of Friday and Monday absences might have raised a suspicion about his absence on June 25, it did not mean that every Friday absence was faked. The arbitrator found the testimony of the grievant and his wife rebutted any presumption of guilt for a Friday absence and that Passell was to be reimbursed for earnings lost.

Discussion Question 1: How could the union have strengthened its case?
The union relied only on the testimony of the grievant and his wife. Being aware that the arbitrator might have viewed the wife's testimony as prejudiced in favor of the grievant, the union might have sought to introduce other independent evidence that Passell was home ill. A receipt from a pharmacy for medication on the day in question; particularly if pursuant to a prescription; a note from the physician's office stating that Passell had telephoned for advice or a prescription; and testimony from others who visited him at home, who were in his car pool, or who had been invited to the canceled party would have further bolstered the claims of the grievant and his wife.

It is important for the grievant to have such witnesses at hand or available in the event the employer challenges the union's prepared witnesses. If they are not produced as witnesses during the hearing, the opportunity for their participation may be lost permanently.

Discussion Question 2: How could the employer have strengthened its case?
Testimony from those supervisors who had imposed the earlier penalties might have been valuable to show that the grievant had been told to secure medical certification during his next absence or to show that he had been warned that an unsubstantiated claim of a cold would not be tolerated. Similar testimony of unanswered telephone calls to Passell on June 25 or of his car being absent from his house might have been sufficient to shift the burden of proof to the grievant to overcome inferences that he had been well enough to leave his house on the days he claimed he was bedridden.

Discussion Question 3: Did Passell's disciplinary record shift the burden of proof to the grievant?
The threshold issue was whether Passell's June 25 absence was legitimate. Although the grievant's record clearly placed him on notice of the risk he ran for an unjustified absence, particularly on a Monday or Friday, it did not prohibit such absences when justified. If, however, the prior penalties had contained a requirement that any future absence be medically substantiated, then the grievant would have been bound by that requirement. Here there was no such requirement. The employer had the traditional burden of proving the particular absence was not justified. The record would have been relevant if the June 25 absence was found to be unjustified. At that point, the record would have been relevant only to the imposition of greater penalties than those levied in the past, consistent with the precepts of progressive discipline.

In discipline cases, the burden of proof is the employer's. While the employer might have presented a prima facie case showing a June 25 call-in consistent with call-ins made on the previously penalized Fridays and Mondays, the grievant effectively rebutted the prima facie case by his testimony and that of his wife. Absent any contradictory proof by the employer that he was seen outside his house those days, that there was no scheduled party, or that he had told others that he was planning to take a June 25 absence, and absent any effective challenge to the credibility of Passell and his wife, the union testimony would have been relied on by the arbitrator.

Discussion Question 4: What if the grievant was told on his return that he needed a medical certificate to return to work?
Most arbitrators would look with skepticism at an after-the-fact request for medical verification. To find that an employee was required to secure medical verification of an absence, that requirement would have had to have been imposed on the employee prior to or, at the very latest, during his absence. In this case, there was no such prior requirement, and given the nature of the ailment—a cold—it would have been reasonable for the employee not to have gone to a physician during his illness. If the absence had been due to a broken limb or a serious malady, both of which normally would be the subject of a medical examination, then the *failure* to follow that normal course of action would have been suspect, even if not specifically ordered by the employer. The grievant in this case returned to work as a normal matter after he felt his cold had run its course.

A visit to a physician might have been required on the grievant's return to work on Monday. In this case, the grievant testified that he was still not feeling well then, so a physician examining him on Monday might have been able to find that Passell's condition on Monday reflected an illness that might have kept him out of work the preceding Friday.

Prescribed Procedures on Absences. To assure that the employer has adequate notice and proof of the legitimacy of an absence and to protect against abuse, employees are expected to conform to the prescribed procedures for reporting and verifying absences.

CASE: ADEQUACY OF A MEDICAL EXCUSE

The company had posted the following notice on employee bulletin boards:

> If you are ill and unable to report to work you must call the time and attendance office at least one hour prior to your scheduled starting time. Failure to report will result in your being considered AWOL. If you are out more than two work days on your return to work submit to your supervisor a medical certificate explaining why you were out and unable to work.

The grievant, Jenny Blue, was scheduled to report to work Tuesday at 7:00 A.M. At 6:45 A.M., she called her supervisor to explain that she suddenly had taken ill with vomiting and would be unable to report for work. She called the time and attendance office the next two mornings, Wednesday and Thursday, at 6:00 A.M., reporting she was still sick and unable to report to work. She returned to work on Friday with a note from her physician, which read, "I examined Jenny Blue on Wednesday A.M., and she had gastroenteritis and was unable to work."

Blue's supervisor read the note and said, "I have to put you on AWOL. You called in too late, you called me instead of the time and attendance office, and the medical note does not say you were too ill to work on the three days of your absence." Blue grieved the imposition of AWOL, and the case was appealed to arbitration.

At the arbitration hearing, the company argued that the posted notice was clear and specific and that the grievant failed to call within one hour as required by the notice and as necessary to provide an opportunity to secure a replacement. It argued that Blue was out on Tuesday, Wednesday, and Thursday, but the medical certificate she secured covered her absence only on Wednesday. The company argued that every employee had specific tasks to perform and that the absence of the employee placed the employer at extreme disadvantage, imposed a heavier work load on the remaining employees, and interfered with production. It urged the discipline imposed be sustained.

The union contended that the grievant was legitimately ill, that the illness came upon her at a time too late for her meet the one-hour advance notice, that despite her vomiting she still made the effort to contact the company as soon as she could, that she contacted the supervisor rather than the time and attendance office to enable the supervisor to secure a replacement, and that the latter was but a minor departure from the requirements. It asserted that Blue was so sick that day that she could not get to the doctor, that she did go to the doctor the next day, and that the doctor did verify that she had gastroenteritis and was unable to work for the duration of her absence. The report from the doctor was consistent with Blue's account, according to the union, which urged the grievance be sustained.

In his arbitration decision, the arbitrator stated that the rules set forth by the company in its posted notice were specific; that the grievant undertook to conform to those rules; that her telephone call at 6:45 A.M., while in violation of the one-hour reporting requirement, was subsequently substantiated as being due to a sudden onset of gastroenteritis and vomiting; and that Blue's notification was an acceptable departure from the one-hour limit as she had no control over when her illness commenced. Blue did act in good faith to advise the employer of her absence as soon as she was able according to the union.

In dealing with the question of the medical certificate, the arbitrator held that the visit to the doctor's office was evidence of the employee's good faith to substantiate the legitimacy of her absence, that the diagnosis of gastroenteritis was consistent with her testimony, that the doctor's finding that Blue was unable to work was consistent with the diagnosis of gastroenteritis, and that the medical certificate covered the absence on Wednesday and by reference to "was unable to work" presumably covered her Tuesday absence as well. But the arbitrator went on to say that there was no reference to a Thursday absence being required by Blue's condition; that it was incumbent on the physician to specify the duration of her absence if it was to continue; and that absent any proof that she was unable to report to work on Thursday, Blue must be held to have been AWOL for that one day of absence. Accordingly, the arbitrator sustained a portion of the discipline attributable to Blue's failing to report to work on Thursday.

Discussion Question 1: Would the foregoing result have been different if the employee had a record of attendance problems?
The case as set forth was confined to the issue of compliance with a posted notice. Arbitrators tend to be more lenient with employees who are unfamiliar with procedures or who have demonstrated good faith and a reasonable effort to substantiate their absences. They, likewise, are more strict if an employee has a history of attendance problems of if the employee has had specific notification in the past of a need to conform to the posted procedures. Thus, in the foregoing case, if the grievant had had a series of three or four disciplines involving her calling her supervisor instead of the time and attendance office, then her failure to do so in this case might have been grounds for the imposition of a heavier penalty. Likewise, if the griev-

ant had a history of tardy notifications just at or after the start of the shift, then the arbitrator might view with greater suspicion a tardy report, as in this case. Finally, if there had been some question in the past of the authenticity of Blue's doctor's certificate, then the arbitrator might have agreed with the employer that the employee had been placed on notice to provide either more explicit documentation or the presence of a physician at the hearing to substantiate the legitimacy of the offered certificate.

Arbitrators will adopt the standard of reasonableness in reviewing the efforts of an employee to substantiate an absence when the employee had been placed on prior notice of the need for medical substantiation. Similarly, when there is evidence that the employee has undertaken to abuse the system or has amassed an unacceptable record of absenteeism, resulting in greater scrutiny or closer adherence to the rules by the employer, then the arbitrator is likely to hold the employee to a higher standard of proof.

Discussion Question 2: What are the proper items for inclusion in a medical certificate?

The purpose of a medical certificate is to show that the employee was unable to work during the period in question. Doubts concerning the legitimacy of an absence or illness are overcome most effectively by a medical certification that would contain several points:

1. A statement of symptoms complained of by the employee

2. A diagnosis of the employee conducted by the physician, with a statement of the physician's physical findings, such as tenderness, pain, and abrasion, and of diagnosis of the condition underlying those findings

3. A prognosis for the future course of the condition, such as the employee being required to rest for a day or being required to take medication for a period of time; a forecast of that condition being sufficiently controlled by a future date; or the requirement that the employee return for examination on a certain date to ascertain the prognosis

4. A statement regarding the impact of that condition on the employee's ability to work such as "This employee was ill and unable to work due to gastroenteritis and is fit to report to work on Friday," or "This employee is unable to do heavy lifting beyond 50 pounds until the first of next month," or "This employee currently is able to work only four hours per day, with one ten-minute rest period per hour."

It is in the final item that the physician is expected to relate the employee's physical condition to his or her job requirements. This is not always within the scope of knowledge of the physician, and the physician in most cases may rely on the employee's assertion concerning the impact of his or her condition on job performance. The problem may be exacerbated by the loyalty that physicians have to their patients, in some cases blindly endorsing patients' or expost facto telephone claims that they are unable to work. These so-called ten dollar notes are often challenged by the company, which is within its authority in seeking verification of any claim of inability to work.

Arbitrators frequently are confronted by disputes in which the doctor's claim of inability to work or work restriction is challenged by the employer. The employer may present testimony from its own or another physician stating that the employee was able to report to work or was in a condition where he or she could have performed the work. That challenge to the employee's physician may require the arbitrator to weigh the positions of the two physicians. Usually these determinations are based on whatever is presented at the hearing, generally the doctor's certificate on the employee's behalf and perhaps a similar certificate or testimony from a physician representing the employer. In some cases, the employee or union may request continuance to bring his or her physician to the hearing, or arrangements may be made to take a deposition from the absent physician. Arbitrators tend to make their rulings on the evidence presented by the parties without asking for the presence of a particular witness, so it is up to the union and the employer to decide whether the evidence they have presented is sufficient to have their view prevail.

In weighing the issue of whether or not an employee was unable to work or was restricted to certain activity, arbitrators are often required to weigh the competency of the medical testimony, not only concerning substance, but also concerning the qualifications of the physician. Thus, a determination by the union's cardiologist that the employee's heart condition would preclude him or her from heavy lifting probably would be more credible than the testimony of the company's physician, whose field of expertise was occupational diseases. Likewise, a statement from a psychiatric social worker employed by the company that an employee's record of violence in the plant could portend future repetition would be more credible than a statement from the employee's family physician that his behavior was perfectly normal and should be acceptable because the employee had no physical ailments.

Discussion Question 3: How would the arbitrator have ruled if the employee had not gone to a physician during the absence?

Individuals who suffer stomachaches generally are not likely to visit a physician under normal circumstances. Thus, an employee who had such an ailment probably would not secure the medical visit and documentation to cover such an absence. In most cases, the employer would be satisfied with an oral report of the employee's absence and reason for the inability to return to work and would not require medical documentation. The need for documentation arises when the employee's attendance pattern demonstrates a suspected abuse of oral reporting or when the enterprise is sufficiently large so that there is a greater need for strict rules on reporting. But even in the latter case, the employer is more likely to be lenient to an employee with a long record of good attendance or to a short-term employee absent for the first or second time. Likewise, arbitrators are unlikely to require strict adherence to prescribed procedures unless there is a need to do so. This may be the case in an enterprise where the absence of one employee would disrupt an entire operation or where there is a history of attendance problems among the employees as a group or for the particular employee in question. Indeed, arbitrators have held that the requirement of an employee to incur the expense of visiting a physician when that employee has a clear attendance record may, in fact, be an excessive requirement.

Discussion Question 4: In the foregoing case, what would be the grounds for reducing the disciplinary penalty imposed by the employer?
If the employer had imposed the penalty (1) for calling within the hour prior to the scheduled starting time, (2) for reporting to the supervisor instead of to the time and attendance office, and (3) for being absent on Thursday without substantiation, and the arbitrator had found that there was grounds only for the third element of the penalty, then the arbitrator might specify that the penalty be reduced to cover that single infraction. The arbitrator might, however, have found that the single infraction was sufficiently grave to justify the retention of the entire penalty. If the arbitrator felt that the penalty imposed was appropriate for that step of discipline, bearing in mind the employee's work record, then it is unlikely that the arbitrator would have reduced the penalty. But if the employer had considered each one of those elements a grounds for a greater penalty, then the arbitrator would have reduced the penalty to conform to the one element of the charges that had been proven.

Discussion Question 5: Under what circumstances would absenteeism be grounds for removal?
An employer is entitled to rely on the attendance of its employees in order to operate its facility. Employers recognize that there will be occasional absences, illnesses, or injuries and adopt rules that seek to protect employees who are legitimately absent while protecting themselves against abuse of that right. Progressive or corrective discipline is used as a tool for seeking to reform the employee suffering from attendance problems. There are times when the attendance patterns of an employee persuade the employer, and perhaps the arbitrator as well, that the employee is unwilling to reform his or her attendance habits and that despite the efforts at corrective discipline, there is no reasonable prospect for expecting the employee to reform. Under

such circumstances, the employer is justified in removing that employee from its roster, rather than having to perpetually disrupt its operations because of an employee's unwillingness to work to provide the necessary services. In many such cases, the arbitrator determining incorrigibility is required to ascertain whether or not an employee is indeed beyond correction or whether an employee has been subjected to such physical problems that his absences have been due to an inability, rather than an unwillingness, to conform to required attendance patterns.

Labor and management have long relied on progressive discipline as the device for bringing employees into approved, acceptable work habits, but in attendance disputes, the arbitrator may not come into the case until the employee has been terminated. The arbitrator then must assess whether termination was justified on the basis of the employer's knowledge of events at the time of the company's action. In some cases, posttermination evidence shows that an employee had indeed overcome problems concerning attendance, such as in the case of an employee whose aged mother was in poor health and dying from cancer or the case of an employee suffering from an undiagnosed illness. Post-termination evidence may show that the aged mother had died, permitting the employee to return to a normal work schedule, or that the undiagnosed condition had, in fact, been diagnosed after termination and that the employee has returned to good health. The prevailing standard is that the clock stopped at the time of termination. But in such situations, the arbitrator may find that conditions giving rise to the removal had changed and that the employee should be given a chance to return to work. In such cases, because the employer had acted properly at the time of the removal, the arbitrator is unlikely to impose any back-pay penalty on the employer, but rather reinstate the employee without back pay. Even that reinstatement may be dependent on the employee's record. An employee with short-term service would not be as likely to be reinstated as an employee with many years of service and with a clear work record.

Discussion Question 6: What protections can be afforded to an employee who has a chronic condition that precludes regular attendance?
The employer frequently is confronted with employees whose medical conditions precludes them either from being regular in attendance or unable to fulfill the complete requirements of the job for which they were hired. In the former case, periodic or regular absences may be so disruptive that the employer is unable to rely on the employee as a team member. The employer may be able to work out a time-sharing arrangement with other employees if the absences are of a foreseeable nature, but if the absences are sporadic and not at predictable times, then the employer may conclude that that employee is unavailable to meet employment obligations. If an employer has a sufficiently large work force, an employee could be assigned to a regular

job with limited duties or to such tasks as he or she could perform within the limits of any medical restrictions. But in small enterprises, the employer may not have positions that can be handled by employees with medical restrictions. These employers may decide that they are unable to continue to employ those who are unable to perform the full range of tasks for which they were hired. Arbitrators may be called upon to determine the reasonableness of the employer's action in terminating such employees, either because there was no job suitable for them to assume on a restricted basis or because their absenteeism deprived the employer of the regularity of service for which they were hired. Arbitrators may review whether an employer acted properly in concluding that there was no suitable work available.

Situations in which an employee suffers from chronic ailments are among the most difficult. The absence may not be the employee's fault, but it is not the employer's fault either. If the employee is unable to provide reasonably regular attendance or to perform the tasks for which hired or tasks required by the employer, then the arbitrator may conclude with the employer that it acted properly in terminating the services of such employees.

Discussion Question 7: If you were the union, how would you have prepared for the foregoing case?
The union might have contacted the physician and secured a letter from the physician stating that he knew the employee was absent on Tuesday and intended the certificate to cover Tuesday and Wednesday or stating that he had told the employee to remain out of work on Thursday and expected the certificate to cover her until her return to work on Friday. The union might have secured the testimony of other employees to show that they had been permitted to return to work without penalty under identical circumstances. The union might have brought into the hearing the members of the employee's family to testify about her condition on the days in question, or it might have brought in evidence of telephone calls to the physician on Thursday, reflecting continued inability to return to work. It also might have brought testimony to show that the rules relied upon by the company had not been on the bulletin board or that Blue worked in an area where she had no access to those notices.

Discussion Question 8: If you were the employer's representative, what evidence would you have secured to present your case?
The employer might have secured its records to show consistent application of discipline for similar situations, contacted the employee's physician to show that he or she had been unaware of Blue's absence on Thursday and not authorized it, or brought in another physician to testify that gastroenteritis runs for one or two days but seldom for three. Both the union and the company might have presented evidence of the employee's record, in the

case of the union to show that she was reliable in attendance and had not been absent excessively in the past, or in the case of the employer that Blue had a poor attendance record, with this latest episode being further evidence of her unreliability.

Discussion Question 9: To what extent are notes from a family member or spouse reliable as proof of an employee's inability to report to work?
On occasion, an arbitrator is confronted with a note from an absent employee's spouse, such as the following:

> This note is to substantiate my husband's illness for October 28, 29, and 30. During this period of time, I observed the following symptoms: cough, slight fever, nasal congestion, and sore throat, along with complaints of muscular aches, including headaches. My husband definitely could not go to work for the reasons listed above. He was probably contagious because my mother-in-law and I came down with similar symptoms several days later.

Such notes raise two fundamental questions. The first is the accuracy and honesty of the alleged observation. Clearly, an employee's spouse has a vested interest in helping to avoid disciplinary penalty. Additionally and perhaps even more important, even if the report were accurate, it lacks the professional analysis needed to reach a diagnosis, prognosis, and conclusion concerning an employee's inability to work on the days in question. Anyone may observe symptoms of an illness, but beyond such lay observations, determinations about the legitimacy of an absence require professional assessment, most desirably by a physician, but perhaps by other qualified medical personnel. The assertion in the note that the employee was probably contagious is a lay conclusion and lacks the credibility of a statement made by medical personnel.

Absence due to Family Problems. The increasing frequency of females working and two-job families raises the likelihood that a family crisis may on occasion interfere with regular attendance.

CASE: THE TARDY BABYSITTER

Sharon Bohnin was a divorced mother who had been working at the plant for eight years. She had a three-year-old daughter, Joyce, and lived alone with her daughter in a community about 30 miles from the plant. Bohnin had been regular in attendance until her husband left her about one year earlier. Since that time, Bohnin had been absent several times because her daughter had been sick or because her babysitter did not report as scheduled. She had been subject to escalating disciplinary actions to the point where she was told that if she was tardy again, she would be terminated. On the date in question, the babysitter had arrived late, and Bohnin had missed her ride to work. The employer accepted the facts as recited, but concluded that because Bohnin was unable to report as scheduled and had such frequent absences, the company no longer was able to continue to employ her. An order of termination was issued. Bohnin filed a grievance against the termination, and the case was appealed to arbitration.

At the arbitration hearing, the union argued that the imposition of discipline was not for just cause, that Bohnin had a record of having been a good worker, that she had responsibilities as a single parent that sometimes interfered with her efforts to report to work, and that she had been conscientious in her efforts and had secured a babysitter to take care of her daughter so she would be able to come to work without any problems. It argued that the reliability of the babysitter and the babysitter's inability to come to work made it necessary for Bohnin to be absent on the day in question. It argued that the absence was legitimate and beyond the control of the employee. The union further argued that female employees have the extra burden of family responsibility that males do not have; that it was discriminatory to penalize a female employee because of those additional responsibilities when a male employee, lacking those responsibilities, would not be so disciplined; and that the penalty should be rescinded.

The employer contended that it was not responsible for the problems arising from an employee's family situation, that it had the right to expect employees to report to work regularly and on time, and that an employee had the obligation of securing a prompt and reliable babysitter. The employer also stated that it was not discriminatory in its disciplining Bohnin, as a male taking care of a child would have been similarly disciplined if a babysitter's tardiness had caused him to be late.

The arbitrator considered the claim of discriminatory treatment, acknowledging that female employees were less likely to have spouses at home taking care of children than were male employees, but noted that the employer's responsibility did not run to such familial situations. The arbitrator held it imposed a heavier burden on a single female parent with a child to assure for that child's care than it would for the average male employee, but asserted that the employer was entitled to regular attendance by both female and male employees. The arbitrator further held that the employee was aware of her reporting requirements and that her choice to live 30 miles from the plant without her own transportation and that her choice to depend on a not-too-reliable babysitter was the employee's burden and not that of the employer. The arbitrator found that the prior warnings issued by the employer regarding the risk of being tardy or absent in the future provided adequate notice to the employee that she would be disciplined for an infraction such as the one in this case.

The arbitrator noted that many employers provide child-care facilities to their employees, but that such was a matter of negotiation between the parties or of the employer's unilateral determination and was not an entitlement on the part of the employee. The arbitrator concluded that the employee opted to work at the plant; that she undertook that position with an awareness of the responsibilities of the job and of her child support; and that while the employer had acted properly in treating her leniently in prior absences, it was within its authority in finally imposing discipline when the grievant was unable to reform her own situation to enable her to meet her employment responsibilities. Accordingly, the arbitrator found the discipline to have been imposed for just cause.

Discussion Question 1: If you were the union, what evidence would you have sought to present in the case?
The union could have investigated other situations in which female employees responsible for child care had been absent and more leniently treated. It could have shown that the employer's treatment of Bohnin was disparate in comparison with treatment of male employees who had to stay home under similar situations. In addition, the union might have shown a change in the employee's home situation that would have assured that this problem would not arise again, such as her having moved closer to the plant, having had another family member move in, or having made other arrangements to assure that the child would be taken care during all work hours.

Discussion Question 2: What evidence would you have secured if you were on the employer's side?
The employer might have secured evidence to show that the grievant's condition had not changed since the imposition of discipline and that the union, through negotiations, had tried unsuccessfully to provide a child-care facility and had withdrawn the proposal. It might have introduced evidence of a clear practice of having imposed discipline in similar situations.

Discussion Question 3: Should the arbitrator seek to alter the employee's work shift to one more consistent with her family responsibilities?
It may appear to the arbitrator, and indeed the evidence may so specify, that the problems confronted by the employee in this case stem from her being on the day shift, that if she were placed on the afternoon or evening shift, her child-caring responsibilities would be eased by more reliable babysitting and not interfere with her attending to her job. Such a shift change may be an ideal way to resolve the problem particularly with a spouse working the same shift, but unless it is set forth as one of the issues confronting the

arbitrator, the arbitrator had best not deal with that issue in the decision. To order a shift change might create a contract violation for some other employee in terms of it being an infringement on the rights of other employees and their access to shift changes.

If the issue of shift change had been raised by the union or by the employer and if the issue was either specified or assumed by the parties to be an issue, then perhaps it would be appropriate for the arbitrator to consider a shift change as a potential remedy. If the parties argued that issue, the arbitrator would be able to base the decision on the evidence and on the contractual arguments raised by both parties. But for the arbitrator to propose such a shift change on his or her own initiative runs the risk of the arbitrator's placing the grievant or the employer in violation of the contract on rules governing shift assignments. Such an overture is appropriate in off-the-record discussions between the parties as a possible solution to the problem if the arbitrator seeks to resolve the conflict without issuing a decision. If raised in that manner, then the parties could deal with the proposal and perhaps even negotiate a special arrangement that would preclude the filing of grievances by others who might be affected adversely by such a shift change assignment.

Tardiness

As in the case of absenteeism, the employer has the right to expect employees to report as scheduled so that the operations of the enterprise can continue smoothly during shift changes or can commence promptly at the start of a shift. As in trying to improve attendance and control absenteeism, the employer is within its authority in instituting a program of progressive discipline for tardiness. Some employers have very strict standards, requiring the employee punch in and be at his or her job location at the time of shift change. Other employers only require employees punch the time clocks by the start of the shift.

In some cases, a charge of tardiness is made for any punch-in or report to work after the scheduled start of the shift, while in other cases a leeway period of up to fifteen minutes is built into the system before the imposition of discipline. Some employers impose discipline based on a single tardiness, with a second discipline after a second tardiness, and so on. Other employers impose discipline after a series of instances of tardiness. As long as the system and its variations are known to the employees and as long as the employer is consistent in its application of discipline, most arbitrators will endorse a system of progressive discipline for tardiness, ruling in each particular case about whether there was just cause for the imposition of discipline or about the propriety of the employer's discipline in light of its practices and the grievant's record.

CASE: A SNOWBOUND ACT OF GOD

John Blau was an employee with a series of disciplinary penalties based on his tardiness. His first warning occurred after his alarm clock failed to go off on time. His second warning came after he failed to reach his car-pool location in time to be picked up, which forced him to take a taxi to work. A three-day suspension was issued for Blau's tardiness on a day when he arrived by bus. In the latest dispute, the area was hit by a heavy, mid-March snowstorm. Blau, who lived 10 miles from the plant in a house off the main road, was snowbound. He testified that he tried to plow his driveway so that he could remove his car, but the street leading from the end of his driveway was unplowed and thus beyond the capabilities of his car. He was scheduled to report to work at 7:00 A.M., but after walking the 2 miles from his street to the main road where he was able to secure a ride, he finally reported to work thirty minutes late. The employer imposed a disciplinary penalty of a two-week suspension for this tardiness. Blau filed a grievance over the discipline, and the case was appealed to arbitration.

At the arbitration hearing, the employer argued that Blau had a serious and continuing record of disregard for his reporting responsibilities, that he had been reminded repeatedly of the consequences of any repeated tardiness, that the snowstorm in question was anticipated at least two days in advance, and that Blau should have made arrangements to be at a location where he could be sure to report to work. It argued that 80 percent of the work force attended work on time that day and that since he had been given so many warnings of the need for promptness, the company was within its rights in imposing a two-week suspension.

The union contended that the snowstorm was an act of God, which made the timeliness beyond Blau's control, and that he had made a serious effort to plow his driveway and would have been able to report on time if the community in which he lived had been able to plow the street in front of his home. It noted that Blau started early from his home, that he walked a considerable distance before be could flag down a vehicle, and that he was strenuously attentive to his employment responsibilities in endeavoring to report on time. It was the act of God, rather than any fault of the grievant's, that led to his being tardy. The union also argued that Blau had made a diligent effort to conform to his prompt reporting responsibilities and that the situation in this case was beyond his control. Thus, he should not have been disciplined for it.

The arbitrator noted that there were two questions to be decided in the case. The first was whether or not there were grounds for discipline. Then, if discipline was judged appropriate, the question was what penalty would be appropriate. The arbitrator noted that absenteeism and tardiness were particularly high on the date in question, that the grievant was in an area where the plowing service was less efficient than in the urban location of the company, that he had gotten up sufficiently early and plowed his driveway in order to arrive on time, and that the tardiness was not due to any failure on Blau's part, but rather was attributable to the failure of his community to plow the adjacent street.

Thus, the arbitrator held that the grievant's tardiness on the day in question was beyond his control. Even though he had full awareness of the importance of his reporting to work on time, his inability to do so was not attributable to any laxity or tardiness on his part. Because the cause of his delay was not of his doing, the arbitrator found that the grievant was not properly subject to discipline for the infraction on that date. Accordingly, his penalty was rescinded, and he was to be made whole for any lost earnings.

Discussion Question 1: Does the obligation for prompt reporting vary because of the employee's living a substantial distance from his workplace, or does it vary because of his reliance on public rather than private transportation?

The employer is not in a position to control where the grievant lives or how the grievant reports to work. The employer's concern begins at the shift's starting time at the plant location. If the employee opts to be dependent on a single alarm clock, to live at a distance far removed from the workplace, or travel by public transportation, then it is the employee's responsibility to assure that he or she is at work at the start of the shift. The employee must assume an obligation to make certain that lifestyle factors do not detract from the overriding obligation of reporting to work in a timely fashion.

Discussion Question 2: If you were preparing the case for the union, what sort of information would you have looked for?

In preparing the union's case, it would have been helpful to secure a list of those who reported to work on time and those who reported to work late. It would have been valuable to determine the number of employees who were able to attend or report to work on time who lived the same distance away as the grievant. It also would have been helpful to determine from weather reports, newspaper reports, and photographs the extent of the storm's impact on the community where the grievant lived as well as at the employer's facility. Some documentation, photograph or eyewitness, of the grievant undertaking to plow his driveway would have been an asset.

Discussion Question 3: What information would you have secured if you were preparing a case for the employer?

The employer did provide information about the percentage of employees who reported to work on time. It might have been more helpful to have information showing the employees from the grievant's community or from communities even further from the plant who were successful in getting to the plant on time, to show that there were streets open in his community, or to somehow determine whether or not Blau got as early a start as he claimed he did. If the employee had called in, for instance, claiming he would be late, the timing of that telephone call might have given some indication of whether he had started to shovel out early enough to arrive at work on time. Such evidence would be helpful to the employer to show that this was merely another case of the employee's error rather than acts of God, and that given the fact this was employee error, it would be appropriate for the employee to bear the burden of the discipline.

Discussion Question 4: Would the results have been different if the grievant was a newly hired employee new to the urban setting and unaccustomed to adhering to time limitations?

Arbitrators may be sympathetic to ethnic, neighborhood, or other group dynamics that impede an employee's reporting to work on time. One of the benefits of progressive discipline is that it provides an opportunity for an employee to learn the requirements of his or her new work environment, including that of being on time, and that it provides the opportunity for employees to reform their conduct to report to work in a timely fashion.

Assault

The workplace brings together individuals of varying backgrounds with diverse interests and attitudes. Sometimes interpersonal relations among employees flare into physical confrontations and attacks. Some of these confrontations and attacks occur between employee and supervisor. The employer is within its authority in trying to maintain tranquility in the work force and to prevent disruptive outbursts that may cause bodily harm or may interfere with the smooth operation of the enterprise. Company rules generally prohibit fights between employees and place employees on notice that they will be disciplined if they fight. Management's effectiveness in preventing altercations is dependent on the strictness of the employer in enforcing its rules against fighting. In most cases, the employer specifies that fights will result in removal, yet the threat of removal as a deterrent works only if that threat is implemented. Once the employer introduces a penalty less than termination, that becomes a precedent.

However, in cases when an employee threatens or physically engages in an altercation with a supervisor, the generally accepted rule is that the offense is so disruptive to the relationship between employer and employee and to the employer's ability to supervise the employee thereafter, that termination is usually considered an appropriate penalty on first offense. Arbitrators are less likely to provide a second chance after fights with supervisors than after fights between fellow employees.

CASE: A RACIAL CONFRONTATION

David Foltz was a black employee of ten years' seniority who had had a series of verbal exchanges with David Bonbright, a white employee of similar seniority. They frequently had exchanged epithets deriding the other's racial background, and they had been separated on more than one occasion by fellow employees and by supervisors. On the day in question, Bonbright passed Foltz's work station, brushed against it, and was told by Foltz to "keep away from my work area, honky." Bonbright tapped his finger against Foltz's chest and said, "I'll walk where I need to, just don't brush with me or you'll never walk again." Foltz pushed Bonbright away; Bonbright responded with a fist to the jaw. Foltz responded by pushing Bonbright to the floor. The two were separated, and management terminated them both for fighting on company premises.

At the arbitration hearing, the employer argued that the two were well aware of the rule against fighting. They had been warned repeatedly to avoid confrontations with each other, and they had voluntarily undertaken to provoke each other. Thus, management argued, both were responsible for the altercation and neither withdrew from the hostile situation to avoid the fight. Thus, the discharge penalty was appropriate in both cases.

The union argued that the penalty was inappropriate, that the exchange was unrelated to work performance and arose from the employees' out-of-work relationship, and that both employees be reinstated. Foltz testified that he had not initiated the incident, that he had warned Bonbright to keep away from his work area, that Bonbright had initiated physical contact by hammering at his chest, and that Foltz's response was natural to having been hit initially by Bonbright. Bonbright argued that the racial epithet from Foltz was insulting, that his pride justified his response, that he approached Foltz to warn him of the risk of further confrontation and epithets, and that it was Foltz who initiated the first blow.

The arbitrator examined the chronology and the history of the antagonistic relations between the parties and concluded that such antipathy was best handled away from the workplace. It was incumbent upon the employees to abide by the rule against such physical exchanges if the employees were to be able to keep their jobs. He noted both parties were culpable for the escalation of the conflict; that both were willing participants in the escalated conflict; that neither one sought to avoid the physical altercation; and that when both were willing participants therein, they did so in full awareness of the rules and of the risks they ran by engaging in fighting in the shop. Accordingly, the arbitrator held that both were equally culpable of breaking the rule, that they were properly subject to discipline, and that the disciplinary penalty was for just cause.

Discussion Question 1: What role should the union play if the altercation is between two bargaining-unit employees?
The union is placed in a difficult position when two of its members are participants in such a conflict. In some cases, the union may request the participants to represent themselves or to secure their own counsel. In other case, the union may find itself in a position of defending one member, the victim against a fellow union member, the aggressor, which may be awkward if the aggressor claims innocence, unless the aggressor has been removed and has declined to process a grievance. The union must be mindful of its duties of fair representation of all of its bargaining-unit members and avoid placing itself in a position where it might be subject to lawsuit by representing one bargaining-unit employee against another.

Discussion Question 2: What role should the employer play in investigating and preparing cases involving fights between two employees?
The employer must be careful to investigate such altercations to determine whether or not both participants were equally culpable or whether one employee was the instigator and the other the responder. In this case, the role of racial animosity was the triggering event. The employer must ascertain whether one of the participants reacted reasonably to a challenge, to a racial slur, or to a challenge to fight. Arbitrators may not agree that mere participation in a fight is grounds for termination, but they may consider the reasonableness of an employee's response to a challenge or provocation. Arbitrators are less likely to impose termination on a victim merely because he was seen participating in an altercation.

Discussion Question 3: What behavior would an arbitrator view as necessary to avoid discipline in an altercation case?
The idealized response of an employee who is challenged to a fight by another employee would be to walk away from the employee or to respond by saying, "We can take care of this outside the plant." More likely, however, is that an employee is going to be drawn into the fight. It is reasonable for an employee to fight back, if only to ward off further blows, if the initial blows of the aggressor are likely to continue. Likewise, the arbitrator will look at the reasonableness of a physical response by an employee who is lured into an attack by provocative language or provocative action. While inducements to fight do not justify or excuse physical hostility, they may be viewed as mitigating factors explaining why an employee has acted aggressively.

Thus, arbitrators are likely to tailor the penalty to the reasonableness of an employee's action participating in a fight. The employee who is the victim and walks away is likely to be exonerated; the employee who is harrassed into a response will be treated more leniently than the employee who is the aggressor. If both employees are aggressive and escalate the conflict, then the arbitrator is more likely to impose heavy discipline on both.

CASE: THE OFF-DUTY THREAT

Supervisor Peter Harris and employee Chris Albertyne had a stormy relationship. The supervisor had sought to reduce the tension, but Albertyne remained hostile toward him. In an effort to reduce their hostility, Harris asked Albertyne to join him for a drink after work in a tavern across the street from the plant entrance. After a few drinks, Albertyne became hostile toward Harris and said that he had had enough of Harris's harrassment, that Harris was a lousy supervisor, and that if he continued to bother him, he would see to it that "Harris doesn't harrass anybody anymore," adding, "Don't forget, I know where you live."

At that point, Harris terminated the visit and left the bar. The next day, Albertyne was called into Harris's office and was issued a letter of termination for threatening the supervisor. Albertyne filed a grievance, and the case was appealed to arbitration.

At the arbitration hearing, the employer argued that Albertyne was the aggressor, that he threatened the supervisor and the supervisor's family, and that such conduct was unacceptable and justified termination on the first offense. The union argued that Albertyne was misunderstood and that he was not threatening the grievant; that he was upset at the harrassment from Harris; and that in any event, the incident occurred off company premises and after work and was not grounds for imposition of any disciplinary penalty.

The arbitrator was required to determine first whether there was a threat. He determined that the language used by Albertyne was indeed a threat; that it was intended to place the grievant in fear of violence from Albertyne; and that in so doing, Albertyne sought to place Harris in a position where he would not be able to exercise properly his managerial and supervisory authority against the grievant. The fact that the interaction occurred off the plant premises, the arbitrator reasoned, did not excuse the attack and was, indeed, sufficiently related to the workplace because it was intended to impact on Harris's performance as a supervisor. The arbitrator ruled that the grievant was guilty of having threatened the supervisor, that the threat was intended to interfere with Harris's supervisory authority over the grievant, and that the exchange having occurred off the premises and off company time was irrelevant in light of the fact that it was intended to have its impact at the workplace.

The arbitrator then ruled that such behavior was unacceptable and was destructive of Harris's supervisory role; that it could not be excused or permitted to occur again; and that because Albertyne's threat had placed Harris in fear of the threatened attack, Albertyne had placed himself in a position where he could not continue in the company's employ because of his disruption of the traditional supervisor-employee relationship. The arbitrator ruled that such a termination penalty was appropriate on a first offense in cases of threats or physical violence against a supervisor and that the grievance was to be denied.

Discussion Question 1: What investigation might the employer have undertaken in the preparation of its case?
The employer might have investigated the details of the relationship; ascertained what contact, if any, Albertyne had made with Harris's family; and tried to document any past hostility that Albertyne had demonstrated against fellow employees or other supervisors. It might have cited other cases of employees who were terminated for threats or physical attacks against supervisors and perhaps secured witnesses to the conversation at the bar in the event of a question of credibility about Harris's version of what had been said.

Discussion Question 2: What should the union have done in the preparation of its case?
The union might have sought to document through evidence or witnesses that Albertyne and Harris had had a bantering relationship and that there had been prior exchanges of a similar nature which had not been taken seriously by either party. The union might also have sought to show that Albertyne had been under the influence of alcohol at the time of his conversation with Harris, that the alleged threat was said in jest, that the grievant had a serious problem with alcohol, and that he did not know where Harris lived.

The union also could have produced evidence that Albertyne had made similar threats against other supervisors or even against Harris in the past, and that these remarks had been disregarded or not taken seriously. The union may have sought to establish that such threats were good-natured "shop talk" and had not resulted in past disciplinary action.

Discussion Question 3: Are different standards to be imposed in cases of physical violence or threats involving supervisors than in those involving fellow employees?
Arbitrators would hold that challenge to supervision and physical confrontation with management are to be taken more seriously and penalized more

heavily than exchanges and challenges among fellow employees. The rationale for such disparate treatment is that while fights between employees may disrupt production, conflicts with and challenges of management are destructive to the employee and the supervisor and place into question the authority of the supervisor. The supervisor could be placed in danger of physical attack or damage due to the legitimate exercise of his or her managerial authority.

Arbitrators therefore may be more tolerant in resolving physical disputes between combatant employees than they would be in physical disputes involving an employee and a supervisor. A threat of violence against the supervisor or his family, whether made on or off the premises, generally would be viewed as grounds for termination on first offense. It should be noted, however, that supervisors may be just as likely to be provocative, threatening, or harrassing as bargaining-unit members. So an arbitrator, in dealing with a case involving a conflict between an employee and a supervisor, will certainly entertain charges by the employee that he or she was provoked into the action or was a victim of a confrontation, threat, or epithet by the employer.

Criminal Conviction

An arbitrator's jurisdiction is confined to the parties' agreement. In questions of discipline, he or she must determine whether there was just cause for the imposition of discipline under the terms of the agreement. In the issue of termination, the arbitrator has to determine whether there was just cause for termination under the contract. In some cases, the arbitrator is confronted with matters that are of a criminal nature and which seemingly may have been resolved in a criminal-justice tribunal before the grievance is appealed to the arbitration forum.

The question remains whether the arbitrator is bound by such criminal rulings or whether the traditional just cause standards concerning the employment relationship can be applied with disregard for the judicial findings. One view is that the arbitrator is bound by the rulings of the court in the jurisdiction in which the incident occurs. The other view is that the arbitrator is not bound by such court rulings because he or she has an independent jurisdiction under the contract to determine if there was cause for an action of removal.

One school of thought makes a differentiation based on the nature of the criminal determination. Thus when an employee pleads guilty to a criminal violation, the arbitrator is bound by that admission, just as the arbitrator would be bound if that admission of guilt occurred in an earlier step of the grievance procedure. That philosophy also extends to employees who plead at the mercy of the court or nolo contendere on the theory that the employee is admitting to the facts of the case and leaving the penalty to the discretion of the court. That same view would exclude from the arbitrator's purview the decisions of a judge or jury that an employee is guilty of the same offense. The rationale used is that if the arbitrator is to be bound by the judge or jury, there is no need for him or her to rehear and redecide the case, since that determination is one by which he or she is to be bound. Some say that such evidence is admissible to help the arbitrator in making a determination. But if such is the case, there is no need for an independent determination of the arbitrator since any doubt as to the crucial final issue is, in fact, disposed of by reliance on the ruling of the judge and jury. The arbitrator's ruling would be extraneous thereto.

CASE: THEFT UNDER THE LAW; THEFT UNDER THE CONTRACT

Dan Roth was a five-year service employee working in a lumberyard. He was found by police with several sheets of plywood in his personal pickup truck. He was brought into court, charged with theft, and in a jury trial was found guilty. The employer then terminated Roth. He filed a grievance against the termination, and the case was appealed to arbitration. At the arbitration hearing, the company sought to introduce the ruling of the court and jury that the grievant was found guilty of the theft.

The union objected on the grounds that the determination of guilt by a jury was not binding on the arbitrator because it involved two different parties, the state and the grievant as defendant, rather than the company and the union. Thus, it should be excluded from the arbitrator's purview. The employer responded that the finding of theft was admissible, that the burden of proof was greater in a criminal proceeding than in an arbitration proceeding, and that the ruling of the jury should be admitted.

The arbitrator held that the finding of the jury was not admissible, that he had a jurisdiction, under the parties' collective bargaining agreement, that involved different parties and a contractual, rather than a legal, determination of just cause for termination; and that the employer had the burden of proof without reliance on the finding of the jury. The case proceeded and the arbitrator found that there had been proof of just cause for termination. The grievance was denied.

Discussion Question 1: Would the result be different if the case involved a felony and if the company rules precluded the company from hiring a person who had been convicted of a felony?
The case involving the lumberyard was, of course, in the private sector. There are employment relationships in which employees who have been found

guilty of various offenses are barred from employment, not only in the federal sector, but in companies such as security firms. In such a case, the ruling of the court would be admissible not for the evidence of the guilty finding, but for the evidence of the grievant's having a felony conviction on his record and thus barred from employment.

Discussion Question 2: Should the arbitrator have taken in the evidence of the jury's finding for whatever it may have been worth?

The employer in a termination case has the burden of proof. If the conviction by a court of law is introduced into evidence, it effectively shifts the burden of proof to the employee or union to defend or explain the conviction. Even in cases in which the arbitrator admits such evidence, as in the case of a pleading of guilt or pleading of nolo contendere, it may be necessary for the union to explain why a certain plea was made. Again, the burden of proof has been shifted. But the ultimate burden of proving just cause for termination must rest on the employer and must be based on evidence garnered from the employment relationship, rather than based on a ruling by a court of law.

Discussion Question 3: To what extent would prior criminal convictions be admissible in an effort to impeach the testimony of the witness?

The employer would be within its rights in introducing evidence of a criminal trial in an effort to impeach the testimony of a grievant. Although the employer might be precluded from introducing evidence of a jury conviction in its direct testimony, it would be justified in introducing it in cross-examination of the witness. Thus, the question on cross-examination, "Have you ever been convicted for this offense?" would be admissible. Evidence of a prior record also might be introduced to impeach a witness in cases involving other matters in which the credibility of the witness's testimony is in doubt. The question, "Have you ever been arrested for any offense?" might be a legitimate question by the employer seeking to discredit or impeach the witness's testimony.

Falsification of Company Records

Employees are expected to be honest in completing company records, including employment applications. An employer has the right to rely on the honesty of its employees in filling out such records. In the case of routine company records, such a falsification may be viewed as theft of time, particularly if the employee is a direct beneficiary because of compensation being based on the data contained in such records. If the data in the records concern the employee's wages and those data are entered by the employee, then it is a legitimate grounds for discipline if the employee has altered such record for his or her personal financial gain. Some arbitrators make a distinction between theft of property and theft of time, but the prevalent view is that if the employee's theft of time is of his or her own making, is deliberate, and is geared to personal financial gain, then it is to be treated as theft.

A more difficult problem arises in the area of falsification of employment applications. It is reasonable to expect that employees applying for a job will place the best light on their records and credentials. Nonetheless, the employer is entitled to an honest presentation by the employee so that the employer, rather than the employee, is the selector of the information necessary to make the determination about whether that applicant will be hired. Sometimes employees are hired on the basis of falsifications or omissions in their applications. This leads the employer to believe that the employee is more qualified for the job than reality dictates. Disputes arise when the employee's falsification is discovered by the employer, who then takes action to sever the employment relationship.

The theory for the severance of the relationship is that the employment was obtained under false pretenses. The issue before the arbitrators is to determine (1) whether the falsification was deliberate, (2) whether the falsification was significant or de minimus, (3) whether, if the facts had been known, the employer would have hired the employee, and (4) whether the time period between the hiring and the discovery of the falsification was sufficient to erase in whole or in part the consequences of the falsification.

CASE: THE FALSIFIED MEDICAL HISTORY

Deborah Gold had applied for a position as a shipper five years ago. In her employment application, she was asked if she had ever suffered from any problems of the back or neck. She answered no to that question. She was hired and worked as a shipper without incident for five years until she began to experience neck pain. She went to the company physician, who diagnosed her condition as a degenerative joint disease in her upper neck, which made it impossible for her to continue to do the shipping work with its lifting component. She was told to apply for disability retirement.

While processing Gold's application for disability retirement, the employer reviewed some records from her personal physician and found that she had been treated for pain in her shoulder three years prior to her filling out her employment application. The employer reviewed the employment application and concluded that Gold had falsified it by answering no to the question of whether she had experienced any problems with her back or neck. The employer terminated Gold on the grounds of that falsification. She filed a grievance and the case was appealed to arbitration.

At the arbitration hearing, the grievant acknowledged that she had undergone extended treatment by her physician for a shoulder problem but said that she had not been aware that the problem involved her neck or back either at the time of the treatment or when she completed her employment application. She testified that it was not until she underwent her disability retirement examination that she learned that the problems might have been interrelated.

The employer argued that the grievant was aware of her prior condition; that she should have indicated the shoulder ailment in the employment application; and that even if a specific question was not asked about the shoulder, it was incumbent upon her to have asked the interviewer whether the shoulder ailment was properly reportable under neck and back disorders. The company asserted that by hiding her shoulder ailment, Gold took unto herself the determination of whether her physical condition permitted her employment and that because she secured employment that she would not have secured if she had fully answered the application question, her employment was obtained fraudulently and should therefore be rescinded.

The union took the position that the grievant had answered the question of neck and back ailments correctly, that she was innocent of any intentional wrongdoing, that she was unaware of the relationship between her shoulder ailment and the back and neck question, and that she had been a conscientious employee for five years without any difficulty before the ailments arose. It asserted that the employer had acted improperly in charging the grievant with falsification and urged her termination be overruled.

The arbitrator in this case was faced with the question of whether the grievant intentionally had deceived the employer by answering that she had no back or neck problems when she was aware that she had been treated for a related ailment in the shoulder. The determination by the arbitrator was made largely on the basis of the credibility of the grievant. The arbitrator believed that the grievant was speaking truthfully in saying that she was unaware of the relationship between the shoulder and the back and neck problem; that the shoulder problem had, in fact, dissipated by the time of the employment application; and that she had answered no to the question of ailment under back and neck because she had never suffered from any pain in the back or neck.

The arbitrator ruled that the grievant's answers to the employment application were honest; that she was not depriving the employer of information it had asked for in order to make its determination regarding Gold's qualifications for hiring; and that since she had demonstrated acceptable service for the intervening five years, there was no grounds for the employer's determination that she had falsified her employment application. Accordingly, her termination was reversed.

Discussion Question 1: What information should the union have secured in preparing for its case?
The union might have secured the full documentation of the grievant's shoulder treatment and it might have secured testimony from those who had treated her to determine whether or not she had been told that her problem involved the back and neck. The union could have secured testimony regarding the type of work Gold performed while in the company's employ to show that she was fulfilling the full responsibilities of her job without any injury to or impact on her neck, shoulders, or back.

Discussion Question 2: What issues should have been explored by the company in its presentation?
The employer might have investigated Gold's employment history to determine from company physicians whether the grievant had had evidence of any problem with the neck, back or shoulders prior to her employment with the company. The employer also could have examined the grievant's personal medical history to determine whether she had ever been told of the relationship between back, neck, and shoulder problems.

Discussion Question 3: What time period would be sufficient to overcome a falsification of employment application?
There is no fixed standard or number of years of good employment service that is adequate or sufficient to overcome any specific falsification on an employment application. In some cases, the arbitrator will say that the falsification is so deliberate that it may never be overcome, as in the case of a money truck driver who was asked if he had ever been convicted of any criminal violations while driving and who answered no, although several years later it was discovered that he had a series of criminal convictions dealing with his driving, any one of which would have kept the employer from hiring him.

In such blatant cases, the arbitrator may find that time does not cure the wrongdoing. However, in cases in which the employee is viewed to have stretched the truth in order to gain employment, the arbitrator may say that several years of a clear record and satisfactory service may overcome such falsifying of information. The standard used by the arbitrator in such cases is whether the employer has enjoyed the satisfactory service of the employee for so long that, if given the choice and the anticipation of such a clear record of performance, the employer would have accepted the employee even with the tarnished record.

Theft of Time or Money

It is widely accepted that an employee discovered to have stolen from his or her employer is to be removed for that single offense without resort to the concept of progressive discipline. The discovery of theft raises the question of whether that employee had been stealing in the past. Termination is regarded as an important signal that any theft will not be tolerated and is, in that sense, a deterrent for other employees. To reinstate an employee guilty or theft, even with a heavy disciplinary penalty, is a sign of condonation and thus would establish a standard that every employee may steal once and receive a heavy penalty before being removed. Such a weak standard is universally unacceptable, and employers, endorsed by arbitrators, have adhered to the standard that theft brings termination on first offense.

Nonetheless, there are numerous cases concerning theft that come to arbitration. One category of these cases is concerned with questions of credibility: Did the employee in fact steal what he or she is charged with stealing?

CASE: STOLEN SOAP

The company had been concerned with theft of materials from its warehouse. A security representative of the company was called in to establish an observation post where employees could be scrutinized as they left the warehouse. At around 6:00 P.M., the company's security lookout observed Max Brown exiting the warehouse, carrying a carton marked with the company's brand and describing the contents as dishwasher detergent. Brown placed the carton in the back seat of his car, returned to the plant, and brought out another carton, which he also placed in the back seat of his car. Brown got into the car and began to drive to the exit of the employee's parking lot.

The security observer radioed to a plant guard to stop the car as it went through the plant gate. However, the plant guard's radio was not working correctly. He saw the grievant come through the gate and motioned him through, although he did notice the two cartons in the back seat. Brown was thereafter terminated for theft. In the processing of the grievance, Brown denied that he had taken any product from the plant and that when he went out through the gate it was during his lunch hour and the back seat of his car was empty. The case proceeded to arbitration.

At the arbitration hearing, the security lookout testified that Brown had taken the cartons from the plant and placed them in his car. Both the lookout and the plant guard testified to having seen cartons in the back seat of the car. Brown testified that he had gone through the gate at the time and acknowledged that he had two cartons in the back seat of his car, but he claimed that they were, in fact, empty and that he had taken them out of the plant because he needed some cartons in which to pack some books because he was moving.

The employer argued that Brown had been seen taking the cartons, that the cartons were heavy and that he would have carried them together if they had been empty, instead of carrying them separately. The company noted that there were two employees who saw the cartons in the car and pointed to the fact that when confronted with the facts, Brown changed his story and acknowledged having taken the cartons. It concluded that because he admitted that he had lied about not having any cartons in the car, it must be assumed that he also was lying when he claimed that the cartons were empty.

The union testified that Brown was a long-service employee with a clean record; that he was upset by the incident and the challenge to his honesty; that he had never been in such a situation before and, therefore, initially denied having taken anything because he thought it would make him suspect if he acknowledged taking out the empty cartons; and that it was not until he was called to testify under oath that he felt constrained to tell the truth that the cartons were empty when he took them. It asserted that Brown had no intention to steal, that he had no need to steal, that he had no need for any cartons of soap, and that he was innocent. It argued that the removal of the two cartons was perfectly appropriate and in conformity with company policy permitting employees to take such cartons. Brown should be reinstated with full back pay because there had been no proof of theft, the union concluded.

The arbitrator in this case was confronted with the question of whether or not there had been theft. The arbitrator had the testimony of the lookout and the plant guard on the one hand, and the testimony of the employee on the other. The burden was on the employer to prove the theft. There was no dispute over the fact that the employee was within his rights in taking out empty cartons. The only question was his credibility: whether or not he had full cartons.

The arbitrator determined that the employer had not proven that the boxes were full. Because the employer had not stopped the vehicle to ascertain its contents, it had not met its burden of proving there was soap or anything else in the cartons. Furthermore the arbitrator found the midhearing admission by the grievant to be credible. Therefore, the grievance was sustained.

Discussion Question 1: What evidence could the union have secured to bolster its case?

The union might have secured witnesses from the plant to show that there was a uniform practice of employees' taking empty cartons, with the employer's acquiescence, from the plant or a witness to show the employee was, in fact, moving and had needed cartons to transport books. The inventories of the plant might have been used to show that there had not been any cartons of soap missing that night or that the employee worked in an area where he would not have had access to the full cartons of soap.

Discussion Question 2: What evidence might the employer have presented? The employer might have secured the testimony of supervisory witnesses who had observed the employee carrying a carton or working in an area where he would have had access to full cartons of soap. The company might have produced testimony that the employee was not in an area where scrap cartons were held or that scrap cartons were broken down and flattened routinely before being given to employees for removal. It might also have shown that the cartons in the scrap area at the time of the incident were cartons that had contained products other than the soap detergent as allegedly observed by the lookout.

Discussion Question 3: What credence should the arbitrator have given to the fact that there were two witnesses testifying to the observation on the management's side but only one on the side of the union, the witness himself?
Testimony that persuades an arbitrator is not necessarily strengthened by the fact that it is repeated by numerous witnesses. It is possible for witnesses to corroborate prior to testimony and coordinate their stories and thus provide the same testimony. The standard the arbitrator employs is whether he or she believes the testimony of the grievant or believes the testimony of the employer. An arbitrator has said, "I don't know who is telling the truth, but I do know whom I believe." The arbitrator makes credibility rulings on the basis of corroborating and circumstantial evidence in many cases. Thus, the observation of the removal of the cartons may not have been disputed. The question is whether or not their contents were known, and in that case, the arbitrator may have reasoned that the testimony that the boxes "seemed" full when they were carried out or that they were carried out separately was not as credible as the employee's statement that they were empty.

Discussion Question 4: What weight should have been given, if any, to the fact that the employee changed his testimony?
Naturally, an arbitrator would be suspicious of an employee who had changed his story, but if the union had established that the grievant was a believer very active in his church, was nervous about the accusations against him, and had a persuasive attitude of his being bound by the oath to tell the truth, then the arbitrator might find the grievant's testimony believable. But absent such ancillary evidence, an arbitrator indeed would be suspicious of an employee who changed his or her story in order to satisfy the questions of the

inquisitor. Nonetheless, even a change in a grievant's account of what happened does not constitute proof that there was a theft of product.

Discussion Question 5: Did not the burden-of-proof concept in this case permit the employee to get away with probable or possible theft?
Unions take the position that the standard of proof in theft cases is guilt beyond a reasonable doubt, as in criminal cases. Employers take the view that there is a less stringent standard of proof. The preponderance of arbitrators take the view that this is not a criminal matter: there is no incarceration involved and there is no duty of proof beyond a reasonable doubt. Nonetheless, the employer does have the burden of proof, proving to the satisfaction of the arbitrator that there has been a theft.

Arbitrators tend to take the position that if an employee indeed is guilty of theft, there is less harm done by permitting him or her to get away with it once and have the employee learn a lesson from the experience than is done by terminating an employee who is innocent. Loss of employment for theft is serious, and this offense on the employee's record is likely to haunt the employee whenever he or she seeks a job. Although termination is the capital punishment of industrial relations, the standard of proof generally is accepted to be the preponderance of evidence, or more accurately what is needed to persuade the arbitrator.

The second category of theft cases that concerns arbitrators involves determining what is theft: Had the employee taken or benefited from taking something? Is theft of time to be equated with theft of property? Is an employee who alters his or her time card to show that he or she worked through lunch and should be paid for that time guilty of theft?

There is little question that falsification of time cards in order to receive wages for time *not* worked is as much a personal windfall to the employee as stealing and then selling the company's product. Nevertheless, arbitrators view theft of time as something different from theft of property and do not consistently apply the rule of termination on first offense as they would for theft of property.

Perhaps more difficult to trace but related to falsification of time cards is alteration of production records. In such cases, the motive for the falsification may be in determining guilt. If it is to cover poor performance or to establish falsely a good work record, the falsification is quite different than if it is to pad the paycheck. If compensation is based on piece rate, a record entry greater than actual output for purposes of obtaining higher compensation could be compared with the falsification of time cards by an hourly paid employee. In both cases, the employee is falsely seeking compensation beyond his or her entitlement. Is that theft? Here, too, there may be credibility questions. Did the employee make the false entry? Was it done inadvertently or intentionally? Was it done to profit from the falsified entry?

Somewhat less direct but still intended to benefit the employee is falsification of an overtime priority list, with the employee placed in a higher priority position. Such falsification doesn't entitle an employee to a windfall but to an out-of-order chance to perform overtime work and hence to receive additional payment. In such a case, the falsification would not likely be considered theft of time or money.

A third category of theft cases focuses on the value of the items taken. Does the rule of termination for theft apply to anything taken, regardless of value? Does the securing of items from a scrap pile constitute theft? Cardboard in a scrap pile may lack economic value, but what about scrap copper in a tube plant or gold dust in a dental laboratory? Most arbitrators would agree that if scrap has economic value, as for salvage or resale, then it should be treated as theft. To hold otherwise would encourage the scraping of valued products in the workplace, permitting employees to take with impunity the material they had earlier placed in scrap bins.

A more troublesome issue arises in the taking of items with minimal or no monetary value. What about company pencils or a ballpoint pen or a few nails to avoid a long trip to a hardware store? Certainly if the act of taking something belonging to the employer constitutes theft, then it should make no difference whether or not the commodity has economic or resale value. Yet no one wants to terminate an employee with years of loyal service because he or she took a carton, a company pen, scrap paper, or a single bar of soap from the employer. The problem arises in trying to draw the line between de minimis theft and "real" theft. If taking one or two pens is de minimis theft, what is taking a box of twelve pens or even a carton of twelve boxes of pens?

Likewise, should a more lenient treatment be accorded to an employee with long service and a clear record? Does that create a balance, with long service justifying theft of greater value than short-term service?

CASE: STORED CASH

A passenger at an airline ticket counter handed ticket agent Doris Hamel an envelope and said, "I just found this here." Hamel opened it and discovered ten twenty-dollar bills. She said "I'll hold them in case the owner comes back." "If he doesn't," said the passenger, "the money should be mine." Hamel agreed and put the money in an envelope with the following note to the station manager: "This $2,000 was discovered at counter 7 at 3:45 P.M. on April 23 by the following passenger:" It then listed the name, address, and telephone number of the passenger and was signed by Doris Hamel.

Hamel placed the packet in her money box, which she used to store cash and ticket stock and which was locked in the company safe when she was not at work. Both the company and Hamel had keys to the box, which Hamel locked. About two months later company auditors discovered the $2,000 and advised labor relations. Hamel was terminated for theft, and thereafter appealed to arbitration. Company rules specified that any items of value found by employees should be turned over to the station manager.

The company contended that the removal was for just cause. It claimed that grievant kept the money in her money box, which was within her possession, and that she violated the rule against personal retention of found items of value.

The union contended that the grievant was innocent of theft. It stated that Hamel was holding the money for the individual who lost it or the passenger who found it, that she did not tell anyone else she had found the money for fear that someone would claim falsely that he or she was the person who left it there, and that she did not hand it over to the station manager because *she* had not found it and because she felt the passenger who did find it was entitled to it. The union concluded that because the company had access to the money box, it was within the employer's control and that there had been no theft.

The arbitrator found that there had been no theft, that the employee had the opportunity to take the money herself or to have someone claim he or she had been the original owner, and that having left the envelope in her money box for so long, she lacked intent to steal it. The arbitrator also found however, that the grievant had failed in her obligation to report the discovery of the money to her supervisor, that her fear that "word would get out" if she told about the money did not override her obligation to comply with the company rule on found items, and that she was properly subject to discipline for her violation of the reporting rule, although not for any theft. The arbitrator reduced the termination to a letter of warning, based on the grievant's otherwise clear record.

Discussion Question 1: If you were the union, what else would you have done in this case?
The union might have brought the passenger who found the money to testify and bolster the grievant's testimony of his claim for the money. It could have shown that the grievant was unaware of the rule or that her training had omitted reference to such handing over of found items.

Discussion Question 2: What could the employer have done to bolster its case?
The employer could have shown that the grievant was specifically told during training to turn over found money. In trying to prove intent to steal, the

company might have reexplored Hamel's prior employment to discover if there was any evidence of related activity, such as theft or falsification of records, in an effort to impeach her credibility. The employer also could have contacted the passenger to determine if he had put in a claim to redeem the money.

Discussion Question 3: Is the operable standard stealing or intent to steal?
Most arbitrators would agree that exclusive possession of the property, unlike the shared control in this case, creates a stronger impression that the grievant is acting improperly. Thus, if the grievant in this case had exclusive control and access to the money box or if the money was locked in her locker or kept in her pocketbook, she would more likely have been found guilty of theft. But if theft were involved, there is always the chance that the item would not have been removed from the premises for the grievant's use. Employers who wait until the employee actually removes the stolen property from the premises or who intercept it at the company gate generally have a stronger case in proving theft because they thus foreclose any claim by grievants that they were holding the materials in the normal course of their duties with intent to return them or to deliver them to the proper in-plant destination.

Incompetence and Poor Workmanship

Corrective discipline may have its greatest impact in the area of correcting poor workmanship. When the employer hires a new employee, it generally is not assured of the success of that employee in the workplace. It may hope and expect that the employee will be a contributing worker, that the employee will justify the hiring and the compensation paid, and that the employee will be a productive contributor to the enterprise. But that expectation is not always borne out. The employer is often placed in the position where it is necessary to stimulate the employee into improved workmanship. Many employees will respond positively merely from a supervisor's urging that the employee become more productive, efficient, or careful. Nonetheless, some employees fail to respond to simple urgings. It is for these employees that corrective discipline becomes an important tool in the endeavor to encourage them to conform to their employment responsibilities.

Through the steps of oral warning, written warning, a three-day suspension, a week or two suspension, and ultimately termination, the employer is able to chart for the employee a clear indication of the consequences of the employee's failure to correct performances or behavior so that he or she is no longer guilty of poor workmanship. If the employee responds to the early proddings of that corrective discipline by adaptation to the needs of the employer, that employee will avoid the heavier penalties and the increasing risk of termination.

If the employee fails to respond to the early warnings and is subjected to disciplinary suspensions, then he or she is made aware of the ever-increasing pressures to reform behavior to avoid the ultimate penalty of termination. In the final analysis, either the employee is able to adapt behavior to the acceptable standards of the employer, thus saving the job, or the employee demonstrates by failure to respond to corrective discipline that he or she is incapable of handling the requirements of the job and thus is no longer suited for employment by the enterprise. The ultimate decision is based on whether the employee will improve or the employer will remove.

In cases of incompetence or poor workmanship that come before the arbitrator, the question usually is confined to whether or not the employer's action was taken for just cause based on the evidence available at the time it took the disciplinary action. The union may argue that the employer failed to place the employee in a position suitable to the employee's experience and background. The union also may argue that the employer acted improperly in denying the grievant a suitable or reasonable period to acclimate to the new job. The union may further argue that the employee, although unsuited to the position, could very easily handle another position or that the employee should be given additional training to assure confidence in the position to which assigned.

In assessing whether the employer's action was taken for just cause, the arbitrator is bound by the terms of the parties' agreement, including specifically negotiated language on job assignment, training period, break-in period, and the like. Unless there are certain contractual guarantees of the right of the employee to spend time in learning the position, the arbitrator will more likely turn to the language of the management-rights clause, which in most cases grants to the employer the right to hire and to assign employees. Thus, in assessing whether the employer's disciplinary action was for just cause, the arbitrator may find that the contract grants the ultimate authority to the employer. The arbitrator must determine whether or not the employer acted within its managerial authority or acted arbitrarily or capriciously in expecting a certain level of competence or production from employees.

The union may request that the employee be assigned elsewhere or be placed in a position under a different supervisor. Unless there is contractual authorization for making such changes, the arbitrator will usually find that he or she is bound by the employer's authority to assign employees and that since such right of assignment is reserved to the employer except for time for break-in or learning periods, it would be beyond the arbitrator's jurisdiction to mandate such actions. If, in fact, the contract grants such determinations to the employer, then the arbitrator may find that the employee has failed to meet the requirements of the job and is suited for discipline.

CASE: PENALTY BASED ON COMPANY COSTS

Max Seymour was hired by the company as a machinist after ten years of prior experience in a similar enterprise. After he had worked for the company for approximately two years, he was promoted to the position of lead machinist. According to the parties' agreement, an employee who is promoted to a higher job shall be given thirty days in which to demonstrate his ability to handle it. During this time, the employee also is free to reject the higher-paying job and return to his former position.

The evidence in this case showed that the grievant completed the thirty-day break-in period and assumed the position of lead machinist. Two weeks later, the grievant was working on a lathe when he dropped a heavy piece of metal on the electronic control box and caused $4,000 damage to the machine and rendered it inoperable for two weeks. The employer was forced to contract out the work during that period at an additional cost of approximately $8,000.

Management imposed a two-week suspension on Seymour, his first disciplinary penalty. In the letter of suspension, the employer advised the grievant that the penalty was particularly heavy because of the cost of the damage to the employer. The grievant acknowledged having caused the damage but challenged the penalty, and the case was appealed to arbitration.

The company argued that the damage done to the lathe was due to the grievant's carelessness, that he had been given specific training in how to carry objects around the lathe to avoid the risk of damage to the electronic controls, and that he was aware of the consequence of damage to those controls and of the employer's inability to rely up the lathe if any damage occured. It asserted that Seymour had voluntarily undertaken the promotion and training program and that his acceptance included the related responsibilities.

The union argued that the grievant was improperly disciplined. According to the union, the work in question was extremely delicate and something that the grievant had not been adequately trained to perform. Therefore, he should either be given additional training on how to work around the electronic controls, he should be given the option of moving into a job more suited to his level of skills, or the arbitrator should hold that the accident was unavoidable and that the imposition of discipline inappropriate. It also asserted that any penalty based on the cost of damage was inconsistent with labor-relations practice and that the penalty for this first offense should be reduced to a letter of warning.

The arbitrator held that the grievant had sought the promotion to the position he was serving, that he had been given thirty days in which to undergo the training or to remove himself from the higher position if he felt unqualified, and that when he failed to take such action, the employer was within its authority in determining that he was qualified and required to live up to the responsibilities of that higher position. The arbitrator reasoned that when the accident occurred, it was something that was within the grievant's control and that he could have avoided if he had relied on his training.

The arbitrator concluded that since the grievant was in a position for which he had bid and for which he had completed the requisite break-in period without protest, there was no grounds for granting either a move to another position or additional time for more training. The arbitrator found that there was grounds for the imposition of discipline, but that the discipline should have been based on a first offense of poor workmanship rather than on the cost of the damage to the employer.

He reasoned that to base the discipline on the employer's economic loss would mean that inexpensive wrongdoings or accidents would be tolerated with minimal penalty because of the minimal loss to the employer, while an employee with but one incident of poor workmanship on expensive equipment would be deprived of the benefits of progressive discipline. Accordingly, the arbitrator ruled that the penalty was to be reduced to a written warning and that the employee was to be made whole for the earnings lost by having to serve the disciplinary layoff period.

Disscussion Question 1: What position might the union have taken in this case?

The union might have searched through company records to learn of cases in which employees had been permitted to obtain extra training. It also might have sought information on employees who were permitted to move into other positions when they proved incapable of handling positions into which thay had been promoted, or it might have provided information on the relationship between disciplinary penalty and cost of damage.It also might have challenged the cost-expenditure estimates provided by the employer, but those variations would not have been significant in light of the arbitrator's decision in this case.

Discussion Question 2: What position might the company have taken?

The company could have provided evidence of how it had handled similar cases in the past. It might have cited prior negotiating history if the union had sought language for retraining or an opportunity to move into other positions. It might have offered testimony that the grievant had been warned specifically against the error he had committed in this case.

Discussion Question 3: Should the amount of damage borne by an employer as a result of an employee's poor workmanship be excluded from the consideration of the penalty in a case such as this?
The theory of progressive discipline is based on increasing penalties because of a series of infractions. To base the penalty on the economic loss to the employer would, in effect, return to the time when employees were readily terminated for accidental damage to company operations or equipment without any of the benefits of progressive discipline. It is particularly true in an era of increasingly costly equipment and machinery that adherence to that precept would cripple the concept of progressive discipline. Consistency, furthermore, would dictate that the employee responsible for poor workmanship that does not cost the employer anything should be free of any discipline because of the absence of financial impact on the employer. Thus, progressive discipline must be based on repeated incidents, and the cost thereof should not be the controlling factor.

Discussion Question 4: Isn't it unfair to employees who may be in positions beyond their competence to deny them the opportunity to pull out of those positions if they mishandle them, as in this case?
Employees have the option of bidding for positions of higher compensation and greater responsibility. They are selected on the basis of their desire to move into higher positions on a permanent basis. The break-in period provides employees with an opportunity for determining whether they are qualified or whether they wish to withdraw from the new position. But once that period has passed, the employee is to be considered responsible for competent workmanship at that higher level. The end of a break-in period may trigger the assignment of other employees into newly vacated positions. To allow an employee to move back into a position previously held after that thirty-day period would cause substantial disruption throughout the network of jobs already filled as a consequence of the upward move.

Furthermore, the employee has chosen to be in a position where he or she is committed to a certain level of job performance and has recognized the possibility of discipline for any inability to conform to that higher standard of job performance. The employee must bear the consequences of the job expectancy in the higher position. In this case, the employee failed to meet that requirement. An imposition of progressive discipline, used to its best advantage, would demonstrate to the employee that he had the ability to continue in the job, provided he was more careful and conformed to his training.

If employees feel they are inadequately trained or improperly placed, their recourse is to initiate a move for additional training or change of position through the contractual procedures involving requests to management. But when employees fail to take such action and employers initiate action based on poor workmanship or poor performance, then employees must bear the consequences of such discipline. The standard becomes whether there was just cause for discipline, not whether an employee was properly placed in a position.

Alcoholism and Drugs

The use of alcohol and drugs among employees in recent years has been of increasing concern to employers and to the unions representing the employees. The performance of employees under the influence of alcohol and drugs creates risks to both the user and fellow employees. It also imposes on the employer substantial risks of damage to equipment and product, interruptions and breakdowns of output, and potential problems in imposing discipline and discharge for violations of company rules against consumption of alcohol and drugs. The use of alcohol and drugs has become an insidious and increasingly pervasive problem in the workplace.

Employers naturally are concerned with maintaining the workplace free from the influence of alcohol and drugs. The traditional standards of the employer's having control over the workplace and over performance of employees when they are at the workplace is presumed to extend to the employer's right to protect itself against alcohol and drugs by excluding them from that workplace.

Thus, it has been held reasonable for an employer to enact rules that prohibit the possession of alcohol or drugs in the workplace. If an employer has the authority to bar the importation of alcohol and drugs into the workplace, then it would follow that the employer also has the right to regulate, control, or ban alcohol or drugs consumed by the employee prior to his or her entrance into the workplace if that prior consumption would result in a continuing influence of alcohol or drugs once the employee enters the workplace. Indeed, there has been stronger self-interest in disciplining employees who report to work under the influence of alcohol than there has been regulating the bringing of alcohol onto the premises. The possession and nonconsumption of alcohol on the premises does not of itself interfere with the employee's goals of work performance or job productivity. Prior consumption of alcohol and an employee's being under the influence thereof once at work clearly does.

Employers have sought protection against these dangers by disciplining employees who violate the rules against possession, use, and being under the influence of alcohol at work. As in other improprieties employees can expect escalated penalties for repeated violations of the rules until ultimately the employees are terminated.

Therefore, the employer has a stake in assuring that employees who come to work do so free of the influence of alcohol and drugs as well as in assuring that alcohol and drugs are not brought onto the premises for possible consumption while at work. It is consistent with that stake for the employer to establish rules concerning the possession and work under the influence of alcohol and drugs.

The conventional wisdom before the 1980s had been that the employer had the right to regulate the conduct of its employees while on the premises and that employees have the responsibility for sufficient control over themselves. They would therefore either refrain from engaging in prohibited conduct or face the consequences of discipline for violating rules concerning alcohol consumption. Over a period of time, the evidence gathered in the medical and psychiatric community established and ultimately persuaded employers that alcoholism is a disease; that consumption and reliance on alcohol even off the premises might be beyond the control of employees; and that disciplinary penalties imposed on employees for coming to work under the influence of alcohol constitute the imposition of discipline for a condition that might be beyond the employee's control.

The more recent and increasingly prevalent standard is to consider alcoholism as a disease and to encourage employees to partake in programs geared to overcoming their dependence on alcohol. In this way, the employer is able to protect the investment of time and effort in the training of employees and place itself in a position where it is able to return the employees to productive performance for its own benefit, for the benefit of the employee and his or her family, and for the benefit of society at large.

Treatment of alcholism as a disease has other benefits to the employer as well. By encouraging employees who are victims of alcoholism to come forward and to enlist in programs of self-help, the employer may be relieved of the policing operation necessary to protect itself against violation of company rules against alcoholism because employees voluntarily identify themselves as willing participants in such programs. Such volunteerism, of course, works only when there is no penalty attached to such volunteering. Discipline for violation of the rules against drug or alcohol possession or use is imposed on those who refuse to take advantage of the available programs of employee assistance or fail to live up to their requirements. Encouragement of employees to identify their problems and to partake in programs of rehabilitation and alcohol control serves notice to other employees that the hiding of their condition will justify the imposition of discipline if they are engaged in that rule violation in this area.

Thus, the punishment ultimately is based not on a violation of the rule as much as on the employee's failure to come forward for treatment as a means of avoiding a punishable violation. Employees who fail to enter into or adhere to programs for rehabilitation thus run a higher risk of discipline up to termination for incidences of violation. The evolution of treatment for alcohol abuse has provided a valued precedent in dealing with what has become an even more invasive problem, the treatment of drug use and drug abuse.

Alcohol is a legal substance, and the possession and use of alcohol is not a criminal offense. However, a different situation occurs when dealing with drug possession, use and abuse. Drug abuse has two added dimensions. One is the illegality of possession and use of drugs; the second is the illegality of the distribution of such prohibited substances. In terms of concern for employee productivity, health, welfare, safety, and benefits, many employers have realized that programs of alcohol rehabilitation are equally applicable to drug consumption.

The illegality of drug possession and use is a matter for government regulation. The employer's prime concern is not law enforcement, but rather assuring that employees are productive and the work place free of the adverse impact of such substances. But in the area of the selling of drugs, the issue becomes more complex. The workplace has become an important marketplace for illegal drugs because it provides the intimacy, privacy, and reliability necessary for sales to be transacted. Use of the job site as marketplace raises the likelihood that the purchased commodities will be used at the workplace and thus creates additional problems of regulation and consumption for the employer.

Drug dealing is thus a threat not only to the employer, but to the work force as a whole. Employers tend to hold that the dealing or distribution of drugs is an offense of such a serious nature that it rises to the list of offenses that are punishable by termination on first offense. Arbitrators frequently will endorse that view on the theory that the impropriety of such dealing is self-evident and that employees who are drug dealers should be well aware in advance of the risk in engaging in such prohibited conduct. The employer who imposes standards of corrective discipline rather than termination for such conduct runs the risk of facing repetition of such violations. In the light of the inability to ascertain whether or not a suspect has been selling drugs to employees in the past, it would be inappropriate and too great a risk to allow the employee to return for the prospects of future sales. In addition, a standard of corrective discipline would place all employees on notice that they may sell drugs at least once without fear of job loss. Thus, the employer's effort to eliminate the selling of drugs on company premises is best facilitated by a clear notice that employees who deal in drugs on company time or premises will be terminated on first offense.

Any program for disciplining employees for being under the influence of alcohol or drugs naturally involves the questions of proof of such influence. In the case of alcoholism, the initial standards of proof had been observation by supervisors of (1) slurred speech, (2) blood-shot eyes, (3) a staggering walk, and (4) other physical observations of the employee's conduct. Such charges traditionally were responded to by employee denials of such aberrational behavior. When cases came to arbitration, the arbitrator frequently was confronted with questions of credibility regarding the grievant's actions on a particular day.

Both unions and management recognized the need for more objective proof. On the part of the employees, it was important to seek objective standards to prove innocence; from the employer's perspective, it was equally important to have objective standards to prove culpability. Increasingly, the parties have resorted to such objective standards as Breathalyzer tests and blood-alcohol tests. Such objective standards, while still subject to challenge, provide a credible measure of the extent of the presence of alcohol within the employee's system. Such evidence also provides a timely documentation of the objective standards that subsequently may be introduced in evidence, with arguments based on the test's reliability, accuracy, timing, and conclusions.

The application of those standards to the area of controlled substances creates a greater problem. The standard signs of alcohol consumption may not be present in cases of illegal drug consumption. And absent such external manifestations, the proof of an employee's working under the influence of a controlled substance may necessitate invasive procedures and testing. The problems are compounded by the illegality and criminality involved in such drug use and possession. In addition, the influence of drugs in one's system is of far longer duration than the influence of alcohol. An employee who has been a consumer of drugs may have the evidence of such consumption within his or her system for a period of days, weeks, or even months. The retention of such evidence also brings into question the impact of the drugs on the employee's work performance.

Some employers have sought to introduce random drug testing as a means of deterring employees from drug use, but the risks of bias or favoritsm in selection of testees raises the risk of challenge to such efforts. More effective and acceptable is an objective standard preferably one developed with the cooperation of the union, for mandatary testing.

Companies and unions are still struggling to establish a fair, objective standard for drug testing, protecting employees while at the same time assuring that the employer is able to operate with employees whose lifestyles do not adversely place the company or the employees at risk.

CASE: THE REFUSED TEST OF ALCOHOLISM

Stanley Oakun had experienced a long period of problems with alcohol. In the course of his employment, he had been warned about reporting to work under the influence of alcohol. He had been referred to programs for rehabilitation and had been considered to be free of the influence of alcohol for the past two years. During that time, he was required to attend routine meetings of the employee-assistance program. The dispute in this case arose on a day when Oakun's supervisor observed the grievant walking down the factory aisle with an unsteady gait. He asked Oakun if he was feeling well. Oakun replied in a slurred voice that there was nothing wrong with him. The supervisor asked Oakun if he had been drinking. Oakun replied that he had not. The supervisor ordered Oakun to report to the labor-relations office. When Oakun arrived there, the director of labor relations requested Oakun accompany him to the clinic for a blood-alcohol test. Oakun refused, saying he was not under the influence of alcohol and that there was no need for such a test. The supervisor advised Oakun that he was ordering him to take the test, and Oakun continued to refuse. Thereafter Oakun was sent home and two days later received a notice of termination. Oakun filed a grievance over the termination notice, and the case was appealed to arbitration.

At the arbitration hearing, the employer argued that there was reasonable grounds from the observation of supervisors to conclude that Oakun was under the influence of alcohol; that it was within its authority to request that Oakun take a blood-alcohol test; and that when he declined that request, it was within its authority to order him to take such tests. The company asserted that such testing is the most objective method of determining whether or not an employee has alcohol in his or her system and that the employer is within its authority in ascertaining whether there is alcohol abuse so that it may ask an employee to undergo treatment or at least to go home so that the employee does not create a risk to himself, to fellow employees, or to company equipment.

In the case of Oakun, the company continued, the grievant had a demonstrated history of difficulty with alcohol, and although the employee had undergone extensive treatment and allegedly had control over his alcoholism, the evidence was clear that he had, on this occasion at least, consumed alcohol in violation of his prior promises to avoid alcohol. Given the grievant's record and his failure to abide by the procedures of the company, the employer felt it was within its rights in terminating him.

The union took the position that Oakun's record showed that he had benefited from corrective discipline; that he had undergone the requisite programs of rehabilitation; and that he had shown the employer that for a period of over two years, he had established a record devoid of any charges of alcohol consumption. It asserted that an employee with such a clear record for such a long time was entitled to the benefit of the doubt. The union took the position that Oakun was not operating under the influence of alcohol on the day in question; that he was the victim of a concerted effort by the employer to remove him; that he was within his constitutional rights in refusing to undergo such an invasive procedure as the blood-alchohol test;

and that, in any event, the evidence of such tests often was subject to challenges to reliability. It asserted that the employer had not met its burden of proving that Oakun was under the influence of alcohol and that any discipline imposed on him was imposed for unjust cause. It urged the grievance be sustained.

In her opinion, the arbitrator held that the threshold question was to determine whether the grievant was obliged to take the blood-alcohol test. The arbitrator reasoned that there was reasonable grounds for the employer to conclude on the basis of the supervisor's testimony that the grievant might have been under the influence of alcohol; that it was within its authority in requesting the grievant to take such a test as long as, in this case, the test was a routine device used by the employer to ascertain the presence of alcohol; and that whether that recourse was couched in terms of a request or an order, the employee was well aware of the risk in failing to take the test. The arbitrator reasoned that there was no imminent danger to the health or safety of the grievant had he agreed to take the test and that since there was no danger to his health and safety, he was obligated to take the test on the traditional standards of obey now and file a grievance later.

The arbitrator considered the grievant's claim that he had a constitutional protection against such an invasive procedure, but asserted that the proper forum for testing the constitutionality of his refusal was within a court of law, rather than in the arbitration forum. The arbitration forum was concerned with the relationship between employer and employee as defined by the collective bargaining agreement, and the jurisdiction of the arbitrator covered only that agreement and not any questions concerning constitutional rights and privileges.

The arbitrator found that the employee acted improperly in refusing to take the blood-alcohol test. She next dealt with the question of whether that refusal justified the imposition of the removal penalty. The arbitrator noted that the grievant had a history of difficulty with alcohol, that he had undergone treatment and was alert to the requirements of adhering to the employee-assistance program and abstention from alcohol, and that he had been successful in adhering to that regimen for an extended period of time.

Nonetheless, the arbitrator continued, that was not proof of the grievant's innocence on the day in question. It was within the employer's authority to challenge the grievant's behavior, particularly in light of his behavior that day and his prior relationship with alcohol, and it was likewise proper for the employer to come to the conclusion, on the basis of the evidence presented by its supervisors, that the grievant was under the influence of alcohol on the day in question. At that point, the arbitrator continued, the employer was within its authority to impose discipline on the employee. If the employer had the right to impose an escalated penalty of discipline on the employee for being under the influence of alcohol on the basis of the evidence of its supervisors, it certainly did not surrender that right when it offered the opportunity for objective verification of whether there was alcohol in the grievant's blood system.

Based on the grievant's refusal to comply with a reasonable order to take the blood-alcohol test and based on the evidence of the supervisors who observed the grievant, it was appropriate for discipline to be imposed. In light of the grievant's record and his failure to conform to the dictates of maintaining himself free of alcohol, the arbitrator found that there was just cause for the grievant's removal.

Discussion Question 1: What issues might have been raised by the union?
The union might have emphasized the arbitrariness of a request for the employee to undergo a blood-alcohol test on the grounds that such a test was an improperly random test, rather than a uniform test applied to all employees. It could have argued that such tests are not infallible and cited evidence to show the extent to which there had been problems with such tests either in their administration, in the chain of custody of the sample when it was sent to the laboratory, or in the accuracy of the laboratory's testing. If the grievant had been of the appropriate religion, the union might have argued that such a test violated the employee's religious rights.

The union might have taken the position that the grievant's two-year period of freedom from discipline for alcoholism was proof that the grievant had not been under the influence of alcohol during that period, because the burden would have been on the employer to prove that the grievant was violating the mandate against any continued use of alcohol that would impact on his job performance. Finally, the union might have presented evidence to show that after the incident in question, the grievant had undergone further rehabilitation, and that even if he had been guilty on the date in question, he was thereafter alcohol-free and thus entitled to being given another chance.

Discussion Question 2: What might the company have presented?
The company could have produced witnesses to testify about the grievant's prior lapses, if any, and about the accuracy of the blood-alcohol tests. The company might also have introduced into evidence pertinent legal or arbitral decisions endorsing the arbitrator's actions in declining to decide constitutional challenges raised by grievants.

Discussion Question 3: What if the grievant had appeared at the facility appearing sober but with a beer bottle in his hand?
If the employers rules prohibited the bringing of alcoholic beverages onto the facility premises, then the mere importation of the bottle of beer would be a violation of the rules. If the bottle was sealed, and the employee claimed

he had brought it because of a party he was going to directly after work, there might be a question of whether the bottle was being brought in for consumption or shortage. The employer would have had the right to suspect the bottle was being brought in for on-the-premises consumption, and the burden might have shifted to the employee to prove he had a different intent. Knowing the rule, it would have been appropriate for the employee to have forestalled any doubt or question by checking the beer with the watchman or by at least advising supervision that the beer was not there to violate the company rules.

A different question might arise if the bottle was empty; the employee claiming he picked it up outside to collect the five-cent deposit. In that case there would have been no violation of the prohibition against alcoholic beverages on the premises, but if the facility was one where customers were present, the mere possession of the bottle might have given an impression contrary to the image the employer sought. Only if there was a notice to avoid such appearances would discipline be in order.

Discussion Question 4: Would evidence that the employee entered an alcohol rehabilitation clinic after a termination for repeated drinking on the job influence the arbitrator on this issue of reinstatement?
The issue before the arbitrator is usually whether there was just cause for the termination at the time it was imposed. After the fact, evidence of rehabilitation would not alter the judgement of the employer's propriety in terminating the employee. To reinstate an employee whose termination was justified because there had been an after-the-fact rehabilitation would in fact create an additional level of discipline. Alcoholics could then look forward to termination coupled with entry into a clinic as the ticket to reinstatement. Such a message would be grasped by alcoholics to the detriment of company/employee assistance programs. Evidence of rehabilitation might however be valuable in cases where the termination was premature, and as an element in determining any remedy that might be due.

Insubordination

The workplace is not a democratic institution. The employer is in authority and has the right to manage, to make assignments, to hire, to lay off, to discipline, to determine the means and standards of production, and to otherwise establish policies for its work force to follow in fulfilling the production goals of the employer. The employee should be free to challenge an order that he or she deems unreasonable at the time it is issued. Such discussions are an acceptable vehicle for exchange of ideas and an opportunity to persuade the supervisor to recant on a particular order. But if the employee is unsuccessful in the effort to persuade a foreman or supervisor to alter an order, the employer retains the right to insist on that order being followed, and the employee has the obligation to follow that order. The parties' negotiated grievance and arbitration system provides the vehicle for subsequent challenge to an order and the facility for establishing a remedy. Thus, the employer has the right to impose discipline on employees who fail to conform to its instructions and orders. The imposition of such discipline is to punish the employee who has been insubordinate, with the discipline viewed as corrective rather than punitive. But discipline for insubordination also serves as a deterrent to other employees.

The one exception to the rule of obey now and grieve later is in the area of compliance with orders that may cause an imminent danger to an employee's health and safety. Thus, an employee ordered to climb a ladder that is in disrepair and that has been a site of prior accidents is correct in declining that order on the grounds that it is a potential cause of injury. Although the employee may be disciplined for such refusal, when cases of that nature are appealed to arbitration, the arbitrator will set as the standard for determining the reasonableness of the order whether, if followed, it would have placed the employee in an unreasonable risk of imminent danger to life or limb.

CASE: A TRIP AGAINST ORDERS

Ken Ratzen was a schoolteacher and was married to Judy Ratzen, a research scientist. Judy was invited to present a paper at an international conference in Paris during the first week of November. Ken asked his principal if he could have that week off to accompany his wife to the conference. The principal checked with the superintendent, and advised Ken that his request was denied. Ken made arrangements with his fellow teachers to cover his classes during the week in question and advised his principal of the arrangements. He told the principal that he would take the once-in-a-lifetime opportunity of going to Europe with his wife. The principal warned him that he was doing so contrary to orders, but Ken did leave during the week in question. On his return from Europe, he was given a two-week disciplinary suspension. He filed a grievance and appealed to arbitration.

The employer argued that because Ratzen's contract required him to teach a certain schedule with adequate time off, he was required to teach on the days in question; that he requested and was denied opportunity for leave; and that he took the time off to accompany his wife contrary to explicit orders. It asserted the grievant's having arranged for coverage of his classes did not detract from the insubordination in directly contradicting an order of management to remain at school during the week in question and that the discipline was justified.

The union argues that Ratzen had a responsibility to accompany his wife to a foreign country, that there were security reasons for his doing so to protect his spouse, that he had given reasonable notice to the employer of his intent to be in Europe and had made arrangements with other teachers to cover his classes, and that there was no interruption of his teaching responsibilities during his absence. The union argued that the employer's denial of permission to join the trip to Europe was unreasonable, arbitrary, and capricious, and that even if the employer's order had been reasonable, the penalty imposed for his absence was excessive. Accordingly, it urged the grievance be sustained.

The arbitrator reasoned that Ratzen was obligated to attend to his classes during the first week of November, that he was within his authority in requesting a week of leave to join his wife on the trip to Europe, and that the employer was within its authority in declining that request. The arbitrator found that there was no threat or danger to the health and safety of the grievant or his wife to justify Ratzen's action in taking the week off. His having secured coverage for his classes did not excuse the grievant's action in contradicting the employer's order. The arbitrator found that the grievant had been insubordinate and that the absence of one week was deserving of a disciplinary penalty.

In dealing with the severity of the discipline, the arbitrator noted that this was the grievant's first incident of insubordination and that although he should have been deprived of a week's compensation for the period of time he was absent from his responsibilities, the two-week suspension was an excessive penalty. The arbitrator ruled that Ratzen was entitled to reimbursement for the second week of denied compensation and ordered that his record reflect that he had been warned of the necessity of conforming to orders of supervision.

Discussion Question 1: What arguments could the employer have made?
The employer might have presented evidence to show that there was no safety risk in the wife's trip to Europe. It also might have shown that it had a practice of never having granted such leaves, that the grievant's teaching skills were unique and could not have been handled by the people he brought in to cover for him, and that it had consistently disciplined those who had taken leave without permission or in direct violation of orders.

Discussion Question 2: What might the union have argued?
The union might have argued that the security problem faced by the wife constituted a health and safety issue within the employee's purview, that the classes were properly taught while he was away, that the provision of substitutes was a common practice, and that the grievant should not have been penalized for his honesty, having made a direct approach when he easily could have called in sick on the week in question. The union might have

argued that the employer was arbitrary and capricious in its denial and that the uniqueness of the opportunity made it more reasonable for the grievant to have gone then to have stayed home.

Discussion Question 3: Could the obey now and file a grievance later policy have provided an equitable remedy?

There is no question that the arbitrator, by creating a remedy to *make whole*, can not always place the employee back in the position he or she would have occupied had it not been for the employer's directive. Clearly a trip of this nature was a unique opportunity that could not be replicated by the arbitrator. Neither can an arbitrator make up for the loss of deposit on a summer vacation home when an employee suddenly finds his or her vacation schedule altered. The standard followed by arbitrators in trying to structure a make whole remedy is confined to replicating as closely as possible the employee's work situation. The arbitrator has complete jurisdiction over the remedy when the parties agree to what the remedy, if any, shall be. Most arbitrators take the position that the parties anticipate that the employee shall be made whole for what he or she would have received from the employer had he or she continued to work. They are less likely to go beyond that context in seeking to make an employee "totally" whole.

Furthermore, arbitrators do not seek to make up for consequential damages arising outside the workplace that are clearly beyond the arbitrator's jurisdiction. Thus an arbitrator would not be likely to pay the cost of a lost vacation-home deposit, let alone a trip to Europe for the grievant. So there is, unfortunately, a shortfall in the effectiveness of a make whole remedy, but because the arbitrator's ruling sets precedent for other situations, there is a positive impact beyond the situation in any particular case.

Discussion Question 4: Is a distinction to be drawn between the principal's denial of authorization to take the trip as contrasted with a direct order not to take the trip?

In relationships in which there is a clear practice of supervisors requesting certain behavior and then disciplining employees for their failure to respond, arbitrators generally will hold that such a request is adequate evidence of an order for an employee to respond. At the other extreme are relationships in which the employer has a practice of specifying "this is a order" before imposing discipline; that notification generally will be relied on by the arbitrator to establish what constitutes an order.

The prevailing standard utilized by arbitrators is thus to determine whether the employee knew or should have known that what was said to him or her was in effect, an order with disciplinary results for failure to respond to that directive. If the arbitrator is persuaded that the grievant was aware that a simple request, "I am asking you to do this," was the last time that request would be made, the arbitrator might conclude that the grievant should have been aware that discipline could result from a failure to respond to that request.

Sexual Harassment

In the past few years, society at large has moved to a recognition of sexual equality and has come to recognize the inappropriateness of discriminatory behavior based on sex. This has been codified in public legislation on both the federal and state levels, making such harassment prohibited conduct. While an employee who believes that she, or sometimes he, has been the victim of sexual harassment has recourse to litigation in the courts for the enforcement of any statutes barring such sexual harassment, those statutory rights generally are not considered by arbitrators to be enforceable in the grievance and arbitration process. An exception may arise if the parties' collective bargaining agreement specifies that there shall be no discriminatory conduct pursuant to the statutes of the jurisdiction. Generally, arbitrators shy away from undertaking to interpret collective bargaining agreements in light of Federal legislation or the legislation of the jurisdiction in which the employer's operation is found.

Far more likely is that the arbitrator will view allegations of sexual harassment as being within his or her jurisdiction in terms of how these allegations relate to the parties' agreement. Thus, an arbitrator would view it as an improper exercise of managerial authority for an employer to impose a requirement of sexual favors upon a subordinate as a condition for continued employment or as condition for access to benefits that would otherwise be unavailable to that employee. Likewise, an arbitrator would view with suspicion a discipline imposed on an employee for failure to respond to sexual overtures, solicitations, or inducements by a supervisor.

CASE: DISCIPLINE FOR REJECTED SEXUAL FAVORS

Susan Sonnel was a clerk working for a supervisor who frequently had asked her to meet him after work for a drink, to come to his home for dinner, or to go out together to parties. She had rejected four or five such requests over the four months that she had worked under that supervisor. Four days after a request that she come to the supervisor's home for dinner, Sonnel came to work ten minutes late. The supervisor said that he was writing her up for the infraction, and she was issued a three-day suspension for the tardiness. Sonnel filed a grievance alleging that she had been the victim of sexual harassment and sought the recision of the penalty and the reimbursement of the three days' pay loss.

The employer argued that the grievant was tardy, that her tardiness was in violation of the rules requiring her to report to work on time, and that the same penalty would have been imposed on an employee regardless of sex and regardless of any prior relationship between an employee and the supervisor. The employer also asserted that there was no evidence of any sexual harassment, that the request to join the supervisor for a meal or for a drink after work was no different than a request to join a male friend for a drink or a meal, and that there was no evidence of any sexual impropriety.

The union argued that the grievant had been placed under constant pressure by the supervisor to comply with his requests; that she perceived that constant pressure to be a form of harassment, placing her in fear of discipline by the employer; that her concern was verified by the imposition of the discipline for a first instance of tardiness; and that that penalty was imposed on her as a means of encouraging her to comply with the supervisor's future requests and was, therefore, a form of sexual harassment. Accordingly, it urged the grievance be sustained and that Sonnel be made whole for the earnings lost.

The arbitrator ruled that the standard for determining the propriety of the penalty imposed on the grievant was whether a similar penalty would have been imposed had it not been for the prior relationship between the supervisor and the employee. The arbitrator took the position that an employee who was tardy was, in fact, in violation of the company's rule against tardiness, but argued that the evidence showed that such a first offense generally was met with a letter of warning. The imposition of a three-day suspension was not in line with a first offense, generally being reserved for a third or fourth offense, and it was reasonable to conclude from the frustrated efforts of the supervisor to meet the grievant outside of the workplace that the heavier penalty was imposed because of the grievant's refusal to have a relationship with the supervisor. The arbitrator found that there were grounds for discipline, but that the discipline imposed on the grievant was excessive and should be reduced to a letter of warning, with the grievant being made whole for the three days of earnings lost.

Discussion Question 1: What arguments might have been used by the employer?

The employer might have brought its record of prior discipline for tardiness to the arbitrator's attention to show that there was a practice of granting more than a warning for the first instances of tardiness. The employer might have brought in the testimony of other supervisors who had witnessed conversations between the grievant and her supervisors if these conversations showed that the grievant had been encouraging the supervisor when the solicitations were made. The employer also might have sought to discredit the grievant by seeking to challenge her character and the credibility of her testimony, while seeking to bolster the character and the family orientation of the supervisor.

Discussion Question 2: What positions might the union have taken?
The union might have brought the testimony of other employees who had been subject to similar overtures by the supervisor or evidence of prior protest by other employees against the supervisor's harassment. The union also might have examined the prior disciplinary records of other employees to ascertain the appropriate penalties for similar tardiness.

Discussion Question 3: How should the union present evidence of harassment against other employees if they are unwilling to testify concerning advances made by the supervisor?
It is unquestionably true that victims of sexual harassment often are loathe to reveal to outsiders the details of such advances. Such victims tend to be embarrassed or fearful of such revelations and feel that they are in some way guilty of being party to such exchanges, even if they reject the advances.

Nonetheless, such testimony is crucial if the supervisors who engage in sexual harassment are to be identified and held to account for their improper behavior. The employees' testimony, crucial as it is, must be subject to cross-examination to establish its credibility and its accuracy. Because the employer should be as interested as the union in identifying supervisors who are engaged in improper conduct, it might not be unreasonable to expect both parties to interview victims through a deposition or at a meeting place away from the arbitration hearing. They might be willing to protect the identity of such employees to avoid future retaliation by the supervisor. But if such arrangements are not made, it is incumbent on the union to bring to the hearing those witnesses who can support the grievant's claim so that the employer's advocate has the opportunity to examine and cross-examine such witnesses and so that their testimony can be established as credible by the arbitrator. Most arbitrators would be unwilling to accept such testimony of others claiming they'd been harassed over the objection of the employer if there were any any question about the accuracy or the honesty of the employee's testimony or if they never before protested the supervisors actions.

Discussion Question 4: Should the arbitrator be empowered to penalize the supervisor for his improper conduct?
The authority of the arbitrator is limited to the question submitted to arbitration. Generally, that question in a case such as this would be restricted to whether or not the imposition of the protested discipline was for just cause. Although framed in the context of the propriety of the discipline

against the employee, it really is a question of the propriety of the action of the supervisor. Nonetheless, arbitrators lack the jurisdiction to impose discipline on nonbargaining-unit personnel unless the parties have agreed in the submission agreement to grant the jurisdiction to the arbitrator.

In this case, the impropriety of the supervisor was a matter for the employer to handle. If an arbitrator finds that a supervisor has acted improperly, then the cost is borne by the employer for making whole the wages lost, and any action taken against the supervisor is within the employer's jurisdiction. Any action taken by the grievant to impose a penalty on the supervisor is best handled through litigation alleging violations of statutory rights of the grievant. In that forum, there may indeed be the imposition of a penalty against the supervisor.

Levels of Discipline

As noted above, the arbitrator in discipline cases is confronted with two questions: (1) whether or not there was any grounds for the imposition of discipline, and (2) if discipline was justified, whether the level of penalty was appropriate. There are, however, no clear, preordained steps of discipline except those used within the particular enterprise. The assumption of progressive discipline is that there will be oral warnings, a written warning, and presumably two or three steps of disciplinary suspension before the imposition of termination, but those standards vary from enterprise to enterprise.

In the case of oral warnings, there is frequent confusion about whether or not an oral warning was given. Many employers abide by the practice of having an oral warning noted in writing, perhaps even initialed by the employee, to avoid disputes about whether the warning was issued.

In cases of suspension, there are a variety of suspensions that may be imposed. Generally, initial suspensions will be one to three days in duration. Second suspensions may last from three to ten days, with the next level of suspension being as long as fourteen to thirty days prior to imposition of the termination penalty.

Because the credibility of the progressive-discipline system is dependent on its notoriety and its preventive nature, it is important that the steps of discipline introduced by the employer, either in the form of company rules, posted notices, or past practice, be endorsed by the arbitrator to maintain credibility of the inevitability of the disciplinary action. If an arbitrator seeks to reduce a disciplinary penalty that he or she finds to be excessive, it should be done in conformity with the expectations of that system. Thus, if the parties' progressive-discipline system calls for a three-day suspension on third offense and a two-week suspension on fourth offense, the arbitrator who reduces a penalty from a two-week suspension to the next lower level should adhere to the practice of a three-day suspension on the third offense. For the arbitrator to impose a compromise penalty somewhere between the third offense and the fourth offense (for example, six days) is to create the expectation that the arbitrator will fashion a level of penalty different from that which had been held out as the routine for that enterprise.

There are situations, however, in which the arbitrator may find that the system utilized by the employer is not reasonable. To go from a written warning to a thirty-day suspension would be viewed by an arbitrator as an abuse of discretion and as arbitary, capricious, and contrary to the purpose and goals of progressive discipline. In such a circumstance, the arbitrator might rule that the thirty-day suspension for a third offense is excessive and that there ought at least to be a three- or five-day suspension before the imposition of that thirty-day penalty. The arbitrator would, of course, be fashioning a disciplinary penalty of his or her own. Unless the disciplinary penalties are set forth in the parties' agreement, the arbitrator's determination about is an appropriate penalty would appear to be within his or her jurisdiction.

In a situation in which the employer has followed a practice of imposing a series of four written warnings but no suspensions before a termination, the arbitrator reviewing that practice would have to determine whether the system was sufficiently known and relied on by the employees to substitute for the traditioned escalated penalties or whether the penalties must be escalated to include a disciplinary suspension. Is it necessary to hit the employee's pocketbook to provide a more effective reminder of the need to conform to the rules than would be accomplished by a series of unescalated written warnings. In such a case, the arbitrator might rule that the continuum of written warnings could lead employees into a false sense of security that if they engaged in similar repeated violations it would result in yet another written warning, rather than termination.

Adherence to the steps of progressive discipline as the incentive for encouraging employees to reform their conduct raises the question of whether an employee has responded to the earlier stages of progressive discipline. Thus, if an employee has been given an oral or written warning and a three-day suspension for prior infractions of the same type and there elapses a period of six months before that employee is tardy once again, does that last tardiness justify the imposition of a two-week suspension or a lesser penalty?

If the series of four infractions occurred within one month, there is no question that the fourth offense would justify the imposition of the heaviest penalty. But what if there had been a significant time lapse between the infractions? In many collective bargaining agreements, the parties have allowed for that prospect through *wash-out clauses* that consider, for example, if an employee's record is clear for a period of two years, then all prior disciplinary penalties are removed from his or her record. In that context, the arbitrator's task is relatively easy. The imposition of the fourth penalty in any period short of the two-year wash-out clause instructs the arbitrator that the parties did not intend a wash-out for a infraction within that period. Therefore, an escalated penalty would be appropriate.

But if no such wash-out clause is negotiated, the arbitrator may conclude it is within his or her authority to interpret the progressive discipline system as providing some reward for those employees who respond to the earlier steps by having a clear record for an extended period of time. An arbitrator may, therefore, reduce a penalty if persuaded that the employee has had an extended period of discipline-free employment.

Arbitrators frequently will challenge the employer's escalated discipline if the penalty under review is based on prior incidents of a totally different nature. For example, if an employee has had an oral warning, a written warning, and a five-day suspension for absenteeism and six months later is disciplined for insubordination, should the discipline for the latest wrong-doing be based on unrelated prior disciplinary penalties? Sometimes the answer to that question is found in the company rules or in the company's posting of disciplinary penalties. At other times it is found in the language of the penalty so the earlier absenteeism or tardness infractions may be couched in terms of failure to attend to responsibilities as an employee, which also might apply to the insubordination incident.

But if the purpose of progressive discipline is to encourage employees to reform their conduct and the problem is, for example, attendance, and the employee has overcome that attendance problem, is it appropriate to impose an escalated penalty for a totally unrelated offense of insubordination? Most arbitrators tend to view the imposition of discipline against a background of a discipline-free work force, so that an employee who becomes subject to discipline for whatever grounds is found by arbitrators to be in need of discipline to restore that person to the general background of a discipline-free work force. Arbitrators with such a philosophy are unlikely to distinguish between types of disciplinary infractions as justifying a whole series of different escalated penalties.

A particular problem arises in the case of terminated employees when the arbitrator finds that the termination was inappropriate. Conformity to the standards of imposing a discipline that should have been imposed at the time of the infraction generally results in the reduction of the penalty to a two-week or thirty-day suspension. Considering that appeals to arbitration may take up to one year, the awarding of a year's back pay minus that two-week or thirty-day suspension pay is viewed by many arbitrators as a penalty on the employer or even a windfall for the employee.

Most arbitrators would find it unacceptable to embrace a disciplinary penalty of one year imposed when the infraction is committed, yet they often are inclined to reinstate an employee without back pay on the theory that the back pay, as noted above, would be a penalty on the employer or a windfall for the employee. To subscribe to that theory places a premium on the employer's delay in the processing of such cases. Furthermore, the awarding of eleven months or eleven months and two weeks of back pay is not a windfall, but rather a restitution to the employee of what he or she would have been entitled to receive as compensation had it not been for the improper actions of the employer. The delay in bringing the case to arbitration is not the fault of the grievant.

In some cases the delay may be due to the intransigence of both the union and the management in processing the case. It also may be due to a unique delay attributable to the union, which, for example, did not process the case until threats of a duty-of-fair-representation lawsuit were brought against it. The delays of either the union or the employer should not be visited on the employee, and the employee who acted promptly in the exercise of his or her rights should be entitled to the penalty appropriate for the infraction. The back pay, therefore, should be afforded in accordance with the dictates of progressive discipline as interpreted by the arbitrator, with the employer having the right to go after the union for reimbursement of any loss due to the unions' tardiness in processing its appeal.

A related situation arises in cases in which the arbitrator finds that an employee's record justified the imposition of a heavy penalty but not one of a two-week or thirty-day suspension. For example, an employee with long service who had a series of infractions within a thirty-day period and who was terminated may have had problems due to an emotional or a family situation that thereafter passed. Other examples include the employee who had a problem with alcoholism, a problem that clearly would be resolved by his going to an alcoholic-reform program or the employee who, by virtue of the imposition of the termination penalty, was jolted into getting into a program of reformed conduct.

In all these cases, the arbitrator might not have imposed a thirty-day or fifteen-day suspension as the appropriate penalty, but may have concluded that the termination was the cause of the reform or may have concluded that the behavior of the employee since the termination justified a different view of the employer's action. In cases of a good record or a record of long service, the arbitrator may find that a reinstatement on a last-chance basis is an appropriate vehicle for providing a return to employment for senior employees or a good employee, while at the same time ruling that the employer did not act improperly at the time it imposed the discharge penalty.

Last-chance returns to employment should be used conservatively. To hold them out as an alternative places a premium on filing grievances that might not otherwise be appealed. In such last-chance reinstatements, the arbitrator may prescribe a series of prerequisites for continued employment, such as being free of discipline for a year, being on probation for a year, or being required to attend employee assistance programs or Alcoholics Anonymous meetings once or twice a week for a year. Last-chance reinstatement should not be used as an excuse for the arbitrator's unwillingness to impose the penalty that the employer should have imposed at the time of the initial termination.

Remedy Questions

When an arbitrator either finds that an employee was improperly disciplined or that the discipline imposed on the employee was excessive, it becomes incumbent on the arbitrator to fashion a remedy to make the employee whole for earnings lost less what he earned while out of work. Unfortunately, neither union nor management usually takes the time during an arbitration to present evidence on what the employee has been doing during the period since the discipline was imposed.

In cases of an employee having a penalty reduced from a two-week suspension to a one-week suspension, there is little cause for investigation about what the employee did during that period. It is presumed that he or she was out awaiting return to work and therefore entitled to reimbursement of the earnings lost during the period in question. But in cases of an employee having been terminated and then returned to work, the question arises about what the employee had been doing in the interim. The employer usually is loathe to ask whether the employee had found other work for fear that it would appear to the arbitrator as though the employer was less than convinced of the merit of the termination.

The employer also might be fearful that evidence that the employee had worked during the entire interim might be viewed by the arbitrator as justifying a return to work that might not otherwise result because there would be no cost to the employer for back pay for the period involved. On the union's side, unions are reluctant explore what the employee has done since the termination because the employee may not have lived up to the duty of mitigating damages by seeking other employment.

The arbitrator might come to the conclusion that an employee who had not made an effort to secure interim employment would be less than reliable or that if he or she had been looking for work and had not been able to find any that reinstatement might impose an excessive penalty on the employer in back pay. But for whatever reasons, the parties are often unwilling to supply the arbitrator with information necessary for determing the remedy due an employee for an excessive penalty.

Employees do have an obligation to undertake to mitigate the employer's loss by trying to find employment during the period following their termination. It is assumed that the employee will endeavor to find substitute employment, will register with an unemployment insurance office, and will respond to job interviews. Although the parties do not present such information at the hearing or ask the grievant about it, neither do arbitrators. Arbitrators are unwilling or reluctant to do so for fear that such questions may prolong or complicate the hearing. Indeed, such questioning may be viewed as demonstrating a bias by the arbitrator toward reinstatement.

So these issues remain unresolved in most arbitration hearings, and the arbitrator is left to fashion a remedy, usually articulated in the phrase of "making an employee whole for earnings lost." By such language, the arbitrator allows the parties to resolve what an employee would have earned if he or she had continued at work. That standard permits for reimbursement of earnings that would have been earned in overtime and in possible promotions.

Frequently there is an issue of restitution of unemployment compensation that the employee may have received, but the variations among the state jurisdictions about whose responsibility it is to claim or to initiate a return of such funds is avoided by the language "making whole for earnings lost." That phrase assumes that if the employee is required to return any unemployment compensation, then the employer will make the grievant whole for that amount.

The concept of making whole for earnings lost limits the liability of the employer to what the employee would have received if he or she had continued to work and had not been improperly terminated. Consequent damages, such as the loss of a house for failure to keep up payments, the divorce of a spouse, or the repossession of a vehicle are not considered within the employment relationship and thus are not made whole by the arbitrator. A somewhat different situation arises in the case of loss of insurance benefits during a period of termination. If an employee has been terminated and has lost health-insurance benefits, the arbitrator may order the reimbursement of the cost of private insurance coverage to replace what the employer had been providing, but may not be willing to pick up the cost of hospitalization that occurred during the time of termination. Here too the employee had a duty to mitigate damages. However, arbitrators are split on the issue of whether the obligation of the employer runs to the bearing of the cost of such hospitalization and medical costs, when the terminated employee is unable to match his prior coverage.

4
Wages and Classifications

Wages

Collective bargaining provides the forum for union and management to establish the rates of pay, how compensation is to be paid, and the jobs and duties to which it will apply. Arbitration provides the vehicle for enforcing the negotiated rights, for resolving ambiguities in the negotiated agreement, and for applying the agreement to unforeseen changes in the parties' relationship.

The traditional expectation of a collective bargaining agreement is that it sets forth the conditions of service expected of employees in exchange for specific wage rates. The negotiation of those wage rates is a crucial element of the collective bargaining process. Generally, the explanation of wage rates is specific, identifying the hourly rate to be paid to certain classifications of employees in exchange for the services they perform and sometimes setting forth the job descriptions of the tasks expected at those negotiated rates.

Despite the best efforts of the parties to resolve any pending or anticipated dispute over wage rates during their negotiations, it is impossible to anticipate the variety of issues that might arise over wages to be paid for services performed. Among the questions that might arise subsequent to the completion of negotiations is the application of the negotiated wage rates to a particular position or job. For example, at the time of the negotiations the parties might have had no employees on probationary status; they might not have contemplated the purchase of new equipment, the operation of which would be unlisted in all job descriptions; they might have expected that all employees would continue to work, without any union officer invoking the provision allowing a six-month union leave, for which no compensation had ever been negotiated.

Questions of that nature involve the application of the collective bargaining agreement to classes of employees or to individuals in order to determine their entitlement to the compensation negotiated between the parties. In handling such cases, the arbitrator is placed in a position of determining whether or not a wage rate is properly payable to an employee, even though the parties had not discussed the applicability of that rate to that position at the time of the negotiations. Indeed, one of the benefits of the arbitration process is that it permits closure of the collective bargaining negotiations by the appropriate deadline. The parties then understand that questions of application of rates to particular positions that had not surfaced at the time of negotiations or thereafter would be submitted to a rational, mutually agreed-upon procedure for their resolution. Presumably, that resolution would be in conformity with what the parties themselves would have negotiated had the subsequent facts been known to them at the time of negotiation.

But in addition to questions concerning the application of the collective bargaining agreement, the sincere and strenuous efforts of the parties to clarify the language negotiated in connection with wage rates nevertheless may give rise to disputes over the interpretation of the negotiated language. After contract signing, it is not unusual for one or more of the employees to examine the language and raise questions about its meaning.

CASE: THE UNDERPAID SOCCER COACH

The school board and the teachers' association had for years negotiated annual collective bargaining agreements in which they established the wage rates for new and experienced teachers within the system. At the time of ratification, every teacher knew exactly the rate that had been negotiated for the position held. In those negotiations, the parties also established stipends to be paid to teachers who volunteered for coaching and directing extracurricular sports and student activities. Although salaries were negotiated annually, the extracurricular stipends were negotiated only every second or third contract.

In their most recent negotiations, the parties devoted most of their efforts to negotiating changes in contract language, and the issue of wages was such a sensitive one that it was not resolved until quite late in the negotiations. But just prior to the contract deadline, the parties reached agreement to provide a 6 percent increase in compensation for each teacher. After the contract was signed and ratified, teachers were paid according to the new salary schedule, for which each salary step had been increased by 6 percent. A grievance was filed by the soccer coach protesting that his extracurricular pay for coaching soccer was at the same rate as it had been the preceding season and that a 6 percent increase in that stipend was due. The grievance was denied and appealed to arbitration.

At the arbitration hearing, the union asserted that the grievance was filed for the increase in coaching compensation and that the grievant, as well as other coaches and club directors, received stipends as part of their compensation. It claimed that all employees were entitled to a 6 percent increase in all of their earnings from the school district, not only in their wage rate for classroom teaching. It asserted that there was no effort made by the board during negotiations to exclude those teachers receiving stipends from the 6 percent increase in compensation and that since the increase was in part a reimbursement for losses of real earnings due to inflation, it was appropriate that the amount be applied both to the salary schedule and to the extracurricular stipends. It noted that in the agreement the parties did use the word compensation rather than wages and interpreted that as showing the intent was to provide a package increase in all compensation.

The school district argued that recompense for inflation was in part a motivation for the parties' negotiated settlement, but that inflation was adequately provided for by the increase in compensation applicable to salaries. It noted that the coaching stipends had not always been increased in prior negotiations to a level commensurate with any inflationary increase and that in the past stipends had been left untouched by negotiations unless the parties specifically negotiated increases in them. It noted that the stipend increases always had been negotiated specifically on the basis of such factors as attendance, victory or loss score, and time consumed, and that such stipends were unrelated to inflationary factors.

The school district noted further that to provide the increase the union sought in this case would obligate it to pay additional money to nonbargaining-unit coaches who were hired just to handle sports and were not even on the teachers' salary schedule. Finally, it noted that the 6 percent stipend increase was not contemplated in the negotiations by either party and that it created a substantial additional financial burden that the board lacked the ability to pay.

The arbitrator held that the intent of the parties in their negotiations was to deal only with the question of the salary schedule; that they had a history of negotiating salary schedules separate from coaching stipends; that such stipends were not raised annually as were wage rates; and that it was incumbent on the union to have raised the issue of the applicability of the 6 percent increase to extracurricular activities at the time of negotiations. Having failed to do so, it could not later apply that 6 percent to extracurricular activities as well. Furthermore, the arbitrator noted that the calculations used by the parties in arriving at the 6 percent figure were based solely on the salary increases for all teachers. To have raised extracurricular stipends by 6 percent would have resulted in a smaller increase in salaries. Thus, she concluded, teachers who did not perform extracurricular tasks would be subsidizing those who did. Accordingly, the arbitrator found that the union lacked merit in its claim.

Discussion Question 1: What arguments might the union have raised?
The union could have cited the negotiating history in that union notes showed the agreements made in earlier negotiations for increases in stipends were, in fact, reflective of increases in inflation. It could have cited the prevailing practices in other districts, relied on by these parties for comparability, in their raising of stipends as an element of salary increases, and it could have

referred to any comments in its notes that distinguished compensation from salary increases. It also could have examined the timing of stipend increases relative to wage increases to determine if there was a pattern or ratio for such increases coming due in the latest negotiation. If the majority of teachers were engaged in extracurricular activities, documentation of the percentage would demonstrate broad distribution of benefits from its claim.

Discussion Question 2: What might the employer have argued?
The employer might have presented the negotiating history and showed the annual increases in salary and the occasional increases in stipends as a comparison to illustrate that even when stipends were increased, they may have been at different rates than the salary increases negotiated in that particular year. It also could have shown that the independent negotiating cycle for stipends was reflective of the practice in neighboring communities. A history of negotiating different increases or adjustments for each extracurricular activity could have been used to show there was no basis for a matched increase of the same percent.

Discussion Question 3: How should the arbitrator have ruled if the union had raised the question of applying that same 6 percent increase to the amount of money paid for insurance compensation?
As in the case of the stipend, the arbitrator probably would have ruled that unless the parties had a practice of increasing such insurance payments at the same rate as the salary increases, their tradition had been to negotiate the matter separately. Although the 6 percent compensation might warrant an effort to provide the employees with 6 percent more money to meet their expenses, the arbitrator probably would have ruled it did not apply to negotiation over insurance contributions which had always been considered by the parties as an issue separate from wages.

Discussion Question 4: How could the parties have avoided this issue?
It is virtually impossible to anticipate every problem when the parties rewrite their agreement. That is why there is a grievance procedure. Nonetheless, it would have been important to the parties to make careful use of words. The term *compensation* rather then *wages, wage rates,* or *salary* implies a broader application than the other three terms, opening the door to the claim that stipends were covered because they were indeed part of the compensation. But if the term *salaries* had been used, it would have been clear that there was a specific limitation to salaries for teaching, rather than a general application to include stipends. When the parties negotiate a collective bargaining agreement, it is crucial that the language be examined carefully and read in the light of the potential for subsequent challenge and misinterpretation.

Operations Changes

At the time of negotiations, union and management have a set of prevailing conditions as the basis for their seeking agreement on wage rates. Recognizing that a collective bargaining agreement will bind the parties for up to three years, they endeavor to develop language provisions that will preclude disputes over foreseeable changes. Their anticipation of language changes is based primarily on changes in conditions that have occurred since the last agreement. Unless there is some forewarning of coming changes in equipment, process, or operations, it is difficult at best to anticipate language that will be so explicit that it will preclude any future conflict.

Nonetheless, management and unions recognize that business conditions do not remain static and that changes in production, equipment, and operations are indeed essential for the continuing success of the enterprise and the efficiency of its operations. There is no challenge to management's right to introduce change. Unions, in an effort to protect themselves against unanticipated but potentially adverse changes in their working conditions, often seek management's agreement to language that permits midterm opportunity to discuss and negotiate changes as they become known and closer to implementation.

Management also is alert to the problems that may arise from the introduction of new operations, conditions, and equipment. It may be placed in a position of being unable to utilize fully new procedures because of constraints imposed by the language of the collective bargaining agreement. Thus, it is not unusual to have unions and managements agree to provisions that trigger renewed midterm negotiations in the event of management's invocation of its authority to introduce changes. But to assure that the opportunity for discussion occurs and to avoid the other party's refusal to discuss such changes, the parties often establish criteria for opening such exchanges.

The negotiated standard for triggering such reopened discussion may be substantial changes in production. It may be the introduction of new equipment affecting jobs, and it may incorporate terms such as *substantial, large,* and *innovative* to describe the degree of change that will trigger renewed negotiations. Grievances often arise over whether or not a change introduced by management does, in fact, meet the test to permit the reopening of negotiations. The general standard, whether specified in the contract or not, is whether the change being introduced in operations, management structure, process equipment, and so on is of sufficient magnitude to have an impact on the work force and substantial enough to justify alterations in the parties' collective bargaining agreement that bring it in line with the new working environment. In other words, does the change in conditions render the previously negotiated terms and conditions inappropriate to the present work situation?

CASE: THE NEW COMPUTERIZED LATHE

The company sought to introduce a computerized lathe to replace its manual lathe operated by an employee classified as a lathe operator and experienced in the operation of the lathe and in working from blueprints explaining the work to be done. The new equipment the company sought to introduce consisted of two electronic lathes that operated from computer discs and had a combined output three times the output of the manual lathe, which the company wanted to sell. The collective bargaining agreement called for discussions should the employer introduce a " substantial change" in equipment that would impact on the equipment already in use. Company officials met with the union to announce that they were planning to introduce the new equipment and to retain the current lathe operator. The company offered to continue him at his present rate after providing him with a two-month course on the use of the computer that would drive the new lathes. The union objected to the employee being required to operate two lathes instead of one and being responsible for greater production at the same pay as received for operating the single manual lathe. The union filed a grievance against the company's proposed action, and the case was appealed to arbitration.

At the arbitration hearing, the union asserted that the lathe operator had responsibility for loading and off-loading the lathe, as well as for its operation. It argued that the introduction of two lathes, even though driven by computers, still necessitated loading and off-loading and that the tripled production expected from the two new lathes placed a substantially heavier burden on the employee, justifying a higher wage rate for the work involved.

The company argued that the loading and off-loading of the parts occupied a small percentage of the employee's work-day, that the operation of the electronic lathe was significantly easier than the work of operating the manual lathe, and that it did not require any output of energy for the three-quarters of the shift when the lathe would function independent of human participation. It argued that the new job would be easier than the old one and that the work could just as efficiently be performed by a machinist's helper, as the primary job function was loading and off-loading the new lathes.

The arbitrator was confronted with several issues. First, was the change substantial enough to justify new negotiations? She concluded that the replacement of the lathe, the alteration to the computer, and the increase in loading and off-loading of the parts justified the parties' negotiating the impact of the change on the existing lathe-operator position.

The second question considered was whether the union's protest was premature because the change had not yet been introduced. The arbitrator decided that because the company had ordered the equipment, because it would soon be installed, and because there was differing opinion between the parties regarding the work load on the lathe, it was timely to consider the case if only to protect the employee from a potentially onerous work load.

The arbitrator claimed that the salary of the lathe operator was appropriate for the task to be performed because the evidence showed that the operation of the electronic lathe did require supervision and responsibility for shutting the equipment down if there was a malfunction. She also found that the physical output requirements of monitoring and operating the lathe were substantially reduced by the new automated equipment. They were, however, offset by the obligation for additional loading and off-loading of product. Accordingly, the arbitrator held that the continuation of the lathe operator on two machines at his present rate was appropriate.

Discussion Question 1: What arguments might the union have raised?
The union could have introduced evidence of the high level of specialized training and education the lathe operator brought to the job and could have introduced evidence of other positions to which the lathe operator might have been transferred. If the lathe operator indeed was seeking to avoid the loading and off-loading work, the union could have introduced evidence of other electronic innovations by the company if such changes brought with them job protection or an increase in compensation. It could have compared the lathe operation proposed by the company with other jobs calling for knowledge of computers, jobs that were paid at higher rates. The union could have further offered evidence of higher rates of compensation paid in other enterprises utilizing the new equipment. It could have sought a higher rate based on the volume of exertion required for the loading and off-loading if such duties were at a higher rate elsewhere in the facility. It could have introduced evidence of its efforts to have the job time studied or revaluated under the company's job-evaluation system as evidence of its conviction that the grievant was being underpaid.

Discussion Question 2: What arguments might the company have relied on?
The company could have provided details concerning the easier computerized monitoring function and could have equated its operation to similar computer-controlled operations elsewhere at the plant and paid at a lower rate. It could have provided evidence of other jobs in the plant where the physical component was more time consuming or more arduous than in a

lathe operater's job, although paid at a lower rate. It also could have made comparisons with the skill requirements in other plants where the new lathe was in operation or compared the position with in-house lower-paying jobs that were similarly computerized.

Discussion Question 3: What if the arbitrator had found that the change was not sufficient in magnitude to trigger a renegotiation of the rate?

Since the employee in this case was seeking an increase in rate, the opportunity for securing it was during the renegotiation. If such renegotiation was not mandated under the arbitrator's interpretation of the parties' agreement, then the grievant would have continued to work at the prior rate without change until the next contract negotiations. Similarly, if the company had sought to reduce the wage rate of the lathe operator on the theory that he was now doing merely manual work, it would have been precluded from doing so absent a showing of substantial change. Thus the rate probably would have continued, even though the duties might have been reduced until the expiration of the contract.

Discussion Question 4: What if the company had merely eliminated the lathe-operator position?

Eliminating the lathe-operator position probably would not have precipitated the renegotiation because that was not a change under the contract and because it was within management's rights to eliminate a position. In that case, the employee would have had the right to move, or bump, into other positions to which his seniority entitled him. Theoretically, in such a situation the rate for the lathe-operator's job would have continued as in the contract, although the position would not have been filled. If the parties had negotiated fixed crew sizes or retained certain classifications despite cutbacks, then those guarantees might have come into play to preclude the attempted elimination of the lathe-operator position.

Discussion Question 5: Does the cost of new equipment automatically constitute a substantive change to justify reopening negotiations?

It is neither the size or the cost of the equipment nor the timing of a change that precipitates a reopening of negotiations. Rather, it is the impact of the change on the employees. That impact may be de minimus if, for instance, a computerized addition was made to the existing lathe without any increase in output or job duties. Then that change in the job might not have precipitated a review, let alone an increase in compensation. But one of the issues for resolution by arbitrators is whether the change is *substantial* or *material* or whether it is, on the other hand, de minimus, or a slight increase or change in work load that alone is insufficient to trigger such reexamination.

Transfers

The parties frequently negotiate language covering the issue of the employer's right to transfer employees on a temporary or permanent basis from one job to another. In addition to the question of the right to make such transfers, negotiations also address the substantial wage impact of employee transfers. The employer who opts to transfer an employee into another position may face no wage impact when that position is of the same labor grade as the position from which the transferred employee was moved. Nonetheless, a wage consequence might arise if the move is into a higher-paying classification or even if the move is lateral but into a classification in which the employee gains skills that may subsequently assist in his or her seeking a higher-rated position. Such moves also may be used as a deliberate effort by the employer to increase the skills of a favored employee and thus increase that person's eligibility for subsequent upward movement, through the bidding procedure, into a later opening.

The wage benefit of that latter type of transfer is, of course, delayed. A more direct wage impact comes when an employee is transferred to a higher-rated job on a temporary basis. The question often arises over whether the employee is entitled to the wage rate of the higher-paying job into which transferred or whether the employee is to continue at the rate of the job previously held. Such transfers may occur during periods of the regular employee's vacation or absence for illness or injury.

The issue of such transfers occurs frequently enough to have led most parties to incorporate into their collective bargaining agreements language governing the company's right to make such transfers as well as the rate at which employees are to be paid during such transfers. Frequently, the negotiated language makes a distinction between short-term and long-term transfers. If the move is to a higher-rated job, some contracts set stipulations about whether seniority prevails in such moves and about when an employee is entitled to recoup the differential between that employee's regular job rate and the rate of the job to which transferred. Some collective bargaining agreements provide that transfers of longer duration are to be based on seniority exclusively or on seniority skill, and ability, while selection of employees for short-term transfers is to remain within the exclusive authority of the employer. Although management certainly has the right to direct the work force, the expanded skill-acquiring opportunities of promotions as well as the direct financial rewards resulting from transfers to preferred or higher-paying jobs have made such transfers a matter for collective bargaining in most agreements.

Thus, while a collective bargaining agreement may guarantee employees certain rights for transfer to higher-paying jobs, it also may set forth the time period for such transfer before the higher-rate is applied. There also may be a question of whether the employee is fulfilling the requirements of the higher-rated job to justify the higher rate of pay. Such may be a factual issue presented in arbitration and based on the duties performed by the employee while serving in the transferred position. Among the issues to be considered by the arbitrator is whether or not the transferred employee is performing the full range of skills upon which the higher-rated job is based or whether the transferred employee is merely performing in a different location for the absent employee those normal duties that he or she might have done before the transfer. The employee's entitlement to the higher rate is therefore dependent on a showing that the employee is doing work not of his or her regular job but tasks that normally would be performed only by the occupant of the higher-rated job. In establishments where there is a substantial movement of employees among different jobs through the transfer process, these movements may entail a substantial element of compensation and thus be viewed as an important component of the employee's wages.

CASE: THE COMPETENT MECHANIC

The job description for auto Mechanic A at labor grade 10 listed responsibility for diagnosing and repairing problems in the company's vehicle motors. The auto Mechanic B job description did not entail diagnosis but included the ability to make such repairs as were directed by Mechanic A or by supervision. Mechanic B was paid at labor grade 9.

On the day in question John Meyers, the Mechanic A, was out sick. He had been working on a truck engine that the company desperately needed to be put back into service. The supervisor assigned Mitch Verter, the Mechanic B, to the truck, telling him to replace the carburetor and distributor cap. Mechanic B Verter did those tasks and left for lunch. When he returned to the work area Verter noticed some head gaskets that had been left there by Mechanic A Meyers and proceded to remove the engine valves. Verter completed that task by the end of the day and returned to his normal duties. On his return, Mechanic A Myers congratulated Mechanic B Verter on all the tasks done so well. Mechanic B filed a claim for the Mechanic A work he had performed on the day in question. The claim was denied, and the case was appealed to arbitration.

At the arbitration hearing, the union argued that Mechanic B Verter had needed to diagnose the work to be done; that he had done the work left by Mechanic A Meyers as expected of him; and that he had not been told not to use his skills in furtherance of the work the company admitted was a rush job. It noted that he had served as the equivalent of a Mechanic A at his last job prior to joining the company.

The employer argued that the work he had been assigned was that of a Mechanic B, that he had not been told to do the Mechanic A work, and that he had done so voluntarily. Thus, there was no obligation to pay the higher rate for that day.

The arbitrator held that grievant Verter was a Mechanic B in this company, regardless of whether he had been the equivalent of Mechanic A elsewhere. The supervisor in charge assigned him to specific tasks consistent with his capabilities and classification, and thus he had no authority to diagnose work beyond what he had been instructed to do. Because the valve work was not assigned to him and because he was not given the discretion to diagnose what work remained to be done after the assigned tasks, the grievant's work in replacing the engine valves was assumed voluntarily and beyond his obligations as a Mechanic B. The arbitrator denied the grievance because Verter had not been given the authority to proceed to replace the valves without direction.

Discussion Question 1: What could the union have presented?
The union could have presented evidence of the grievant's prior experience as a Mechanic A and could have argued that once that level of diagnostic expertise had been reached, the assumption of tasks became automatic. It could have argued that the grievant had routinely done diagnostic work in his regular job, that his position was improperly classified, and that the supervisor had assigned him to the vehicle in question specifically because the company wanted to utilize his expertise in fully repairing it.

Discussion Question 2: What could the company have presented?
The company could have shown that the grievant identified the need to work on the valves from the presence of the gaskets, that he had discussed the overhaul with Mechanic A before the latter got sick, or that there were notes or invoices that showed the tasks to be done and therefore served as instructions. It could have shown the grievant had less than Mechanic A skills or perhaps that he had been told by the supervisor to report back for further instructions after having done the carburator and distributor-cap work. It could further have detailed the possible scenario of the grievant having made the wrong assessment or having improperly done the valve change with the financial consequences to the company of such volunteering.

Discussion Question 3: What would have been likely to happen to the Mechanic B if he had not done any work after the two tasks?
The Mechanic B classification removed from Verter the responsibility of looking for tasks to perform, particularly if filling in for a Mechanic A. The Mechanic B's obligation would have been to report to a supervisor that the assigned tasks had been completed and to report availability for additional

tasks. Although the supervisor was not constantly present, Mechanic B still was obligated to seek out the supervisor or to report his completed tasks to another supervisor and thus be available for further assignment.

Piece-Rate Incentive Pay

A commonly negotiated standard for compensation is payment on the basis of productivity or effort. The rate of compensation for jobs on incentive or on piece rate generally is based on an examination, called a time study, of the time needed for various elements of a job. Generally, the management may perform a time study for a job subject to challenge or review by the union's time-study expert, or there may be time studies conducted jointly by company and union experts. Disputes over whether a particular time study is an accurate reflection of the various components of a job often are appealed to arbitration. Generally, however, the rates reflected by the time study and the incentive-pay arrangements are a matter of direct negotiations between the parties. There are few problems during the life of the contract in such matters unless there is a change in production technique, equipment, or standards. If that occurs, the contract generally will provide criteria for a new time study. Such matters are frequently appealed to arbitration if the parties' time study experts are unable to resolve them.

Arbitration of such technical matters frequently is performed by arbitrators with prior experience in handling time-study and incentive questions. Many of the arbitrators who do time-study cases are engineers, although the parties frequently utilize more generally educated arbitrators for such disputes. Some arrangements provide for the parties training their arbitrators in the time-study techniques used under their contract. Some parties provide time-study consultants to serve with a lay arbitrator on a tripartite panel to assure that the arbitrator gets full presentation of the parties' two views on the disputed time study. The objective of such revised time studies generally is to assure that the employee, even though subject to more strigent production standards because of equipment or process change, is at least to be paid commensurate with the new demand of the position and in compliance with the wage patterns established by the agreement.

There is no question of the company's right to set production standards, whether those production standards be the amount of work an employee is to produce on an hourly-paid basis or the amount of production an employee is to be paid on the piece-work basis by compensation under the incentive system. But just as the employer has the right to set the production standards on incentive or hourly work, the employees have the right to challenge the reasonableness of the compensation for meeting those job standards and to assure that changes in the job content, method, or performance are accurately and adequately reflected in the revised wage rates.

Job Evaluation

A different procedure for the establishment of a wage rate for a particular job is through the traditional system entitled *job evaluation*, which either may be negotiated or unilaterally introduced by the employer. This job evaluation system determines the wage rate for a particular job based on its component elements, as distinguished from the tabulation of time spent for every task or motion that makes up a job, as in a time study. The system of job evaluation also provides a rational basis of the job relationships that determine the relative rates of a universe of jobs within an establishment. Job evaluation examines the same factors common to every job and thus provides comparisons among jobs based on the demands of the various elements in the job.

Evolving from the early system of job evaluation as developed by the National Metal Trades Association, the parties to collective bargaining have adapted the job evaluation point system to the unique requirements of their particular operation. Under the system, a number of factors are identified, such as manual skill, mental skill, education, physical demand, hazards, responsibility for equipment, responsibility for safety of self, training, and responsibility for safety of others. All factors are common to every job being rated.

Each factor is then subdivided into a number of levels based on the intensity of that particular factor in that particular job. The levels, in turn, have points within them and may range from none or minor to the most demanding or the highest. These levels are uniformly applied to the various factors. A point system applies certain point values to each level of each factor. The jobs are then analyzed in terms of the level of intensity to be applied to each one of the factors that are called upon in the performance of a particular job. Thus an A level for education with 2 points may read, "requires no formal education beyond ability to read and write." An F level for education with 12 points may read, "Requires a bachelor's degree in engineering." The points within the levels are added, and the total point value of the job is then the basis on which that job is compared with other jobs. The parties then negotiate wage rates based on certain cut-off points in the total point system, assigning labor grades to each one of the jobs. They are guided by certain benchmark jobs requiring varying degrees of skill; these jobs are used as a basis of comparison among the various factors.

Jobs falling between 100 points and 120 points might be negotiated at labor grade 1. Jobs falling between 121–165 may be negotiated as falling in labor grade 2, and so on. The rates are negotiated for the labor grades and applied to whichever jobs fall therein. Thus a sweeper or a janitor with relatively limited point assignments on the factors of the job might only accumulate a total of 102 points, resulting in a placement within labor grade 1. A tool-mechanic job having higher requirements and encompassing such factors as education, skill, responsibility for expensive equipment, risk of danger to others, and high responsibility for expensive product might require an accumulation of 200 points and thus be slotted in labor grade 7.

Under the job evaluation system, any newly added duty might lead to a claim that the job should be moved up to the next level. Thus, any new or changed job could be subjected to scrutiny under the job evaluation system, which would examine its components as well as any changes to ascertain whether such changes would be enough to raise the point level. If the total point increase for the job is high enough, the job would be moved from one labor grade into a higher-paid labor grade. Parties generally resolve such disputes on their own, but there remains the right to appeal an allegedly improper factor determination or factor grading through the grievance and arbitration system and to resort to an appeal to arbitration.

The system is viewed as a relatively easy and understandable system for rationalizing job rates and job relationships. Yet many problems continue to arise from the employee's perception that the requirements of a job are sufficiently onerous to justify allocation or placement on a higher point level with a greater point total for the job. This may be asserted even though the protested factor or level may not call for the increase in points that the grievant thinks appropriate. The problem is further exacerbated by the point range within labor grades. An employee, even though proving that his job entitles him to a point rating of 119 instead of 100, might still find his wage rate unchanged if the cut-off point for labor grade 2 is 120 points.

An advantage of the job evaluation system is that once in place, it provides an orderly procedure for examining alleged changes in jobs and for integrating new jobs into the existing wage structure. At the same time, it facilitates wage negotiations by confining them to increases of wages at the labor-grade levels without the need to tamper with individual jobs or be subjected to the pressure of employees seeking disparate increases for their particular classifications. The system evaluates the job, rather than the incumbent holding it.

CASE: THE OVERQUALIFIED TOOLMAKER

Richard Reilly was a college graduate with a bachelor of science degree in engineering. After his prior employer went out of business, he applied for his present job as a toolmaker. He was assigned to a job as toolmaker that previously had been evaluated in the job evaluation system as having a 187 point total, placing it in labor grade 9. Reilly filed a grievance over the factor rating assigned to his job. The factor of education, which was rated as 18 points called for a high-school shop-training education, while an engineering-degree requirement would have produced 20 points, the highest rating in the education factor. Reilly said the work required an engineer's knowledge. Reilly also challenged the experience rating for the position, noting that he had previously held a toolmaker's job all through college and had an excess of four years of experience, while the job evaluation system for the position to which he was assigned called for only three years. According to Reilly's calculation, increases in those two factors alone would have raised his point total sufficiently high to move the position into labor grade 10, the highest-paid category in the job evaluation system. The company denied the claim, and the aggrieved appealed to arbitration.

At the arbitration hearing, the union argued that the proposed changes were valid; that Reilly was indeed a person with superior qualifications, experience, and education; and that the job as currently rated was an inadequate reflection of his competence. The union argued that to upgrade the job factor to the level requested by Reilly would enhance the status of the classification, would provide a greater incentive to workers to aspire to the classification, and would be an important factor in not only improving the quality of the work done in the classification, but also constitute an inducement to retain employees of Reilly's competence.

The employer argued that the job evaluation system did not evaluate or score the competence, experience, or qualification of any incumbent, but rather established the expectations of each position in order to compensate properly and fairly incumbents in a manner consistent with requirements of other jobs within the job evaluation system in the enterprise. It also argued that granting the increases sought by Reilly would result in downgrading the other toolmakers who lacked engineering degrees or a fourth year of experience and would entail reevaluation of the education and experience factors in all the other jobs in the company.

The arbitrator ruled that although there was no question about Reilly's exceptional qualifications or his possession of a level of competence beyond that negotiated by the parties as being required for the position he held, his competence did not justify the dislocation or destruction of the symmetry and rationale of the entire job evaluation system. The objective of the job evaluation system was to provide a framework of expected skills, and the several factors that go into the job were rated on the basis of the demands of the position. To depart from that system for one highly trained incumbent also would justify reductions in rates for others in that classification possessing only the current requirements and lacking the upward qualifications.

This would destroy the negotiated standards of comparability agreed to by the parties as the basis of their system.

Discussion Question 1: What might the union have argued?
The union might have argued that the factor ratings on the items that Reilly challenged were too low for the position, rather than just too low for Reilly. It could have sought an increase therein, noting that all employees in that classification were being underrated for the particular factors challenged by Reilly. That assertion, when buttressed by evidence of higher levels of performance expected by incumbents, might have led to a reexamination of the number of points attributed to the particular factors without changing the qualifications for the job. That could be accomplished by increasing the points for high-school shop education—with that increase in points applying to all jobs within the system.

Discussion Question 2: What position might the employer have taken?
The employer might have relied on examination of prior grievances resolved by the parties or decided by arbitrators, which would have reflected the futility of prior challenges and would have endorsed the overriding need for preservation of the system despite the occasional superior qualifications of a job incumbent. It could have presented data on the impact and cost of raising the points for high-school shop education or three years' experience when applied to all jobs requiring those levels of attainment. It could have cited a negotiating history of factor determination for the toolmaker job to show how claims similar to those raised by Reilly had been rejected by the parties in negotiations.

Discussion Question 3: Does the permanence of the job evaluation system deter or prevent its adjustment to meet external job-market changes?
There are three ways in which compensation for jobs falling under the job-evaluation system can be adjusted to reflect changes in the labor market. One is by changing the wage rate to be paid for jobs falling within the various labor grades. Those changes may be made by percentage or they may be made by flat, across-the-board increases for the individual job or, more likely, for the entire range of labor rates. Increases in the need for highly skilled personnel to fill more complex jobs can be answered by percentage increases, which provide larger amounts of money to those at the higher labor grades.

The second method of change in rate is to lower the cut-off point on the spectrum of point totals so that lower point requirements would be necessary for placement into the next higher labor grades. This compression of the labor grades results in occupants of a greater percentage of positions being paid at higher labor grades.

The third prospect for change is through restructuring of the point system to grant greater points for various levels of accomplishment of a particular factor, either by negotiation or, as in the case cited above, by filing a grievance that the point level attributed to a particular level of accomplishment in a factor is inadequate. It is the prospect of such adjustment that gives vitality and acceptability to the overall system and permits its continuity and survival. Such negotiated or even arbitrated changes in point or in labor-grade allocation tend to preserve the more general framework of rationality and equity that pervades the system.

Job Classification

Management is acknowledged to have the right to establish, to change, to combine, or to eliminate job assignments. The parties may negotiate the impact that such managerial decisions have on the employees. The impact is reflected in the wage rates negotiated for a particular classification. That impact includes an employee's entitlements and rights to a particular job within a classification when there is a change, elimination, or transfer that affects that employee. The contract may include procedures for achieving agreement on a job classification, including the duties, equipment, skills, and qualifications required of employees to fill that classification in order to be entitled to the negotiated rates.

Not all collective bargaining agreements have negotiated job classifications. But even if job classifications are unilaterally promulgated by the employer, they come to be accepted by both parties as the framework for determining the rights and entitlements of the employees assigned to or removed from those classifications, as well as for determining the rates pertinent to employees performing the required duties. There is a generally accepted correlation between the duties required for a job classification and the rate of pay negotiated for the performance of those tasks.

The varying wage rates subject to contract negotiation are generally tied to the job titles and job classifications in use at the enterprise. In some situations, the classification or title is so specific that it may, for example, refer to the work done by employees on a particular machine. However, the more general approach is to enumerate a series of duties that, when performed by an employee, places him or her in that job title or classification and entitles him or her to receipt of the negotiated rate.

As long as management assigns employees to perform tasks within the classifications covered by certain job titles and pays the appropriate rate, there is little challenge to such action. Challenges do arise over the entitlement of one employee over another to such assignment by virtue of seniority or other qualifications for promotion or transfer. They also arise when there is a change in duties for a job, which may lead to challenges over whether the job is, in fact, a new or a changed job.

As long as the employer does not make assignments that are inconsistent with the correlation between title and rate of pay, there will be little dispute. But if the employer should take tasks that belong in one job classification, say at a grade 5, and assign that work to an employee with a lower-rated title paid at labor grade 4, then there is grounds for the filing of a grievance protesting the assignment as a violation of the contractual commitment to pay the rate of labor grade 5 for tasks covered by the correlated job classification.

The fit of a job assignment need not be a perfect one. An employee need not be expected or required to fulfill all the requirements of his or her job, but if there is a reasonable relationship between a job assignment and the covering classification and if the core work expected under that classification is performed by the employee assigned to it, then it is to be expected that the appropriate wage rate for that core work will be extended to the employee performing it.

At one time, job descriptions may have been very specific when allocated to unique trades. The more recent tendency has been for employees to have more diversified skills with less rigidity in terms of skills being reserved for a specific job description. Indeed, it is far more prevalent to find skills that are common to a number of classifications. The appropriate classification for a particular skill thus is dependent on the unique characteristics of one classification that may be absent from other classifications, although many elements may overlap.

CASE: THE UPGRADED GARDENER

The university department of grounds had a classification of gardener, paid at labor grade 5, and a classification of landscaper, paid at the higher labor grade 6. The job description for gardener included responsibility for applying fertilizer, planting seeds and shrubbery, and maintaining the university grounds in an attractive manner. The job description for landscaper held that employee responsible for purchasing and selecting fertilizers and insecticides, for supervising gardeners, and for maintaining the areas in an attractive condition. Gardener Ruth Reardon filed a grievance asserting that her role in selecting fertilizers and insecticides as well as in applying them entitled her to compensation at the rate of landscaper.

At the arbitration hearing, the union argued that the grievant's work in selecting and applying insecticides and fertilizers was performed by her for a number of years and that it was the core element of the landscaper's classification. Because she had been doing that work with the acquiescence and approval of the department, she was entitled to be paid at the higher rate.

The employer took the position that the work performed by Reardon was a gardener's and not a landscaper's work. The selection of insecticides and fertilizers was from those in stock, which had been purchased by the supervisors within the department; thus, it did not constitute an exercise of discretion sufficient to justify payment at the higher rate. Additionally, the employer argued that the grievant did not perform any of the supervisory duties of landscaper, which were inherent in the higher labor-grade job description.

The arbitrator found that much of the work performed by Reardon was work that indeed overlapped both jurisdictions; that the use of insecticides and fertilizers was work done by both landscapers and gardeners; and that even though Reardon may have been the one who selected the insecticides and fertilizers to be used, whereas other gardeners only used those insecticides and fertilizers that were assigned to them, such selection and ordering, whether from the stockroom or from outside, was not the core element of the landscaper's classification. That core element, the arbitrator found, was supervision of other gardeners. Because the grievant had acted under the supervision of a landscaper, as did other gardeners, and because selection of insecticides and fertilizers was only one element in the landscaper's classification and not the key or core element of that classification, the grievance was denied.

Discussion Question 1: What issues might the union have raised?
The union might have produced evidence to show that the grievant did not do the same work as other gardeners; that she acted independently without the supervision of the landscaper, compared with other gardeners who acted under the supervision of the landscaper; and that the selection and purchase of insecticides and fertilizers was performed solely by her without any interference by or, indeed, even without the approval of the landscaper and without his exercising control over that function. It could have used the testimony of the landscaper that Reardon was doing the same work he was, assuming the landscaper also was a member of the union and willing to testify.

Discussion Question 2: What position might the employer have taken?
The employer might have provided testimony of times when the grievant had been issued orders by the landscaper, either in terms of notes written to the grievant or via log entries assigning tasks to be performed during an upcoming shift. Negotiating history of the parties in determining the wage rate and the tasks expected of the employees in that wage classification might have been of assistance to the employer's assertion that the grievant was a gardener and not a supervising landscaper.

Discussion Question 3: What if the landscaper had been absent and the employer had assigned the grievant to a temporary assignment to fill in his position? What rate would have been appropriate?

The parties in negotiation recognize that employees are on occasion absent from work and that there are positions vital to the functioning of the operation that must be filled on a temporary basis pending the return of the incumbent. In cases in which the person assigned to the temporary vacancy is performing functions that are covered by his or her permanent job description, there would be no justification for an increase to the rate of the position being filled. If, however, the employee is performing work that is unique to and a core responsibility of the higher-rated vacant position, then compensation would be appropriate for the difference between the rates.

In the above case, the transfer of Reardon into the landscaper's job may have been merely to order supplies, to answer the telephone, or to perform routine functions covered by Reardon's own job description, even if not continually performed by Reardon in her regular job. Thus, if there were not other gardeners at work during the day of the landscaper's absence, it would follow that Reardon was not doing supervision of other gardeners and would not be entitled to a higher grade.

If, on the other hand, while filling in for the landscaper Reardon did not order supplies, insecticides, or fertilizer, but rather directed the work of other gardeners, then that higher rate would be appropriate because that was determined by the arbitrator to be the crucial distinguishing element of the landscaper's job description. The fact that such assignment or direction of gardeners might have occurred just at the start of the shift or for a portion of the shift does not lessen the fact that the responsibility and the supervisory role were exercised. Supervision is determined not merely by the amount of time taken to issue orders, but includes as well the time span during which those orders are being implemented. Employees might return to the supervisor for further instruction, or the supervisor may need to ascertain the progress of the work he or she had ordered to be done.

Discussion Question 4: What if the landscaper had called Reardon and said, "An emergency has arisen; I must leave. Would you come and cover my job for the next couple of hours?" Assuming Reardon, on filling in the landscaper's job, did supervise employees and perform the full range of duties of the landscaper's position, would she have been entitled to the compensation?

Most collective bargaining agreements contain language defining the period of time during which an employee may be assigned to a higher-rated job before triggering the transfer clause procedures or securing the rate for the job to which transferred. Sometimes the time span is one hour, one day, or one week before the higher rate is triggered. To hold otherwise would lead to multiple claims for extremely short periods of time when employees were, in fact, doing work that may have been merely one component of many tasks performed by a supervisory employee during the course of the normal workday.

In the absence of strict time minimums of work performance for entitlement to upgrade, arbitrators can use a rule of reasonableness in determining whether the upgraded employee performed tasks anticipated by the description of the temporary job or whether employees indeed were filling in for brief periods when none or few of those tasks were being performed. Additional restrictions on the payment of higher compensation for such limited periods of time also might be found in the language or practice permitting the company to assign employees to other positions on an emergency short-term basis. If such emergency assignments are made in good faith and for short duration and do not involve a range of duties of the higher-skilled job, then arbitrators may permit such moves without additional compensation being paid.

Job Classification Changes

If the right of management to assign tasks and to determine equipment and methods of production is to be respected, management also must have the right to establish new classifications, to adjust the content of the work performed under such classifications, and to combine or eliminate classifications. The impact of such actions generally is subject to negotiation through the collective bargaining process. In some instances, that negotiation results in language restricting or prohibiting the company in its effort to change job classifications. Thus, in some collective bargaining agreements there is negotiation of classification titles, with the understanding that those classifications are to be preserved throughout the life of the agreement without elimination, combination, or adjustment.

Collective bargaining agreements usually recognize negotiated classifications as unchangeable, distinguished from the more general practice of classifications being more flexible and recognizing tasks to be performed. Arbitrators are sometimes confronted with the question of whether the listing of a job classification (particularly if its job description has been negotiated) constitutes an automatic guarantee of retaining the classification and its duties. This is a problem when technological change may justify changing tasks, combining tasks, or eliminating the classification.

When the employer seeks to make such classification changes under contract restrictions, the changes become matters for negotiation. If such negotiation is unsuccessful, the classifications generally are viewed as continuing in effect for the duration of the collective bargaining agreements.

Specific retention of such contractually recognized job classifications also may be viewed as prohibiting the employer from unilaterally establishing new classifications. But the more prevalent view of arbitrators is that unless the parties have negotiated that classifications are to be frozen for the life of the agreement, they are to be viewed as the basis for compensation for a group of tasks in effect when the agreement was signed. They do not detract from the employer's right to respond to change and maintain its competitive position through changes in job assignments, work methods, or new equipment. Thus, the existence of negotiated classifications or negotiated job descriptions is not generally viewed as a restriction against making changes in classifications.

When such changes do occur, the prevailing view is that they must be reasonable, they must be made in conformity with existing employee rights, and they must be subject to negotiation with the union because they have an impact on employees' wages, hours, and working conditions. The same standard applies in the case of changes in individual assignments. Employees are presumed to meet the requirements of the job to which they are assigned and are therefore entitled to the agreed-upon compensation for that job.

There are occasions in which the employer may exercise particular authority to order assignments, even though such assignments may appear to be in conflict with an employee's individual rights. Such conflicts over the employer's right of assignment may come to arbitration.

For example, an employee ordered to work his assignment on a religious holiday may protest a freedom-of-religion infraction. Such an assignment may raise a question of discrimination under Title VII of the Civil Rights Act. The employee may seek to be moved to a different assignment. Arbitrators dealing with such problems frequently identify that there may be a particular legal remedy available to the employee outside the collective bargaining agreement, but that the company has the right to direct the work force and to maintain efficient industrial operations under the contract. Although trying to accommodate employees' religious beliefs, arbitrators generally are reluctant to endorse the legal entitlement to profess or practice that belief at the expense of the employer's authority to make assignments consistent with the essential operations of the enterprise.

Even under the Civil Rights Act, the employer must make reasonable accommodation for the employee's religious belief in the scheduling of work. The employer is protected against any result that would impose an undue hardship on the conduct of the employer's business. A similar situation may arise in the case of employees with physical limitations as a result of injury or illness. Employees may have the right to perform tasks within their physical restriction, but only provided there is work available that can be performed effectively within that restriction. Most arbitrators would endorse the employer's effort to provide limited or light-duty situations, while upholding the employer's right to restrict the number of such limited or light-duty assignments. The alternative, to guarantee all limited or light-duty requests, risks causing irreparable damage to the employer's ability to run its enterprise.

Such a situation might arise if an employee, because of a physical disability or illness, is unable to be sufficiently regular in attendance to enable the employer to be dependent on the employee's availability to handle a job in regular need of that employee's attendance. Although the employee may not be responsible for the absences due to a legitimate illness or injury, that physical impairment may make the employee so unreliable that the team on which she works can't operate reliably. In such situations, arbitrators have held that the employer is not required to continue in its employ an individual who is unable to provide an adequate level of availability. Thus although employees may have religious, health, or illness entitlement that the employer should endeavor to accommodate, the right to operate the enterprise will usually be held to prevail in the event of conflict.

5
Leaves and Other Benefits

C ollective bargaining provides the basis for unions to secure as contractual rights certain benefits, such as leaves, which had previously
been matters of unilateral grant by the employer. Among these benefits are wash-up time, bonuses of various types, leaves of absence, personal
leave days, bereavement leave, call-in pay, and sick leave.

Wash-up Time and Other Unpaid Benefits

Despite the history of collective bargaining agreements having been negotiated to cover all wages, hours, and foreseeable working conditions, there is
a category of conditions that may not have been negotiated by the parties,
but that nevertheless have remained in effect. These may have originated
from the employer's magnanimity in providing such benefits as a Thanksgiving turkey near the end of a profitable year. If that gift was repeated the
next year and continued thereafter, it evolved as an employer's expected
grant to the employees and as a past practice.

Such benefits may have been unilateral grants by the employer or may
have originated as an assumed trade-off for contract language in earlier
negotiations. For example, the union may have asked for paid coffee breaks
and lunch periods, and the employer succeeded in having the union withdraw that demand in exchange for an assurance that it would provide paid
coffee breaks or even paid coffee without it being written in the contract.
The issue of wash-up time is a similar type of benefit that may have come
into use by expressed or tacit understanding between the parties or by the
employer's acquiescence once it recognized that employees were washing up
while still on their shift, rather than after they had punched out.

All of these benefits over a period of time become established working
conditions. They also usually reflect a cost to the employer and sometimes
a financial benefit to the employees. The wash-up time may cost the employer perhaps ten minutes per employee per shift in lost production. While
that does not translate into an economic benefit or windfall to the employees,
it does permit them to leave from work directly after punching out and saves
them the need to spend ten minutes at the plant on their own time washing
up. The Thanksgiving turkey is a cost to the employer and a financial savings
to the employee. Free coffee or free meals provided through this same tra-

dition are likewise a cost to the employer and a financial benefit to the employees. Thus, these past practices rise to the level of financial benefits, relieving the employees of the need to expend money for such benefits, and may become an appreciable addition to their wages.

Furthermore, it could be argued that having consistently received such a benefit over time, the union had no need to make it a part of its collective bargaining proposals. In a sense, the union acts in reliance on the continued receipt of that benefit as part of the status quo.

The issue comes to arbitration when the employer ceases to provide the benefit. The dispute frequently focuses on evidence of periodic renewal of the benefit, such as an annual October vote by the company's board of directors to provide the Thanksgiving turkey. It also might depend on whether or not the employer had placed the employees on notice that the particular benefit was to be viewed as a bonus, rather than as a condition of employment. If the employer had advised the employees on every occasion of granting the benefit that it was, in fact, a bonus that could be rescinded at any time, then the employer would have a stronger case when it invoked its authority to rescind that benefit.

If, on the other hand, the employer had not kept alive the knowledge that the benefit was a periodically renewed bonus and had led employees to believe, by its silence, that this was an accepted condition of employment, and during intervening negotiations the employer had made no effort to eliminate the benefit, the benefit would have continued to be an entitlement and would have become an established condition of employment. It constituted a part of the established environment that the union accepted as an ongoing condition. If the benefit was repeatedly and routinely provided, there would be no need for the union to demand the formalizing of such accretion.

Faced with this situation, if the arbitrator finds that the benefit was, in fact, repeatedly assured as a renewed and cancelable bonus, the employer generally would be allowed to rescind it. That recision may be made more attainable on the employer's part if it is able to show that there has been a change in conditions that necessitates the revocation of the benefit, such as an economic decline that would preclude continuation of the practice of granting the Thanksgiving turkey.

But in most cases, if the arbitrator concludes that the benefit has become part of the working conditions, then the arbitrator will say that having been continued in effect over a period of time during which there had been negotiation and opportunity for the employer to announce its cancellation, the working condition should continue until the parties negotiate a change. The cost to the employer in such a situation is a temporary continuance until those negotiations. Then the employer may announce the recision.

CASE: THE DAY BEFORE CHRISTMAS

Prior to unionization, the company gave employees the day before Christmas as a paid holiday. When the union negotiated its first contract, it secured an agreement with seven paid holidays, but it did not discuss the day before Christmas as a holiday. Nonetheless, the company continued to let employees have that day off with pay if it fell on a workday. That practice continued without any change in the contract language during the four intervening negotiations. Last year, the company announced that the day before Christmas would be a regular workday. Eliza White objected to the company's action, but worked on December 24 and filed a grievance for the lost day's pay.

At the arbitration hearing, the union argued that the day before Christmas had always been recognized as a holiday and that there was, therefore, no need for the union to negotiate it as a separate holiday. It argued that such a firmly established practice could not be unilaterally eliminated and that any change therein must be a matter of collective bargaining. Accordingly, it urged the grievance be sustained.

The company argued that the employer was obligated only to provide the paid holidays negotiated in the parties' agreement and that its unilateral grant of the day before Christmas had been a matter of annual determination by the employer. It noted that the benefit was only granted when the day fell on weekdays, and thus it had not been granted every year. It concluded that the grievance should be denied.

The arbitrator acknowledged that certain prior practices often continued as benefits, even though not specifically negotiated into the collective bargaining agreement. That standard was applicable, however, only if both parties had accepted that external practice and had not discussed the issue in negotiations. In this case, with the contract guaranteeing seven paid holidays, it forced the conclusion that the parties considered but rejected the inclusion of other holidays, such as the day before Christmas. The subsequent negotiation of President's Day and Martin Luther King's Birthday as two additional holidays confirmed that the omission of the day before Christmas was intentional. The Latin concept of *inclusio unis est esclusio alterius*—to include one is to exclude others—coupled with the fact that the holiday was not provided or paid when it fell on a Saturday or Sunday, forced the conclusion that the disputed day was not assured to employees as a paid holiday. It was a unilaterally granted benefit. Therefore, the employer was within its rights in canceling it without negotiating that cancellation with the union.

Discussion Question 1: What could the union have presented?
The union could have presented its notes from prior negotiations to show that the day before Christmas had not been the subject of negotiations. It

could have shown that the employer at some point had made a commitment to continue the benefit; that might have occurred if there had been worker protest over a proposal to delete it. It also could have drawn up a list of comparable extracontractual practices that had been continued or that had been subject to negotiation before cancellation. It could have argued that the benefit was a past practice to be continued pending negotiation. It also could have offered calendars of earlier years in which negotiations had occurred to show that the disputed day occurred on a weekend, obviating the need to discuss it as a holiday during those years.

Discussion Question 2: What could the company have presented?
The company also could have offered calendars of the years in which prior negotiations had occurred to show the number of years in which the day before Christmas had fallen on workdays as support for its view that it was deliberately excluded from the contract. Management also could have examined its own negotiation notes to see if the day was ever mentioned in negotiations and could have introduced those notes into evidence if the union had asserted it was mentioned. The company might have produced data to show how other pre–collective bargaining benefits had been negotiated if they were to be continued once the agreement was negotiated.

Discussion Question 3: Would the result have been different if the employer had announced it was suspending or eliminating the holiday just for this year because of a particularly heavy work load?
Such an announcement would have shown the employer considered the suspension a temporary interruption in an otherwise permanent benefit and probably would have led the arbitrator to endorse the union's view that management understood the benefit to be guaranteed. Had that been the case, the arbitrator would then have needed to consider the employer's right to suspend such a guaranteed benefit. If the employer did have the right, the issue would then have been to determine the appropriate remedy, either through holiday compensation for those having to work on the lost holiday or through provision of a substitute day off. The employer's need to have employees work on that holiday, if proven, would lead to the creation of a suitable remedy for the loss of that right.

Discussion Question 4: What would have occurred had the grievant declined to work the holiday and taken it off instead?
Most arbitrators would hold that the employee was required to do work as assigned and would view the case as one of insubordination and self-help. It thus would not be necessary to resolve the issue of whether the day was a protected holiday. Unless there is a showing that following an order to work constitutes an imminent danger to an employee's health or safety,

employees are expected to conform to an order and file a grievance thereafter. Failure to follow that course is viewed as insubordination, justifying at least the loss of the day's pay and obviating the need to determine the holiday issue.

Leaves of Absence

The traditional expectation that wages are negotiated for services performed has been expanded in most collective bargaining agreements beyond that narrow expectation into a range of compensations paid for situations in which there is actually no performance of services. The amount of compensation may run from full pay to negotiated levels of partial pay, depending on the nature of the negotiated benefit.

Jury Duty

It generally is accepted that the performance of jury duty is not only a community responsibility, but also an unavoidable call upon an employee to be away from his or her job for what might be an extended time. In order to lessen the financial impact of such jury calls and to encourage employees to live up to and not evade their public responsibility to serve as jurors, employees frequently are provided with financial guarantees to make up the difference between the minimal amounts of money they receive as jurors and the compensation they would have received had they been working.

It should be noted that there are some state statutes that mandate that employers pay the difference between the statutory jury fee and the employee's regular compensation. But absent such statutory requirements, any entitlement to payment for the time spent on jury duty is a matter of contract language. Arbitrators will not be likely to imply a duty to pay full reimbursement up to the level of an employee's normal wages unless there is contract language supporting such an obligation.

The general precept is that employees are entitled to be made whole for earnings lost by serving as jurors, provided the parties have so contracted. Under this theory, an employee who works the night shift and tends to his or her jury responsibilities on his time off during the day would not be entitled to jury-duty compensation because the jury duty was not performed on normal shift time.

Employers may seek to regulate against abuse of the jury-duty benefit by requiring documentation that the employee had served on the jury for the days in question. It therefore follows that if employees have falsified their claims in order to secure compensation for the time they are otherwise absent from work, then the employer would be entitled not only to recoup the amount of money paid, but also to impose disciplinary penalties on the employees for either falsification of company or public records or for seeking compensation for work not performed. Such fraudulent claims may be viewed by the employer as tantamount to theft of time and accordingly may be penalized by termination on first offense.

Furthermore, the contract language usually is restricted to pay only for jury duty. If an employee is called as a witness at a court proceeding, most arbitrators would say that such is a matter distinct from jury duty and should be negotiated separately by the parties. Reimbursement for jury-duty compensation is not extendable to employees who take time off to serve as witnesses in legal proceedings.

CASE: THE SLEEPY JURIST

Janet Devine worked the 11:00 P.M. to 7:00 A.M. shift. She was called to jury duty, which required her to report to the courthouse at 9:00 A.M.. Her jury assignment ran for three weeks. Her employer told her that jury compensation applied only if the jury duty precluded reporting to work. The parties' agreement provided as follows: "Employees who are unable to work because of being on jury duty will be reimbursed the difference between jury duty pay and their regular earnings."

Devine complained that she could not work her shift and then serve on the jury until 4:00 P.M. without it interfering with her efficiency in both tasks. She advised her employer that she was going to be out on sick leave until the end of her jury stint. She filed a grievance asking for jury-pay reimbursement, which was denied. She then appealed to arbitration.

At the arbitration hearing, the union argued that the jury-duty reimbursement provision was not negotiated just for those on the day shift who were required to serve, but that it was a benefit to which all employees were equally entitled, regardless of the shift on which they were working. It asserted that to require employees on other shifts to continue to work their regular hours while also serving on jury duty was discriminatory, onerous, and of risk to their health and safety. It urged the grievance be sustained, that Devine be granted the compensation differential, and that the sick-leave time she took off be restored to her credit.

The company took the position that the parties negotiated specific jury entitlement, that the contract was clear and that it specifically entended jury-duty reimbursement only to employees who were "unable to work because of being on jury duty." It argued that Devine's shift hours did not prevent her from being on jury duty while also working her shift, that she had the option of taking time off if she felt the jury duty made it difficult for her to work her normal hours, and that there was no contractual obligation to extend the differential reimbursement to employees who served on jury-duty during their own time and for which they were being paid the statutory jury pay.

The arbitrator held that negotiation of a benefit such as jury-duty reimbursement presumably anticipated that all bargaining-unit employees would have equal access to its entitlement. If that were not to be the case, it was incumbent on the parties, and specifically on the company, which would have benefited from such a restrictive interpretation, to incorporate that limitation into the contract provision. The language as drafted did not specify the application of the reimbursement only to day-shift employees or employees whose shift hours overlapped jury-duty hours. Rather, the language stated the reimbursement applied to those "unable to work" because of the jury duty.

The arbitrator found that the evidence supported the conclusion that an employee required to serve on jury duty for what could well be a long day commencing at 9:00 A.M. would have worked long hours of intense mental concentration. To require that employee to then provide another eight hours of work to the employer would certainly result in performance at less than peak efficiency to the point that a conclusion of being "unable to work" could readily be supported by the facts. Devine could not have been expected to work her 11:00 P.M. to 7:00 A.M. shift at the level of efficiency and concentration expected of her if she also had to serve on jury duty. Such lowered operating ability might well have courted inefficiency, poor workmanship, and the risk of disciplinary action therefor. Under the circumstances, the arbitrator found there was merit to the grievance and sustained it.

Discussion Question 1: What evidence might the union have presented?
The union could have produced evidence of negotiating history showing an intent of equal application to all shifts or at least showing neither party proposing the benefit be restricted to day-shift employees. The union could have examined the records of prior cases of jury duty to determine if only day-shift or all shift employees had shared therein. It could have shown that Devine's efficiency would have been impaired by being required to work the night shift. This could have been done by expert testimony on the impact of working nights and days. Evidence of practice in other companies with the same or similar language would also have been helpful.

Discussion Question 2: What position could the employer have taken?
In addition to similar surveys of comparability, of negotiating-history notes, and of past practice, the employer could have introduced evidence to show that living routines can be adapted to double tours of duty or cited the extent to which employees in the plant worked double shifts or long overtime with-

out their work efficiency being affected adversely. The company also could have argued that if the union's interpretation had been considered in negotiations, it would have been incumbent on the parties to develop different language because employees from other shifts would have lost eight hours and could reasonably have been expected to ask for full-reimbursement, eight hours lost. The union proposed language for payment of the differential contemplated being on jury duty only during the employee's regular shift.

Discussion Question 3: What would have been the result if Devine had insisted on working her regular night shift while claiming the differential reimbursement for the day shift?

Most arbitrators would have reasoned that the reimbursement was triggered by the employee being "unable to work." If the grievant had been able to work her night shift as well as attend to her jury-duty responsibilities, there would have been no grounds to reimburse her for the loss of work, since she had entailed none.

Discussion Question 4: If Devine's invoking of sick-leave time had been challenged by the employer, what would have been the result?

Once Devine invoked the sick-leave provisions, she placed herself in the position where she had to conform to procedural and verification requirements. If the employer had challenged the bona fides of her sickness claim, it might have been incumbent on Devine to provide medical documentation of illness. This could have been provided in the form of a doctor's certificate that the disruption of her sleep or other hours to serve on the jury made her so sleepy that she was medically found unfit to fulfill her job requirements in a safe or healthy manner.

Discussion Question 5: What if the employer had refused the claim of sick leave at the outset and had ordered the grievant to continue on the night shift while also serving on the jury?

The doctrine of work now and file a grievance later, if applied to the company's order that she continue on the night shift, could properly have been circumvented by invocation of the right to withhold services if there is a reasonable risk of danger to health and safety. If the grievant were able to provide medical verification of her condition and of the risks she ran while working when tired from jury duty, her position could prevail.

Discussion Question 6: What if refraining from night-shift duty entailed loss of overtime? Would Devine have been entitled to that while on jury duty?

Entitlement to lost overtime, whether earned on the day shift or the night shift, is a question of the language of the jury-duty compensation provision of the parties' agreement. If the language cited reimbursement of regular earnings and the negotiating history showed an intent to reimburse for regular compensation exclusive of overtime, then no lost overtime would be reimbursable. The practical reality is that once the jury duty was completed, Devine would have been comparatively low in overtime hours compared with those who continued to work overtime while she was on jury duty. She thus would have been in a prime position to work more overtime hours under the parties' contract provision guaranteeing equalization of overtime.

Personal Leave

Many collective bargaining agreements have incorporated provisions guaranteeing compensation to employees who take time away from work to perform personal tasks that they are unable to perform during their normal off-duty hours. The provisions granting personal leave may require the employee to give specific reasons for taking the day of leave or may require the employee to provide generic indication of the reason for absence, such as personal business, legal business or medical need. Sometimes the leave entitlement is based on the need to perform a task that cannot otherwise be performed during the employee's free time, such as a visit to a medical clinic, a son's college graduation, an appearance in court, or a meeting with lawyers. In enforcing the provision, the employer has the right to assure itself that the employee indeed is taking the leave for the purpose asserted before granting the compensation provided under the contract.

For those contracts stating that written requests for leave must precede the granting of the leave, disputes occasionally arise over the type of documentation required by the collective bargaining agreement. But once the legitimacy of the leave request is established, the days of leave may run from one to as many as are specified as the maximum in the parties'agreement.

Among the problems that frequently arise between the parties on the issue of personal-leave entitlement is whether the leave day must be used for one of the reasons stated in the contract. This problem is particularly acute when the contract calls for general reasons for leave and the employer is thereby prevented from inquiring about more specific reasons. Another problem arises over whether the task for which the leave is taken is one that can be performed on the employee's own time.

Management frequently is determined to avoid abuses of the personal-leave entitlement by requiring substantive evidence of the reason for the employee's taking the leave, either in the form of explicit documentation of the reason for which the time was taken or in the form of an advance statement about the reason for the leave. Unions frequently respond to such requests by noting that the parties had negotiated the listing of only general reasons for taking leave and that the employee therefore is only required to provide a general explanation. The union asserts that such a general explanation is adequate and is essential to protect the privacy of the employee, who may be utilizing personal leave to handle delicate situations that if known to the employer might jeopardize his or her employment position. Among the examples of such sensitive matters might be meeting with an attorney to discuss divorce proceedings, being required to attend a court proceeding on an assault or molestation charge, or securing treatment at an abortion clinic.

Also related to the employer's concern for learning the reasons for an absence may be the employer's fear that an employee is working for another employer. The issue of moonlighting frequently will come under scrutiny if an employee is routinely tardy, requests leave on a routine basis, or leaves regularly ahead of the scheduled shift end. Employees are recognized as having the right to engage in personal business as long as it is on their own time and does not interfere with their responsibilities to their principal employer. But on occasion there is a conflict between personal business interests and employment interests, and arbitrators frequently are faced with the question of whether an employee is entitled to take personal leave for conduct of a business activity unrelated to that of his main employer.

Arbitrators generally look askance at employees taking advantage of a personal-leave benefit in order to moonlight for another employer or for their own enterprise. The taking of such leave days for essential extracurricular business activities is not usually a matter for discipline by the employer. The grant of compensation for such days is not likely to be viewed with favor by arbitrators, who would more likely support the idea of leave without pay for the conduct of such extracurricular business activities. Discipline might be in order if the business absences were repeated after admonitions not to use leave days for conflicting business commitments.

CASE: THE MARITIME LEAVE

Roger Frisch was a teacher working under a collective bargaining agreement with the following personal-leave provision: "Teachers may be granted up to six days of personal leave per school year for medical, legal and personal matters that can not be taken care of during nonteaching hours. Teachers shall submit a request for such leave forty-eight hours in advance, specifying the reason for the leave."

Frisch was an avid sailor and owner of a sailboat, which he had been advertising to sell for three months. On April 15, his ad was answered and arrangements were made to transfer title to the boat. Frisch tried to schedule the transfer on a Saturday or Sunday, but the purchaser insisted on a weekday so his lawyer could be present. Frisch gave in and met the buyer at 2:00 P.M. on Friday at the marina, a one-hour drive away. On the previous Tuesday morning, Frisch had submitted the following note to his principal: "I would like to take a personal leave day on Friday to handle a personal matter that cannot to done during non-school hours." The principal granted the leave request, but several weeks later learned through a friend who also was the buyer of the boat that the day of leave was for the sale of the boat. Frisch was docked one day's pay. He filed a grievance, and the issue went to arbitration.

At the arbitration hearing, the union argued that Frisch was improperly deprived of the day of leave, that the transfer of the boat was indeed a personal matter, that he tried unsuccessfully to have the transfer occur on a nonschool day, that Frisch properly applied for the leave, and that the school district lacked the authority to rescind the leave once it had been granted. Accordingly, it sought to have Frisch reimbursed for the lost day's pay.

The school district contended that its action was appropriate, that Frisch acted fraudulently in invoking as a necessity for personal matters a day off to engage in a business transaction that was well beyond the intent of the contract clause, and that it was a transaction that readily could have been taken care of when school was not in session. It argued that grants for leave were discretionary rather than mandatory and that when the fraud was discovered, it was within its authority in rescinding the leave and charging Frisch for the day's wages.

The arbitrator held that the personal-leave article was negotiated to provide teachers with time off to attend to matters that could not be attended to during school hours and that the parties recognized the privacy of such matters and agreed to exclude them from the scrutiny of the employer. In this case, the arbitrator continued, the employer granted the request for the day's leave on the basis of the grievant's assurance that it was for a personal matter that could only be handled during school hours.

The arbitrator concluded, however, that the sale of a boat was not the type of personal matter that was contemplated by the provision and that because it was beyond the type of activity the parties agreed should be kept private, it should have been revealed to the school prior to its being taken. The arbitrator further concluded that even if it had been a protected activity, it readily could have been conducted during nonteaching hours on a school day without the necessity for a day away from teaching responsibilities. The arbitrator concluded that because the employer lacked the authority to challenge the request prior to the day of leave, it acted properly in denying the leave once it discovered that it had been improperly invoked.

Discussion Question 1: What position could the union have taken?
The union could have offered testimony concerning the negotiating history to show that a wide application of "personal matters" was intended and could have sought evidence of past instances when the school district know-

ingly permitted days off to handle commercial affairs. Although it would hardly call to testify those employees who had clandestinely used personal-leave days for business, it might have been able to secure such evidence through testimony of principals and other management personnel who had known of the commercial nature of the business conducted during personal leaves.

The union also could have sought to establish an analogy to a house closing, which would be more likely to have occurred on a weekday and necessitate absence from school. Teachers might have been willing to testify that they took leave days for house closings, including testimony that their principals knew or should have known of the reasons for the leave. The union could have brought the lawyer for the purchaser of the boat to testify that there no opportunities for the sale to be completed except at 2:00 P.M. on the Friday in question.

Discussion Question 2: What position could the employer have taken?
The employer could have shown a consistent practice of refusing leave days for similar purposes, stating that most teachers seeking leave tended to be more open and explicit in their reasons. The employer could have solicited its principals to establish that there had been consistent denials of leave for such reasons. The employer could have offered testimony concerning the negotiating history and shown a goal of protecting employees from the embarrassment of revealing reasons to take an occasional leave day for medical or legal problems. Testimony of union assurance that it would not agree to or tolerate taking of leave for commercial activity might have been included to show that the parties did not contemplate using the leave for frivolous reasons such as selling boats. The employer could have cited past instances of leave withdrawal upon after-the-fact discovery of improper use.

Discussion Question 3: Did the use of the phrase "teachers may be granted" instead of "will be granted" mean that the grant of leave was not a right that teachers had?
The use of the phrase "may be granted" in conjunction with the phrase "up to six days of personal leave" limited the employer's discretion to the granting of leave when the contractual requirements had been met. The right to the leave was established when the teachers had filed the proper request in timely fashion for an approved form of leave. But the phrase "will be granted" would have deprived the employer of its control over the granting of leaves when prerequisites had not been met. Thus, the parties used the phrase "may be granted" as recognition of the employer's inherent right to grant the leave and its right to withhold the leave if tardily requested or if the employer knew in advance the reason was impermissible. The negotiating history of

the parties in agreeing to the language would shed light on the intent of the parties in their choice of terminology.

Discussion Question 4: Doesn't the short lead time and the vagueness of the categories open the door to abuse of such leave days?

This is a matter of joint concern. It is of concern to the employer, which seeks to restrict the payment of compensation for leave days and which is restricted by time and by ignorance of the true reason for the leave because of the vague benchmarks. It is also of concern to the union, which has the primary goal of protecting the privacy of employees who need the time for matters that might place their jobs in jeopardy if revealed. The union, too, is concerned about abuse of the clause, because revelations of improper usage will certainly trigger a request for more information on the reasons for the leave or even a reduction or elimination of personal leaves in forthcoming negotiations on grounds of abuse.

Management is at a disadvantage in not being able to determine whether the request for leave is legitimate and deserving of privacy. Certainly an employee who is being tested for AIDS would not want that fact known to management and is entitled to the assurance of privacy when taking the day off for that test. Mere knowledge that the test was being taken might well be fatal to his or her continued employment. Given the countervailing rights to privacy and to protection against abuse of the leave entitlement, most arbitrators would assume legitimate compliance with the leave provisions absent evidence of abuse, even as here, after the fact.

Bereavement Leave

Unexpected absence of employees from work due to death of relatives is neither certain nor foreseeable except in the aggregate. Employees and employers recognize that the death of parents, spouses, children, and other relatives causes both emotional disturbance and need for the employee to attend to family matters. In anticipation of such a category of absences, the parties frequently negotiate bereavement leave in order to establish in advance the entitlement of employees to such leave when the need arises.

The parties negotiate three aspects of such leave. The first aspect is the relationship of the deceased to the employee. This relationship would justify the invocation of the right to bereavement leave. The most common relationships included in collective bargaining agreements are spouse, mother, father, sister, brother, and child. Beyond that, the parties may negotiate for aunt, uncle, grandparent and perhaps even the "significant other" with whom an employee may have been living.

The second area of negotiation is over the duration of the leave. Leaves run from one to three days or more under special circumstances, such as unusual distances to be traveled.

The third area of negotiation is the amount of compensation to be provided during the period of leave. Some leave days are granted without pay, while in other collective bargaining agreements, such bereavement leave days are funded by subtracting the time from the employee's sick-leave accumulation. A more general practice is to pay the employees their normal earnings for the days covered by the collective bargaining agreement.

CASE: FUNERAL LEAVE WITHOUT A FUNERAL

Employee Tom O'Brien announced to his foreman that his father had died and that he wished to take off the three days provided in the agreement. The employer granted permission, and O'Brien took the time off.

The parties' collective bargaining agreement provision was entitled "Funeral Leave" and was applied to absences of up to three days for attendance at funerals. The negotiating history of the parties' agreement showed that the union had proposed the term *bereavement leave* for a large number of categories of relatives and that the parties ultimately agreed on *funeral leave* with time off to attend funerals for a restricted group of relatives, including fathers.

During O'Brien's absence, the employer learned that the employee's father had died in the Philippines and was being buried there. When O'Brien returned to work, his supervisor advised him that he was being denied the requested funeral leave and was being docked the three days he was off because he had not attended his father's funeral. O'Brien filed a grievance, which was subsequently appealed to arbitration.

At the arbitration hearing, the union argued that the parties' intent was to provide time off to attend to family affairs occasioned by the death of anyone in the listed classifications of relatives. O'Brien was the sole son of his father and spent the three days ministering to his grieving mother, who lived in the same town as O'Brien, and trying to make arrangements to assure that she would have income from the dead father's estate. It argued that although it initially requested *bereavement leave* during negotiations, it had agreed to the term *funeral leave* because of its more direct and understandable meaning. To limit the benefit to employees who actually attended funerals would deprive a substantial number of employees the opportunity to invoke the benefit when their relatives were at such distant locations that they could not attend the funerals. It concluded that the restrictive interpretation encouraged by the employer was contrary to the parties' intent and that the grievant was entitled to the three days of leave payment.

The employer argued that the parties clearly had agreed in negotiations to a change from the proposed *bereavement leave* to *funeral leave* and thus to a requirement of attendance at a funeral in order to justify receipt of payment. It argued that the type of activity engaged in by the grievant could have been done during his off hours, during weekends, or by taking leave without pay and that he did not use the time to attend a funeral, which was the goal of the parties in drafting the language.

The arbitrator agreed with the company concerning the reason for the language change from *bereavement* to *funeral* and that the narrowing of the language was to permit employees to take time away from their work to attend funerals that would be held during their working hours. The arbitrator acknowledged that although attending to grieving relatives, particularly parents, was an integral component of the leave, the negotiating history reflected the employer's and union's commitment to restrict the absence for funeral attendance. The arbitrator concluded that to provide the three days of leave requested when there was no attendence at the funeral in effect would rewrite the parties' agreement and substitute three days for mourning and bereavement for the parties' agreed-upon three days for funeral attendance and related activities. Accordingly, the grievance was denied.

Discussion Question 1: What arguments could the union have raised?
The union might have produced evidence of the negotiating history to show that its intent was articulated in using the simpler word *funeral* in place of the more ponderous *bereavement*. It might have been able to cite cases in which employees had been given time off under the funeral clause but had not attended funerals or in which employees had told supervisors that the funerals were at distant places and were granted the time off without being required to attend the funeral. The union could have argued alternatively that because only one of the three days granted, in any event, could have been devoted to funeral attendance, the remaining two days were, in effect, bereavement leave to which the grievant would have been entitled, regardless of whether or not he had attended a funeral.

Discussion Question 2: What positions might the employer have presented?
The employer might have similarly researched the negotiating history to cite any notes showing that the employer had proposed the narrowing of the language and the requirement of funeral attendance as well as any comments from union participants. It might have cited past requirements of evidence of funeral attendance as a condition of the payment of leave, and it might have pointed out that there had never been a known grant of leave that did not include funeral attendance.

Discussion Question 3: What if the parties' agreement had specified leave for the death of a father, but the deceased had been the grievant's stepfather?

The determination of the various classifications of relatives becomes very complex and may be used to contrive expansions or restrictions on the list. If the grievant's natural father had been alive and his mother had been married to the new stepfather who died in the Philippines, most arbitrators would tend to preclude his invoking the leave for a stepfather because he also would have entitlement to invoke the leave for his natural father, thus permitting that one employee to expand the agreed-upon list of relatives to two fathers. But if, on the other hand, the stepfather had been the person with whom the grievant had spent most of his life, who had filled the role of his natural father, and who had been recognized as the male who brought up the grievant, then an arbitrator might be more receptive to granting the leave for that individual, particularly if the evidence showed that the grievant's natural father had no contact with the employee or was deceased.

Some collective bargaining agreements specify that the relationship between the employee and the deceased must be a blood relationship. Thus, an employee's mother's sister, an aunt, would be included as an eligible relative, while the aunt's husband, an uncle, who had no blood relationship with the employee, would be excluded from such an eligibility list. Some collective bargaining agreements have relied on the traditional term, husband and wife, and have been challenged by employees whose living companion may have been a common-law spouse or perhaps even another individual of the same sex. The prevalence of divorces and remarriages, the prevalence of stepsisters, stepbrothers, and stepparents, and the multitude of new living arrangements makes this a fertile area for grievance arbitration.

Discussion Question 4: What is the appropriate standard for such determinations?

During negotiations, the parties invoke certain classifications of relatives for applicability of a funeral or bereavement and look for objective and general standards. It is perhaps cumbersome, although it may be more exact, to delineate whether the relationships be by consanguinity, by marriage, by the duration of time spent with the employee, or by a physical or geographical proximity to the individual. But the parties do not take the time during negotiations to foresee the myriad variations that might arise during the life of their agreement.

It therefore becomes necessary for arbitrators to resolve such issues, and the prevailing standard of arbitrators is to look beyond the language to the intent, which is to provide an opportunity for the grieving employee to attend the funeral of that individual whose relationship would inspire the employee to take the time off to attend the funeral or to grieve. The arbitrator in the case above felt inhibited in going beyond the negotiated words because the parties had specifically faced the issue of bereavement versus funeral attendance and, for whatever reasons, agreed upon *funeral,* meaning attending the funeral.

Thus, in the case of a grandmother who had remarried one year earlier and whose second husband had just died, arbitrators would inquire about the closeness of the relationship between the stepgrandfather and the employee and about the whereabouts of the employee's real grandfather. If that individual was still alive and had a closer relationship with the employee than the stepgrandfather, the arbitrator would be faced with the question of whether the employee would be entitled to two periods of leave for the grandfathers. Would both or only one leave be justified if the purpose of the bereavement was for the employee to console the grandmother? This, in turn, raises the question of whether the arbitrator should perserveer as to the emotional ties of the living or the ties of the employee to the dead. In any event these are cumbersome issues for which arbitrators seek to apply emotionally reassuring enforcement, although perhaps hindered by the parties' strict contract language.

Call-in Pay

When the parties negotiate a work schedule, it is assumed that the employees will report to work and perform the tasks assigned them for the hours of the shift to which they are assigned. The parties assume that once an employee reports to work, he or she has made a commitment to work the full scheduled shift. There are times, however, when an employee reports to work yet is unable to work because of weather, a lack of supplies of product, an equipment breakdown, or some other catastrophe that denies work to that employee or keeps him or her from working during that shift. As a means of assuring protection of an employee's income, the parties in most collective bargaining agreements negotiate for call-in or report-in pay, through which an employee is entitled to a partial shift payment for having undertaken the effort to report to work and for being able and willing to work. The theory is that once an employee has reported to work, any reason for not working is usually not the fault of the employee, but rather the fault of the employer.

Arbitrators tend to hold the employer responsible for most situations in which a reporting employee is unable to work, with the possible exceptions of weather or other so-called acts of God. Thus, an employee who reports to work on time is usually the beneficiary of a report-in pay provision, even though he or she may not be permitted to work for the full shift. The general standard would be that the employee would be entitled to four hours call-in pay for having reported. That same standard would also apply to an

employee who came and worked for three hours, since the four hours is usually a contractual minimum. To permit the employer to escape that four-hour minimum payment by having the employee work for any shorter period would erode the contractual commitment and place a premium on making work available for an hour or two to evade the four-hour liability.

CASE: THE MIDNIGHT DRIVER

At 11:00 P.M. the regular truck driver had not reported as scheduled. At 11:15, the company called Brian Harries, who normally worked the 7:00 A.M.–3:00 P.M shift and lived fifteen minutes away, to come in at midnight to substitute for the regular driver and make delivery. Harries, who was asleep at the time, got dressed and left his house at 11:20 P.M. At 11:30, the regular driver appeared, after having been delayed by a washout of the bridge he had to cross to get to the factory area. He was sent out with the emergency delivery. The supervisor telephoned Harries to cancel his need to report, but his wife advised that he had already left.

Harries reported at midnight as requested and was sent home. The company denied him four hours call-in pay on the grounds that he did not report promptly and that because the regular driver had been delayed by an act of God, it was not obligated to pay him.

At the arbitration hearing, the union argued that the four-hour call-in pay was due anyone who was called in off-shift and reported to work; that the grievant had reported to work as rapidly as possible and at the time due; and that once he reported, the call-in pay was due. It asserted that the reason the regular driver was late was irrelevant to the grievant's contractual entitlement.

The company argued that Harries should have left his house at 11:45 to get to the factory at midnight. His leaving so early deprived the employer of the opportunity to reach him to cancel the call-in, and the call-in was occasioned only by the regular driver having been delayed by an act of God in the bridge washout. Therefore no call-in pay was due, the company stated.

The arbitrator ruled that the parties agreed to provide a minimum of four hours pay at the regular rate for any employee called into work on off-shift hours, that the act of God exception to that liability applied to unavailability of work when the employee arrived at the work site, that the lack of work for Harries at his midnight arrival was due to the regular driver's reporting prior to Harries's arrival, and that the fact that that driver may have been delayed by a bridge washout did not relieve the company of the obligation to pay Harries. The grievance was sustained.

Discussion Question 1: What position could the union have taken?
The union could have turned to notes of the negotiation of the call-in provision and, in particular, to any discussion of the act-of-God exception. It
could have produced evidence of prior grants of call-in pay under similar
circumstances, and it could have provided a detailed chronology of Harries's
trip to work from the time of the call until midnight to show that his actions
had been reasonable, entitling him to the pay.

Discussion Question 2: What position could the company have taken?
The company could have argued that Harries left home early deliberately in
anticipation that a call might come that the regular driver had reported. The
company also could have shown a past practice not to provide call-in pay
when the absent employee reported before the called-in worker. It could
have argued that the call-in was an honest error and therefore the company
should be exempt from any penalty.

Discussion Question 3: What if the company had reached Harries prior to
 his departure for work to cancel the call-in?
The call-in pay is based on the employee reporting for work and then finding
none available. It is not triggered by the initial telephone call. Thus, if there
is a later cancellation call, the employer would have no liability even if the
employee initially had prepared to leave or canceled other commitments.

Discussion Question 4: What if the company showed four prior instances
 in which the tardy employee reported before the call-in and no call-in was
 paid?
If the contract was clear that a called-in employee was entitled to compensation, the fact that four other employees had been denied it would not have
had any impact on the above case unless it could be shown that (1) the prior
denial had been denied in arbitration, (2) that one or more instances had
involved union officials who had acquiesced in the company's view that no
call-in pay was due by their failure to file a grievance over the nonpayment,
or (3) that there had been a proven understanding between the company
and the union that pay was not due in such cases. Absent such exceptions,
the contract language mandating call-in pay would prevail.

Sick Leave and Sick Pay

When the parties negotiate their contract, it is not uncommon to negotiate
a protection against wage loss resulting from an employee being sick and
unable to report to work. The objective of such a benefit is to assure a
smooth flow of income to the disabled employee. Even though a physical
condition may preclude him or her from being able to work on the day in

question, the parties generally negotiate an arrangement whereby an employee is given a bank of workdays on credit. Then, when the employee is sick, he or she is able to draw on that bank and remain out of work while being paid for such days up to the amount of credit available to that employee. The size of the credit will depend on the annual accumulation of sick days, the legitimacy of the absence for illness, and any negotiated right to carry over the unused credits from one year to the next.

In order to protect against abuses of the sick-pay provision, the employer often will require that the employee provide medical verification of illness if there is belief that the employee is abusing the sick-pay provision. As discussed in chapter 3, documentation to avoid abuses may be a matter of dispute between the parties regarding its authenticity, its adequacy, and the employee's responsibility to provide it. Although the objective of sick pay is to protect earnings, many parties have negotiated provisions to permit employees to recoup a portion of the value of unused sick leave on an annual basis or on retirement. The theory of such right to cash in unused sick days is that they represent money that would otherwise have been available for sick-leave pay and money saved by not having to call in substitutes or ask employees to work overtime. Thus, even if an employee is able to recoup one-half of the value of the unused sick-leave day, that would provide an incentive to the employee to work rather use the sick leave and would assure the employer of a reduced rate of absenteeism. Employees would prefer to get at least half a day's pay for each day of unused sick leave, rather than take sick-leave days when physically able to work.

An element of sick leave that is becoming a matter of growing concern is maternity leave. Although statutory protections provide assurances that employees will be entitled to grants of maternity leave without prejudice or discrimination under the Civil Rights Act and the Federal Pregnancy Amendments Act of 1978, many collective bargaining agreements are negotiated without regard to those statutory rights. Such matters are, on occasion, appealed to arbitration.

CASE: THE UNSUBSTANTIATED ILLNESS

Tom Ivy called in on May 3 prior to the start of his shift to announce that he was not feeling well because of a stomach disorder and would not be reporting to work. The next morning, May 4, he again called in and reported he wasn't feeling any better and would be out again. The supervisor to whom he spoke advised him that in order to to collect sick-leave pay for the days he was out, it was necessary to bring in medical documentation to excuse the absence. Ivy went to the doctor that afternoon for an examination and was told to stay out a third day and to report to work on May 6. Ivy requested a medical certification and was given the following: "To whom it may concern: Tom Ivy was seen in my office today for stomach problems. He should be out tomorrow and may return to work on May 6."

On May 6 Ivy returned to work, handed the note to his supervisor and went to work. He was later told that he was being given sick-leave pay for May 4, when he was at the doctor's office and for May 5 when he had been ordered to stay home, but not for May 3, because there was no medical verification of his inability to report to work. Ivy filed a grievance over the denial of that day's sick leave. The grievance was denied, and the case ultimately was appealed to arbitration.

At the arbitration hearing, the union argued that Ivy was legitimately ill, that he had called in his absence, and that it was not until the second call-in that he was told to bring medical certification. It asserted that the first day absent would have been allowed as sick leave had it not been for the later days and that the doctor's note showed that on May 4, Ivy still had the same ailment he had complained of the day before. It asserted that the denial of the first day's leave was arbitrary and capricious and that the grievance should be sustained.

The employer argued that there were clear rules governing the grant of sick leave if an employee was absent two or more days. Those rules, it continued, required medical verification of the legitimacy of the entire absence, which was not provided in this case because only two days were excused. The employer noted that the rules calling for medical documentation for absences of two or more days were reasonable and an essential protection against abuse of sick-leave entitlement and that Ivy was made aware of the rule when he telephoned on May 4. It concluded that he therefore was bound to adhere to the requirements.

The arbitrator held that the issue in this case was not the bona fides of the grievant's illness or even his inability to return to work. Rather, the arbitrator held, the issue was the grievant's failure to conform to the procedural requirement of medical substantiation for each day of a medical leave. The arbitrator noted that the procedure calling for medical substantiation was not contractual, but rather unilaterally promulgated by the employer as an effort to control the legitimacy of leaves of absence.

The failure in this case was the omission from the medical certificate of the fact that Ivy was also out ill on May 4. That omission was a procedural one which, if there was doubt, could have been remedied by either the company or the union asking the physician to revise the note, or asking Ivy to have the physician issue a corrected note, or even by the company's waiving its right to insist on a note for May 4, as the ailment was the same the next day and as there was no question of Ivy being ill on May 4. The arbitrator ruled that the employer's procedures should be reasonably implemented and should not stand in the way of granting sick leave for what was clearly a substantive entitlement. Accordingly, the grievance was sustained.

Discussion Question 1: What position could the union have taken?
The union could have argued that because Ivy would have been excused for that single-day absence, there was no rational justification for denying such leave when the illness dragged on longer. It could have offered testimony about the parties' negotiation of the sick-leave provision, particularly as it related to assuring that leaves were not abused. It also could have provided evidence of any role it had taken in the development of the employer's procedures, particularly as they affected requiring medical documentation for one or more days of illness. The union could have offered evidence of prior comparable situations in which leave was granted despite faulty documentation or at least of opportunities being afforded to revise such documentation.

Discussion Question 2: What position could the employer have taken?
The employer could have shown the history of the negotiations over sick leave, particularly if such discussion focused on the employer's right to establish procedural rules or on the union's acquiescence to the employer's authority in such matters. It also could have offered testimony to show the reasonableness of the rules, the union's failure to challenge them at any earlier time, and the necessity of such rules being adhered to as a deterrent against abuse. It could have shown the procedure for advising employees of the note requirement, such as reading a statement to them on the second day of any absence, to confirm the fact that Ivy was told of the requirement for documentation covering all three days of the absence.

Discussion Question 3: Would the union be bound by procedures it had not negotiated?
Assuming as here that the contract was limited in providing the extent of the sick-leave entitlement and that the procedures covering entitlement had been unilaterally developed by the employer, any exercise in procedure development assumes that the rules are reasonable and reasonably enforced. The union and the employees are bound to conform to reasonable rules that are consistent with fair implementation of the contract language, but that does not force either the union or the employer to conform to unreasonable or irrational rules. Thus, if the employer were to require extensive and costly medical tests with the employee to bear the cost thereof, most arbitrators would find such a requirement to be unreasonable and void it from the procedures.

*Discussion Question 4: What if the employer had challenged the determi-
nation of medical incapacity as rendered by the employee's physician?*
As discussed in chapter 3, the employer is not bound to accept the finding
by the employee's physician of incapacity to work. The employer may view
that finding as wrong or as a conspiracy to assist the employee in a plot to
stay out of work. But merely denouncing the doctor's report is not proof of
its fallacy because in any grievance protesting the failure to provide sick
leave, the medical holding of the employee's physician would prevail. Thus,
in order to rebut an employee's physician, the employer must provide a
medical opinion supporting its position that the employee was not sick. The
employer has the right to have the employee examined by a second physician
of the employer's choice, either a company physician or an outside physician
paid for by the employer.

Disputes often arise between the contrary findings of the two physicians
if the employee's physician disputes the employer's physician or if the employee does not accept the findings of the employer's physician. Such conflicts are then appealed to arbitration, and the arbitrator has the responsibility
of weighing the conflicting medical evidence or perhaps even the competence
of the two examiners. Some arbitrators make the judgments on the basis of
the evidence presented. Others ask permission to consult expert medical
authority in rendering their verdict, while others urge the parties to have the
two doctor's agree on a third physician to serve as a medical arbitrator
rendering a final and binding medical assessment.

6
Hours and Schedules

T he collective bargaining agreement is accepted as covering wages, hours, and working conditions. The term *hours* refers to the amount of time employees are to provide services to the employer for the wages that are paid. One theory has been that management makes the hours of work available, and employees are required to work them in exchange for compensation. That theory prevailed before collective bargaining; employees either worked the hours that were available or were deemed unsuited for employment. But with the advent of collective bargaining and the concept of employees having the right, through their union, to negotiate over hours, several aspects of the subject of hours came under the purview of the collective bargaining agreement as being clearly negotiable. These aspects include the time to be worked, the structure of work hours, breaks in the workday, and scheduling of work hours.

Time to Be Worked

Collective bargaining negotiations incorporate not only the rate to be paid for the hours of work, but the number of hours to be worked as well. The subject of the workweek is one that has long been a focus of union interest and federal legislation. The Fair Labor Standard Act of 1938 set the framework for wages in collective bargaining by establishing a forty-hour workweek at regular rates before time and a half is required for work beyond that forty hours. Collective bargaining agreements negotiated following the enactment of that standard in 1938 focused on a normal or regular workweek of forty hours.

Negotiations and management practice since that time have dropped the figure below forty hours as the normal workweek. The determination of what is a regular or normal workweek depends on a particular collective bargaining agreement or on company practice. Most collective bargaining agreements establish the number of hours after which overtime is to be paid. In some collective bargaining agreements, overtime is paid after the forty-hour week provided by statute. In other collective bargaining agreements, arrangements are made for overtime payment after normal workweek hours, which may be as few as thirty-five hours. In other collective bargaining agreements, overtime may be triggered on completion of an eight-hour day or on completion of the normal workday if it is less than eight hours.

Collective bargaining agreements frequently describe a normal workday of eight hours and a normal work load of forty hours, including paid break time and lunchtime. Disputes arise between the parties over whether that eight-hour day or forty-hour week described as normal or regular is, in fact, protected or guaranteed to the employees. Most arbitrators hold that because the parties have agreed to provisions for overtime payment, there is an expectation that work hours may exceed those described as the norm. Similarly, because the parties generally agree to some provision for reporting-in pay, arbitrators reason that provision of reporting-in pay in the event of a plant shutdown, or unavailability of work suggests that there may be abnormal situations when the workweek is reduced from the weekly norm of forty hours or the daily norm of eight hours. In order to determine what is a normal or regular workday or workweek, it is important to examine the parties' understanding of that term from their negotiating history and more importantly from their prior practice. Most enterprises continue for extended periods with a well established work schedule. The parties come to accept that schedule and it remains unchallenged because it remains unchanged. Problems arise when the employer seeks to alter that schedule.

CASE: THE SHORTER SIX-DAY WORKWEEK

The Ajax Widget Company for years had worked on a five-day week of eight hours per day. That figure was never specified in the parties' collective bargaining agreement, but it had come to be accepted as the routine workweek. Overtime was paid after eight hours per day or forty hours per week. A dispute arose when the company posted a notice that commencing the following week, the workweek would be changed from five days of three shifts of eight hours each to one of six days of three six-hour shifts per day. The union protested the change, and the case was appealed to arbitration.

At the arbitration hearing, the employer testified that the change was undertaken to provide a break between shifts, which previously had been eight hours each and therefore contiguous, in order to supply stock and prepare for the next shift arrival. The new arrangement also would utilize more effectively the company's equipment on a six-day, rather than a five-day, basis.

The union testified that there was no stock preparation, cleaning, or equipment movement necessary between the shifts, that the operation had been conducted for at least ten years with contiguous shifts without a problem, and that the company's action constituted a severe hardship to employees who were to be permanently deprived of the opportunity of spending

Saturdays with their families. The union argued that there was no legitimate business reason for the change and that the alteration was to permit employees to work extra hours on a daily basis without having to pay overtime.

The company argued that the change was a legitimate business necessity. It had never committed itself to negotiated starting times or to specific hours of work per day, and there was no provision that precluded its scheduling straight time work on Saturdays.

The arbitrator agreed with the company that there was no specific requirement of an eight-hour day in the contract and that there was no contractual prohibition against Saturday work at straight time, but noted that the employer's action constituted a direct repudiation of what the parties had accepted to be a normal workweek for the past decade. The arbitrator reasoned that the employer's action was a substantial change in the normal workweek, and that such a matter was properly subject to negotiation. The arbitrator recognized that there were times when changes in the normal workweek or workday might have been justified for business reasons, but that the burden of showing that the change was a legitimate business reason was on the employer and that there had been no proof by the employer that such was the case. Accordingly the grievance was sustained.

Discussion Question 1: What factors could the union have stressed?
The union might have provided evidence concerning the amount of overtime that was being worked, showing that much overtime was worked on Saturdays to suggest that the change was made to avoid Saturday overtime. It might further have shown evidence from the negotiating history of the employer's assuring there would continue to be an eight-hour day and forty-hour week or evidence of other provisions negotiated on the employer's assertion that the schedule would continue, as for example in negotiating the overtime provisions: after eight hours in a day or forty hours in a week.

The union might have provided evidence of personal hardship resulting from employees being required to work a normal six-day week as well as evidence of continuity in the employer's receipt of supplies and continuity in the employer's production output and customer shipments to show there was no economic necessity for the change. It could have provided testimony of the employees' need for and reliance on Saturday as a day off for personal and health reasons. The union should have been prepared to rebut the employer's assertion that there was legitimate business interest at stake by providing evidence that there had been no unusual changes in the employer's business or customer dealings. Testimony of an expert witness, such as a bargaining-unit front office employee or even astute cross examination of the company business manager could have established this.

Discussion Question 2: What evidence might the employer have produced?
The employer might have shown stronger evidence of Saturday demand for its products on a six-day basis due to the flow or the disposability of the product or to the short lifetime of the items. In particular, it could have shown that the Saturday work demands could not have been met through normal Saturday overtime. It might have produced a history of similar changes in the past that had been acquiesced to by the union and never protested in negotiations. Customer representatives testifying to the need for Saturday shipments could have bolstered this point.

Discussion Question 3: If the employer had shown that there was a recent change in customer demand requiring product completion on Saturday, would that have constituted a legitimate business reason?
If the company had been able to show that it was required to produce product on Saturday that could not have been produced Monday through Friday and that it had been unable to secure or provide sufficient overtime personnel to perform that work, it might have established the legitimacy of the change, although that, in turn, would have required a showing that routine work on Saturday was required. The employer's case might have been strengthened by showing that Saturday overtime was voluntary and that the company had been unsuccessful in securing people to work on Saturday. Even if the employer claimed that Saturday work was unattainable under the former schedule the arbitrator might have found that problems could more readily have been resolved by requiring Saturday overtime.

Discussion Question 4: Under what circumstances might the employer have shown that the six-day schedule was a legitimate business interest?
One way might have been by showing that the normal influx of raw materials was inadequate on a five-day basis to provide eight hours of work per day, but that the supplier had changed the influx of raw materials to a lower daily volume on a six-day basis and under conditions beyond the control of the employer. While the arbitrator might have viewed the change as acceptable if it were forecast to be in effect for a limited time, the prospect of such schedule change on a permanent basis would strengthen the likelihood that the arbitrator might urge the matter be negotiated between the parties and might prohibit such change absent such negotiation. That conclusion would be based on the assumption of a normal eight-hour day, five-day week, having been unilaterally adjusted by the employer without the showing of a legitimate business requirement.

Discussion Question 5: What if the employer had been scheduling a five-day week and introduced a four-day week of eight hours per day?
The same issue of a normal workweek comes into question when the employer seeks to reduce the normal five-day week to a four-day week. Here

again there would have to be a showing of a legitimate business reason for the change.

In reducing the workweek from five days to four days, even with a legitimate business reason for the reduction, the employer faces the additional question of whether the reduction is in conformity with the parties' agreement governing layoffs. If the parties had an expectation of a normal workweek of forty hours, the reduction to thirty-two hours might be interpreted as triggering the layoff clause since most layoff provisions grant senior employees the right to continue on a full-time or normal workweek basis at the expense of junior employees, who would be laid off to protect those full-time hours. The same argument might have been raised in the above case, in which the workweek had been reduced from forty to thirty-six hours.

In addition to the question of whether the employer may unilaterally adjust the work hours absent legitimate business reasons, there is also the question of the employer's ability to adequately staff its operation during the normal workweek. Because contractual commitment to overtime pay implies that there will be overtime work, the question arises over the amount of overtime work an employer may assign.

CASE: THE EXCESSIVE OVERTIME

The Bloch Manufacturing Company had achieved a very rapid increase in work orders. Its reliance on specially trained electronics technicians had made it difficult to secure additional employees to handle the increased volume. In order to meet production demands, the general manager Richard issued an order telling employees that until further notice, they would be required to work one hour daily of overtime on weekdays and eight hours of overtime on Saturdays. The union filed a grievance on the employer's requiring steady overtime and the amount of overtime required, and the case was appealed to arbitration.

At the arbitration hearing, the union argued that overtime always had been voluntary and that there was nothing in the parties' agreement requiring employees to work overtime when requested to do so. It argued that in any event, the amount of overtime that was being demanded of employees was excessive and was a substantial detriment to the employees' lifestyles and potentially to their health and safety. It urged that the employees be given the freedom to decide whether or not they wanted to work such overtime as well as the number of hours such overtime was to be worked by them.

The employer argued that it had provided voluntary overtime as long as it was sufficient to meet its business needs, but that the sudden influx of orders made it essential for the survival of the company that it have adequately trained personnel to perform its tasks. It recognized the pressures that it placed on employees and their families but asserted that the survival of the company required that everyone work the extra hour per day and the extra day per week. It derided the unions' claim as being self-serving in order to reduce the amount of overtime work, and asserted that there was no evidence of any risk or injury to an employee's health or safety.

The arbitrator reasoned that although overtime needs had been adequately met by volunteers in the past, there was nothing in the parties' agreement that restricted the employer from requiring employees to work overtime when there were legitimate business reasons to do so. Thus, on the issue of whether overtime may be mandated, the arbitrator found that the employer did have the right to require overtime in the absence of a specific contract provision in which the employer had agreed that overtime was to be only voluntary.

On the second issue of the amount of overtime being required of employees, the arbitrator noted that employees were entitled to their own lifestyles and worked for the company on the basis of an expectation that they would have Saturdays to themselves and have the option of voluntarily working overtime. In this case, the prognosis of the work being continued indefinitely on the new schedule was viewed by the arbitrator as an excessive requirement. The arbitrator asserted that the employer had acted unreasonably in requiring employees to work a routine thirteen hours of overtime per week. He found an overtime requirement of half that amount to be more reasonable since it provided employees at least an alternating weekend basis for performing the mandatary overtime, while still leaving the other weekends for personal needs.

Discussion Question 1: What evidence should the union have produced?
The union might have produced evidence of employees earlier having been told to report for overtime work and having declined to do so without any penalty being imposed on them. It might have shown evidence of discipline for declining to work being rescinded on appeal. The union also might have produced evidence of discussions during negotiations as to whether the overtime was to be voluntary or involuntary. On the issue of the amount of the overtime work the union might have shown that the employer had not made a reasonable effort to secure any additional workers or that the problem could have been alleviated by shifting work to a second shift, with experienced personnel divided between the shifts and less specialized personnel called in to assist them.

Discussion Question 2: What might the employer have argued?
The employer might have produced evidence to show the extent of its effort to secure additional personnel and to show the need for highly skilled em-

ployees, who were largely unavailable. It might also have shown financial data pointing out the excessive cost of the overtime to underscore the fact that the change was necessary for business reasons. The employer might also have shown evidence that employees had been callous or whimsical in declining overtime work in the past to show that reliance on voluntary overtime was totally inadequate.

Discussion Question 3: What if the employer had shown that the overtime demand arose from just one order, which was of short duration lasting for one month?

Had that been the case, then most arbitrators would agree that a sudden influx in work would justify the assignment of employees to overtime to complete that order and to save the employer from the burden of hiring new personnel on a short-term basis. Most arbitrators would recognize that the employees were entitled to leisure time with their families, but that if there was a legitimate reason for a short term excess of overtime, the employees were obligated to meet that as a condition of their continued employment.

Discussion Question 4: What would have been an appropriate remedy in this case?

This case differs from most overtime cases that come to arbitration because the claim is not based on employees being deprived of earnings opportunities. Rather, the consequence of the employer's action is substantial additional income to the employees. What they seek in this case is the recouping of lost personal time, which is beyond the ability of an arbitrator to grant.

Many arbitrators have taken the position that overtime may be a justification for self-help, as are orders declined for reasons of imminent danger to health and safety. Personal family time or personal time commitments may be so fleeting that they cannot be recreated. The appropriate remedy in a situation such as this would depend on whether the mandatory overtime was of a short-term duration or whether it was a continuing action, as in the case above.

If the mandatory overtime had been of short duration and the company had returned to its former level of overtime, it would have been possible to provide some measure of remedy by providing employees with additional chances to turn down voluntary overtime without adverse company action against them, provided the refusal of such voluntary overtime did not cause the company renewed adverse impact. However, such a remedy would have been difficult to achieve because the employer had mandated the excessive overtime because of need and was already bearing an additional financial penalty for ordering such overtime. Thus, even if the overtime demand had returned to its normal level, it would have been unreasonable for an arbitrator to provide employees the opportunity to decline overtime in the future if all employees, in declining such overtime, were to create a new economic pressure on the employer. This might have triggered a legitimate business interest for again mandating overtime.

If the overtime requirement had been a continuing situation, the remedy would have been easier. The employees would have gained financially from the employer's business difficulties, and the goal in that case would have been to order the employer to reduce mandatory overtime to a level that would be consistent with the arbitrator's perception of both parties' interests.

The arbitrator could have ordered that all mandatory overtime cease, which would undoubtedly have created excessive economic disruption to the employer and perhaps even a loss of business, to everyone's detriment. One alternative might have been to provide the employer with reasonable time to make a concerted effort to hire additional personnel or to readjust the work schedule with, perhaps, the implementation of the second shift suggested by the union.

Structure of Work Hours

In addition to the issue of determining the number of hours employees should be required to work, a second area of concern to both parties is determining which hours are to be worked. Issues such as the hours, scheduling, and duration of rotating shifts; the scheduling of shift breaks and lunch breaks, and the scheduling of shift starting times are all matters traditionally resolved through collective bargaining. Determining the number of shifts is conceded to be a matter of management discretion, but unions have asserted the right to negotiate the hours of such shifts and, in particular, their starting times. In the case of rotating shifts, negotiation frequently addresses the duration of time employees are to spend on the shifts, as well as shift starting times and days of working the shift.

As in the case of negotiations over the normal workweek, the parties frequently negotiate normal starting times as well as specific shift starting times. Disputes arise between the parties over whether the employer may vary the starting time from the specified hour set forth in the contract or from the "normal" shift starting time that has come to be accepted over time. Arbitrators use the reasoning that normal shift starting time implies such times are not fixed and that there may be occasional abnormal starting times when undertaken for legitimate business reasons.

CASE: THE SHIFTING SHIFT START

Since its initial collective bargaining agreement twenty years ago, the company had followed the normal shift starting times of 7:00 A.M. for the first shift and 3:00 P.M. for the second shift. The company posted a notice that for the following week the shift starting times were to be changed. Employees were to report at 8:00 A.M. for the first shift and at 4:00 P.M. for the second shift. The union filed a grievance challenging the change, and the case was appealed to arbitration.

At the arbitration hearing, company witnesses testified that the time change was necessitated by the change in the train schedule for the arriving product. It had tried to adjust to that change by finding other work for employees in the first hour of the day shift, but there was inadequate work to justify continuing with the 7:00 A.M. starting time, as the incoming product did not usually arrive until close to 8:00 A.M. The union witnesses testified about the inconvenience that the change brought and noted that it broke up available car pools, as employees frequently came to work with employees from a neighboring company that also began work at 7:00 A.M.

The union argued that the 7:00 A.M. shift starting time was a tradition that had existed prior to collective bargaining. It was viewed as a fixed condition of employment from the initial negotiations, and the union had seen no reason to negotiate anything about shift starting time since the employer had always followed that 7:00 A.M. shift schedule. It argued that having so firmly adhered to a 7:00 A.M. starting time, the company acted improperly in unilaterally altering that shift starting time to 8:00 A.M. without negotiation and agreement of the union. It cited the disruption that it caused to employees and urged the grievance be sustained.

The employer argued that it had sought to adhere to the 7:00 A.M. starting time. It had found that time to have been preferable ever since the company had been organized, and it tried to adjust its receipt of incoming product to permit continuance of that starting time. However, the schedules of deliveries from the company's suppliers made continuance of the 7:00 A.M. starting time an uneconomic alternative to the adjustment that took place.

The arbitrator held that long-term adherence to a "normal" 7:00 A.M. starting time, even though not set forth in the parties' agreement, created an expectancy that the shift would begin at 7:00 A.M. and obviated the need for the union to demand a 7:00 A.M. start. However, the arbitrator ruled that even if there had been a specific 7:00 A.M. starting time, the parties adopting 7:00 A.M. as the normal starting time recognized that there might be abnormal starting times other than 7:00 A.M. The employer had the right to adjust that starting time when required to do so by legitimate business needs.

The arbitrator found that the employer had tried to adapt the suppliers' schedules to the 7:00 A.M. starting time, that its inability to do so resulted in an uneconomic first hour of the workday, and that the one-week change undertaken by the employer was for legitimate economic reasons. The arbitrator recognized that the change in schedule constituted an inconvenience for a number of employees, but reasoned that their convenient arrangements for transportation to work did not constitute a restriction on the employer's right to assure efficient operation of its enterprise. The grievance was denied.

Discussion Question 1: What evidence might the union have presented?
The union might have produced evidence to show that the employer had never altered its shift starting time. It might have shown that there were measures that the employer could have taken to secure the necessary product the evening before or to secure a similar amount of product from other suppliers. It could have offered testimony of the volume of work that was required during the first shift to show that the employees were fully occupied despite the late arrival of incoming product and that there were other tasks that could have been done if there had been any idle employees during the first hour of the workday.

Discussion Question 2: What might the employer have asserted?
The employer could have provided documentation of its output prior to the supplier's change of schedule, showing that production was at a certain level prior to the change and that first-shift production dropped thereafter. If the employer had shown a drop in first-shift production with the advent of the tardy supplies, the arbitrator would have been able to ascertain whether the drop was attributable to the men working a seven-hour shift rather than an eight-hour shift. The employer also might have shown evidence of its effort to convince the supplier to bring the product in earlier or evidence that such product was not available from other sources.

Discussion Question 3: What would have been the result if the employer had first notified employees of the shift change when they arrived for work at 7:00 A.M. on the Monday in question?
Most arbitrators would take the view that if the employer had advance knowledge of its need for change, it was obligated to recognize the personal transportation arrangements made by employees and should not have so precipitously mandated the schedule change. If the notification was to go into effect immediately and employees were told to report to work at 8:00 A.M. thereafter, it would not have been unreasonable for arbitrators to hold that employees were entitled to a reasonable period of time of at least one week or whatever was called for in the contract to readjust their travel arrangements.

Discussion Question 4: If employees normally had reported to work at 7:00 A.M. and then been told that their work that day was to begin at 8:00 A.M., would they have been entitled to compensation from the 7:00 A.M. time when they arrived until the 8:00 A.M. shift starting time established by the employer?

The answer to this question depends on the language of the report-in pay provision, but under most such provisions employees who reported in good faith with expectations of being able to work would be entitled to compensation for four hours for reporting to work, whether or not that time was worked. It might be reasoned that since the employees did work more than four hours once they began work, there would have been no grounds for the payment of report-in pay if the purpose of the provision was to assure employees of at least a half-day's pay when they made the effort to report. But another view of report-in pay is that if employees were entitled to begin work at the time they were asked to report and they did report on time and were then required to remain eight hours plus that additional hour, they should have been granted report-in time for the first hour plus the eight hours worked.

A different question is whether the employees were entitled to overtime for the last hour during the time they worked. The reasonable resolution of this issue would appear to be to grant report-in time for the first hour. Because they only worked eight hours, although reporting for an additional hour, they probably would have been entitled to pay only on a straight-time basis for eight hours of work plus the additional hour of report-in pay.

Breaks in the Workday

Another aspect of the hours of work reflected in negotiations is that of interruptions in work during the shift, such as coffee breaks and meal breaks. The parties generally negotiate when such breaks are to take place, the duration of the breaks, and the conditions under which they are to be taken. In some cases, the parties negotiate restrictions on leaving the facility during the work break or during lunch and may permit or prohibit employees from being in certain areas during their breaks.

CASE: THE SILENT RADIO

The company and union agreed to a morning and afternoon ten-minute break period as well as to a lunch break, with the understanding that employees were to remain in the break area during the lunch and break periods. The company had a rule against the use of personal stereo-type items during the workday because it feared that employees with earphones would be unable to hear sounds of approaching equipment. It also banned reading material on the work floor for similar fears of injury due to distraction. The union demanded the right to permit employees to have newspapers and radios with headphones during their break periods. The employer refused, saying that employees would need to go to their locker rooms to secure such items during the breaks. It would take up to ten minutes, the duration of the break, for employees to go back and forth to their locker to get and return radios and reading materials. The union filed a grievance, and the case was appealed to arbitration.

The union asserted that employees were on their own time during lunch and breaks and that they were entitled to listen to the radio or read. Although it recognized the safety reasons for prohibiting employees from wearing earphones on the work floor, such prohibitions should not prevent employees from utilizing their radios during their breaks and lunch periods. It asserted that the requirement of the items being kept in the lockers was an abuse of management's authority because it deprived employees of the right to use them on their own time.

The employer argued that it had no objection to the use of radios or newspapers during break periods at break facilities but pointed out that the parties had negotiated that such breaks were to be limited to ten minutes in the morning and afternoon and a half-hour at lunch. It asserted that employees were free to do what they wanted during those periods, and that although it had no objection to the employees going back and forth to their lockers, they must be required to do so on their own time and not use time in addition to the negotiated breaks. It stressed the danger of employees possessing radios, not only because they might be listened to during the workday, but also because the wires connected to the radios might cause an additional safety hazard. It argued that the possession of reading material during the regular workday was likewise a danger, as employees might pay attention to the reading materials rather than to their jobs, creating an additional safety risk.

The arbitrator held that the purpose of a break was to permit employees to relax from the pressures of their jobs, that the employer recognized that such time belonged to the employees, that they were entitled to use it as they wished, and that the use of personal radios and tape recorders and reading material was consistent with the proper use of employees' breaks and lunchtimes. The arbitrator further held that while the employer was within its authority in prohibiting the use of radios and reading materials during normal work hours, its requirement that such materials be kept in the employees' lockers made it virtually impossible that they could be used by employees during their break periods.

Accordingly, the arbitrator held that employees were permitted to have reading material and radios on their person, provided that the items did not protrude or cause any hazard and provided that neither radios nor reading materials were used during the period on the work floor. The arbitrator found the employees were entitled to use those materials at the break site and break time.

Discussion Question 1: What arguments might the union have used?
The union could have produced evidence of small books or small radios that easily could be pocketed and not be observed by employer representatives to show that the employer was not consistent in policing the prohibition against radios or printed material on the work floor. It might have provided a map of the work area with a description of distances from the locker room to the break area and from the work stations to the locker room. It could have requested the arbitrator visit the work floor to time the length of time it would take to walk from locker room to break area. It might have provided evidence of supervisory personnel carrying radios or reading material to show that the employer was inconsistent in its application of safety concerns.

Discussion Question 2: What arguments might the employer have used?
The employer might have produced evidence of accidents caused by employees using earphones and not having heard approaching equipment. It might have produced similar evidence of tangled earphone wires causing injury or evidence of employees having been disciplined for reading at the work area. The employer might have introduced evidence of precipitating incidents that resulted in injury, as well as the posted notice explaining the change and the reasons for it. The employer also could have introduced a map of the work area and shown the work location of the grievants if they were indeed close to the locker room and break areas to show there was no inconvenience or loss of break time by leaving the radios and reading material in their lockers while working.

Discussion Question 3: How should the arbitrator have responded to a claim that the employer's action was an infringement on freedom of the press and free speech?
Most arbitrators would have taken the position that although employees are entitled to the full exercise of their constitutional rights, the arbitration forum is not the correct arena for their enforcement. Such claims of constitutional right and constitutional right infringement are properly matters for legal procedures because arbitrators have no enforcement power other than of the parties' collective bargaining agreement. Although arbitrators may be required to interpret and apply contractual protections of civil rights, the jurisdiction under which they do so is limited to the contractual relationship

between the parties. Some arbitrators have held that although there may be a constitutional right to freedom of press and speech, there is no constitutional right to employment and that the surrender of employment may be a prerequisite to the exercise of the constitutional rights.

Assignment of Work Hours

The assignment of hours of work to individuals or groups is of concern to both labor and management. The parties negotiate the assignment of employees to rotating shifts based on such factors as seniority and skill. They negotiate language providing access to overtime work based on theories of equalization, seniority, and expressions of interest, and they may negotiate language covering the right of employees to decline to work overtime.

CASE: THE MISSED OVERTIME

The parties' agreement called for an overtime-desired list, on which employees quarterly indicated their interest in working overtime hours. The contract provided that the employer was to notify the employee at work or by telephoning the employee at the telephone number listed in the employment office no later than eight hours prior to the scheduled overtime. In this case, the employer contacted six of the nine employees needed for the overtime assignment while they were on their normal shift the preceding day. Three employees were absent that day. The company telephoned them at the numbers listed last on their employment records. One of those three said she would work the overtime. A message was left with the family of the second employee, Flavia Cindy, while the number called for the third employee, Heidi Stutz, was reported by an operator as having been disconnected.

The next day, the employees who had been contacted reported to work. Stutz and Cindy filed a grievance asserting that they had not been called for overtime although they were on the overtime-desired list and were thus entitled to the work on the day in question.

At the hearing, Stutz testified that she had recently moved, that she had notified the employment office of her changed telephone number, that she had fulfilled her obligations, and that any failure to contact her was the fault of the employer. The company clerk testified that the new telephone listing had been submitted a week before the incident but had not yet been entered in the telephone log.

Cindy testified that she was away from her home at the time of the telephone call, that the message had been taken by her eleven-year-old daughter, and that the child had failed to relay the message to her. She asserted that the employer erred in leaving the message with a youngster and that she was entitled to have been called and advised of the overtime work. Both employees claimed that they were entitled to compensation for the overtime hours denied them.

The union argued that the contract required the employees be contacted and that the employer failed in its obligation to update telephone numbers (in the case of Stutz) and in its obligation to contact Cindy directly. It argued that the responsibility for contacting the employees was absolute, and that having failed to do so, the employer must bear financial responsibility for the inability of Stutz and Cindy to work the overtime on the day in question.

The company argued that it could not be liable for the failure of employees to provide timely notification of telephone-number changes or for the failure of family members to report telephone calls to employees. It asserted that it had acted reasonably in utilizing the telephone listings it had, that the responsibility of keeping the telephone listing up-to-date was the employee's, and that it could not be held responsible for an employee's telephone number not having been recorded immediately in employment office records or for the failure of a family member to transmit a message. In any event, the employer concluded, even if the company was held responsible, the appropriate remedy would have been to provide substitute overtime.

The arbitrator held that although the parties had negotiated for the employer to provide employees with notificiation of available overtime, the obligation was not absolute and that a standard of reasonableness was appropriate. In the case of Stutz, the arbitrator continued, the evidence showed that she had submitted a revised telephone listing to the employment office one week prior to the attempt to contact her and that the failure to revise the employment record was not attributable to any wrongdoing on her part. The arbitrator asserted that the delay of one week in changing the telephone listing in the employer's records was the proximate cause of her having been denied the overtime and concluded that Stutz was entitled to overtime pay for the work she had missed.

In the case of Cindy, the arbitrator ruled that the employer had fulfilled its obligation in leaving a message at the grievant's home, that there was no contractual requirement of actual contact and notice to the employee, and that the proximate cause of that failed communication was not with the employer but with the grievant's child in the failure to convey the message. Accordingly, the arbitrator found that Cindy's claim was without merit.

In establishing the appropriate remedy for Stutz's denial of overtime, the arbitrator noted that the overtime deprivation had occurred six months prior to the issuance of his decision. The overtime-desired list was made up on a quarterly basis and included different names in the present quarter than had been on the list involved at the time of the case. Thus, the offering of an additional overtime opportunity to Stutz would have placed at a disadvantage other employees on the new overtime-desired list employees who had not benefited from the earlier error but who would be harmed by granting Stutz an out-of-sequence overtime assignment. Because the original overtime-desired list could not be recreated, the appropriate remedy was to pay the grievant for the overtime hours denied her.

Discussion Question 1: What might the union have argued?
The union might have shown evidence of prior employer omissions in transmitting new telephone numbers. It might have called as its witness the person who had received notification of telephone-number changes, and to show the company's procedure was tardy, it might have provided testimony of other employees who had been reimbursed for earnings lost in overtime by virtue of the failure of the employer to contact them. In the case of Cindy, the union might likewise have offered evidence of cases in which family nontransmittal of messages had occurred and employees had been reimbursed. Concerning the remedy, the union might have provided evidence of instances in which employees had been granted reimbursement of earnings lost rather than another opportunity at overtime. It could have provided evidence of the different composition of the overtime-desired list during the intervening time taken to process the case to support its view that a make-up opportunity would deprive different employees than those who'd worked the overtime in her absence.

Discussion Question 2: What might the employer have presented?
The employer could have provided information on prior telephone calls, in particular the absence of grievances due to tardy phone listings and to family transmission of messages. It might have shown that these matters had been the subject of prior negotiations, and it could have presented the overtime-desired lists of the last five quarters to show that make-up time was the appropriate and traditionally accepted remedy for such infractions.

Discussion Question 3: What would have been the result if Stutz had not had a telephone at her new location?
Most arbitrators would hold that Stutz was obligated to advise the employer of her not having a telephone at her new location. Under such circumstances, the employer could not be held responsible for failure to reach the grievant. The burden would have shifted to the employee to contact the employer in order to assure that she was given access to available overtime.

Discussion Question 4: What standard would be appropriate for leaving a message with a family member?
If the employer had reasonable grounds to believe that the person receiving the message at the employee's house was competent to transmit the message,

it would be relieved of responsibility for the failure of that transmission once the message had been left. That burden would not be met in the case of a message left with a child of so young an age as to preclude the expectation that the message would be transmitted properly. In the case of an eleven-year-old child who understood the message and was capable of transmitting it, then the burden of transmission beyond that point was no longer the employer's. If the employee had a belief that family members were incapable of properly transmitting such messages, it then would be incumbent on the employee to so notify the personnel office or at least notify the supervisor of the need for a more personal delivery of any message.

Discussion Question 5: Under what conditions would make-up time be appropriate?
The objective of the remedy in overtime cases is to equalize the hours and to assure that employees are not disadvantaged by any employer error in assigning overtime. Thus, if the parties' agreement called for equalization of overtime by the end of the year and the group of employees working overtime had remained constant and fixed, a remedy granting the grievant the next overtime availability, even though out of order, would result in a re-establishment of equity among those in the group. But if the time had expired for equalization or if the group mix had changed, then any remedy granting the grievant another opportunity for overtime would have had a deleterious effect on other employees in the group by depriving them of their access to the make-up overtime.

Discussion Question 6: What if the awareness of the overtime need had occurred at the end of a shift and there had been insufficient time to comply with the notification procedures of the parties' agreement?
If the overtime that occurred on short notice was of an emergency nature necessary to protect the enterprise from loss or damage, then the employer would have been within its right in assigning such employees as were then available to perform the task, perhaps relying on the overtime-desired list of employees already at work at the time to show intent to follow the contract. If additional personnel were needed at that juncture, most arbitrators would hold that the employer would be justified in calling on those at work who were not on the overtime list, rather than to attempt to telephone employees at home who would not be able to arrive in time to perform the work. The negotiated eight-hour notification would not be required in such an emergency situation, but if the evidence showed that the sudden overtime was not an emergency causing potential damage to the employer, arbitrators generally would hold that the employer had erred in not advising the employees earlier of the need for overtime or in not postponing the overtime until it could be performed in accordance with the overtime provisions.

In the emergency overtime situation, those employees who were on the overtime-desired list and were not called would not be entitled to make-up time or reimbursement for the overtime work denied them. In the situation of the nonemergency overtime, most arbitrators would rule that employees who were on the overtime list and could have been called would be entitled to reimbursement for the company's failure to conform to the contractual language of due notice. The result of such a case thus would hinge on whether there was a need for the overtime that could await the contract notification period or whether there was language allowing an emergency exception.

Although the parties may negotiate on the rights of employees to secure work opportunities in various positions, they may also negotiate language retaining to the employer the right to make assignments to specific shifts. Sometimes the legitimacy of such are brought into question.

CASE: THE REVENGE ASSIGNMENT

Ike Taylor was a police officer. When the town's police chief discovered a letter posted on the police officers' bulletin board attacking him as being anti-union, arrogant, and corrupt, the chief called the officers together and asked each one if he or she had written the letter. All denied having done so except for Taylor, who laughed and said he was pleading the Fifth Amendment. Two days later, Taylor was removed from his headquarters detail on the day shift and assigned to a high-crime area on the night shift. He was assigned to work in a single-officer vehicle, although other officers previously assigned to that neighborhood had been assigned to two-officer vehicles.

Taylor filed a grievance claiming he was being discriminated against because of the assumption that he had written the letter, that the assignment was disciplinary, and that he should be returned to his former assignment. Article 6 of the parties' agreement provided the following: "Notwithstanding the seniority provisions of the assignment clause, the chief may make such temporary assignments as he deems necessary for the good of the service."

At the arbitration hearing, the union argued that the employer's action was a disciplinary reprisal for the grievant's allegedly having written the letter and that there was no proof to support that assumption. The change of assignment was obviously in retribution for the chief's supposition that Taylor was at fault, the union argued, and it urged the grievance be sustained and that Taylor be returned to his former assignment in the station house on the day shift.

The employer asserted that the contract granted the chief the right to make assignments notwithstanding the principle of seniority in choosing shifts and that such a right was exercised when the chief believed the need for police officers in a particular location during a particular shift was justified. The employer further asserted that the chief did not take the action because of any belief that Taylor had written the disputed letter. The assignment of Taylor was irrelevant to that incident and was within the chief's authority under the parties' agreement.

The arbitrator held that the parties had negotiated a collective bargaining agreement calling for reliance on seniority in shift assignment. While that precept was not immutable, when the employer sought to invoke the chief's right to make shift-change assignments for the good of the service, the burden was on the employer to show that the assignment was one that would not otherwise have been made through the negotiated shift assignment by seniority.

The arbitrator noted the spontaneity of the assignment and the absence of any evidence of an immediate prior need, and in light of the grievant's statement two days earlier concerning the letter, found that the employer's action was not an appropriate or contractually justifiable invocation of the chief's right to make an assignment for the good of the service. Accordingly, the arbitrator ordered the grievant be returned to his day-shift operation in the station house.

Discussion Question 1: What issues might the union have raised?
The union might have asserted that the employer had the burden of proof. The union also might have provided evidence of the length of time over which the neighborhood had been patrolled by a two-officer car, as well as evidence to show that there had been no change in coverage or situation involving the neighborhood, the shift, or the central-office operations to precipitate a change in assignment. It might have offered as witnesses those employees below the grievant on the seniority roster who would have been subject to call-up for the assignment to the night shift, had the contractual bidding process been followed, to testify that they had never been approached about any changes.

The union also could have been prepared at the hearing to deal with the question of the grievant's responsibility for the disputed letter, perhaps with evidence of his handwriting or with evidence to show that he was not in the station when the notice was posted. Finally, it might have produced witnesses from the confrontation between the officers and police chief to testify about the comments and attitudes of Taylor and other officers.

Discussion Question 2: What might the employer have provided?
The employer might have provided evidence to show that the change of assignment was dictated by other changes in the distribution of the work force, that the assignment to a one-person car was dictated by the shortage of available personnel at the time in question, or that the movement of other

officers from the high-crime area had been necessary because of needs for their services elsewhere. The employer also might have provided evidence of the grievant's record if it showed that he had been antagonistic toward the supervisor, and it might have argued that the assignment was for the good of the service. In any event, because of the employer's need to de-emphasize the jocular attitude demonstrated by Taylor at the confrontation, it could have reasoned that the chief's interpretation of "for the good of the service" was not properly subject to review by any arbitrator.

Discussion Question 3: Was the chief's judgment of what was for the good of the service subject to review in arbitration?
A distinction has to be drawn between language that says that something shall be done for the good of the service and language that says that something shall be done that in the chief's judgment is for the good of the service. In the former, an objective standard is introduced that is properly subject to review by the arbitrator to determine if that standard was properly implemented. In the latter, the parties shift the responsibility to a subjective standard to be invoked in this case by the chief.

The issue given to the arbitrator would thus be quite different from an objective assessment of whether the action was appropriate or reasonable to an assessment of whether the employer acted in an arbitrary or capricious fashion, as the chief had the jurisdiction, under the parties' agreement, to determine whether the action was for the good of the service. That determination would not have been an absolute authority unless the contract so specified. Rather, the standard of arbitrariness and capriciousness would have been the one the arbitrator could have utilized to determine if such a grant of authority had been properly exercised within the meaning of the parties' agreement.

Discussion Question 4: Under what circumstances would it have been appropriate to examine the issue of Taylor's culpability for the letter?
Inasmuch as Taylor was not subjected to discipline for the letter or for his invocation of the Fifth Amendment, there was no basis for the arbitrator to determine whether he was guilty or innocent of such charges of wrongdoing. The issue in this case was not whether Taylor had acted improperly in writing the letter or in invoking the Fifth Amendment or whether the employer had acted properly on its belief that he had done either or both of those things. Thus, there would have been no need to prove the guilt or innocence of Taylor on either or those charges. Rather, the incident and the chief's reaction were the factors introduced to establish a motive for an allegedly improper transfer.

7

Holidays and Vacations

P rior to the advent of collective bargaining, employees lost a day's pay when the company shut down on legal holidays. Any compensation they received was a matter of the employer's discretion. Regarding vacations, employers had no legal obligation to provide paid vacations but did so as a matter of discretion and as a reward for loyal service. Indeed, vacations initially were considered to be a bonus. With collective bargaining, the unions undertook to regularize provisions for both paid holidays and paid vacations. Any rights that employees have to these benefits are recognized to be a consequence of collective bargaining.

Holidays

There are several issues over which disputes tend to arise in the area of holidays. The issues may occur because of careless drafting of language in the parties' contract negotiations or because of inability of the parties to agree on the most precise language, opting instead for less precise language and hoping the agreed-upon terms will cover all eventualities. In such situations, the signatories recognize that a conflict might arise over situations not quite covered by the language, but they fall back on the ready availability of the grievance and arbitration procedure to enable them to resolve such unforeseen disputes. Sometimes issues arise over the failure of the parties to recognize that they have not confronted a potentially explosive topic. For these conflicts as well, the parties may rest assured that any unanticipated problem areas will be sorted out by the grievance and arbitration procedure.

Disputes tend to be grouped into several areas. These include the number of holidays, the compensation for the holidays, and holiday eligibility.

Number of Holidays

In the period before collective bargaining, employees generally were restricted to taking off those holidays that were legal holidays pursuant to the laws of federal, state, or sometimes local governments. In a few cases, employers unilaterally went beyond the statutorily prescribed holidays to provide other holidays as well such as the day before Christmas or the employee's birthday. Many initial collective bargaining agreements merely incorporated those holidays that previously had not been mandated within that jurisdiction.

Subsequent negotiations over holidays generally expanded the list of contractually recognized holidays beyond those in effect in the community. Some of those holidays reflected pressure from bargaining-unit members, who advocated adoption of generally recognized, although at the time not legally recognized, holidays, such as Martin Luther King's Birthday. Unions frequently negotiated for employees to invoke a religious day as a holiday, particularly if the employee belonged to a religious group that recognized holidays other than legally recognized religious holidays. For example, under such provisions Jewish employees may be able to invoke Rosh Hashanah or Yom Kippur as religious holidays, while Catholic employees may be able to invoke Good Friday as a religious holiday.

Employee demand for the day before Christmas as an extra holiday or for personal birthdays as holidays also helped to expand the list. Employers, such as retail enterprises with operation requirements geared to the local economies on the day before Christmas, naturally resisted such expansions. Similarly, employers with team or crew operations tended to fend off birthday holidays, which would deplete the work teams and necessitate extensive rescheduling and overtime assignments to replace absent employees. Similar to the right of an employee to take a holiday on the occasion of his or her birthday is the more recent phenomenon of a floating holiday, which an employee may invoke with requisite notice to the employer.

CASE: THE FLEXIBLE HOLIDAY

Liz Steinfeld advised her supervisor that she intended to invoke her contractual right to a religious holiday on the day after Christmas, December 26, the birthday of the founder of the Society for Free Religious Worship, of which she claimed she had been a devout adherent. The employer denied her request on the grounds that the negotiated clause for a religious holiday did not apply to such a cult. A grievance was filed and appealed to arbitration. The pertinent provision of the parties' agreement read as follows: " In . . . addition to the foregoing holidays, each employee will be entitled to take one additional holiday for religious observation of his or her choice."

The union argued that the Society for Free Religious Worship was a recognized religion and that it recognized the birthday of its founder as one of its days of religious observation. The union stated that Steinfeld was recognized and active member of the religious group and thus was entitled to take the day off as her religious holiday.

The employer argued that the Society of Free Religious Worship was not recognized as a religion and that it was not one of the religions discussed in negotiations as justifying a special day of worship. According to the employer, the request was merely a device to stretch the Christmas holiday period, and thus the grievance should be properly denied.

The arbitrator noted that the clause was aimed at providing employees with the opportunity to participate in religious observation of the employee's choice and that there were no fixed or agreed-upon religions that had to be subscribed to as a prerequisite for invoking the holiday. The fact that the claimed day for religious observance occurred the day after Christmas did not invalidate the claim, provided it could be shown that (1) the society was a legitimate religion, (2) that the society recognized the founder's birthday as a religious holiday, (3) that there was a religious observation on that day, (4) that the grievant was a member of the religious group, and (5) that the religion anticipated participation in the religious observation on that day.

Based on the evidence presented at the hearing, the arbitrator concluded that the society did have a structure and a following, but that it had applied for, yet was denied, tax-exempt status. The arbitrator concluded that the body encouraged prayer without any strict requisite of worship on any particular days or in any specified forum or religious facility. The arbitrator noted that the birthday of the founder was a day of secular gathering of society members but not a requisite day of *religious* observation. Finally, the arbitrator found that the grievant had only recently joined the organization and had been an active participant in a local Bahai Temple until the month before her request for the religious holiday. Under the circumstances, the arbitrator denied the grievance.

Discussion Question 1: What position could the union have pursued?
The union could have provided witnesses from the society and flyers, leaflets, or other publications detailing its religious observances, particularly those scheduled for December 26. It could have provided documentation explaining its application for tax-exempt status. In the event it was unable to have Society personnel present to testify as witnesses, it could have arranged with the employer for depositions from such individuals. The union should have been prepared for the employer's evidence of the grievant's prior Bahai Temple allegiance and had available rebuttal to show the long-term evolution of the grievant away from the temple and toward the society. The union also could have produced evidence of the negotiations to show that the list of religions used was not inclusive and that other groups had been excluded during those discussions.

Discussion Question 2: What might the employer have presented?
The employer might have presented evidence of the rejection of the tax-exemption appeal, testimony from the participants in the negotiations concerning the absence of reference to the society as a religion, and witnesses

to testify about Steinfeld's attendance at Bahai services. It might also have introduced documentation from the society to diffuse the claim that December 26 was a holiday, or it might have offered other evidence or testimony to strengthen the position that the society was a social group rather than a religious group. The employer might also have shown that other society members in the plant or elsewhere did attend work on the founder's birthday to support its contention that December 26 was not a recognized day for religious observance.

Discussion Question 3: What if the grievant had been an avowed atheist, claiming the right to a day off for nonreligious or antireligious observation?
Most arbitrators would probably confine their reasoning to what the parties had negotiated—a day off for religious observation. Clearly, the claim of an atheist would be a challenge to the propriety of the provision. Because the arbitrators would be confined to interpreting and applying the agreed-upon language, the provision would not be applicable to an employee who planned to take a day off for reasons other than those defined in the contract. Rather, the atheist's claim would expand the language to include a day off for those who did not intend to use it for any religious purpose. If arbitrators were to grant such a claim, they would be substituting their judgment for that of the parties by rewriting the agreement to provide an extra day off for religious and nonreligious observation, which would be beyond their authority. The arbitrators might opine that the appropriate procedure for assertion of the atheist's right would be through renegotiation of the contract clause or through a legal appeal on a First Amendment challenge to language contained in the agreement.

Discussion Question 4: Would the result differ if the society were found to be a tax-deductible organization?
If the society had been a tax-deductible organization that still would not prove its legitimacy as a religious body because it could have been an educational charity. The arbitrator would still have needed to rule on whether it was a religious entity and, if it was, to rule on whether the day was one of religious observation. The grievant's claim of being a devotee would still have needed to be considered. Even if the courts held it was a religious entity under tax laws, the arbitrator's responsibility would be to determine if it was a religious entity under the collective bargaining agreement. The tax court ruling would not be controlling on that issue.

Discussion Question 5: If the grievant had won, what would had have been an appropriate remedy?
Accepting the standard that an employee is obligated to obey now and file a grievance later, it would follow that Steinfeld would have been obligated

to work on December 26. If she did, the appropriate remedy would have been to provide an alternative date of religious observation that she could take as her day off. If December 26 had been unique as the annual day of religious observation, then a more appropriate remedy would have been to provide the employee with a paid day off of her choice. She could have asked for permission to take the day off without pay, pending resolution of her grievance.

Compensation for Holidays

The contractual recognition of holidays implies not only that the employee will be able to remain away from work to enjoy the holiday, but also that the employee will be paid his or her normal compensation for the day as though he or she had been at work. No problem arises when the holiday falls on an employee's normal workday, nor is there a problem for a legal holiday that falls on a Sunday and generally is observed on a Monday. In fact, the more recent emphasis on Monday celebrations for most legal holidays lessens the problems of holidays falling on normal workdays.

A somewhat different situation occurs for holidays falling on Saturdays or for employees working on other than a Monday through Friday schedule when the holiday falls on the employee's nonscheduled workday. Most collective bargaining agreements confront the issue by providing that the employees will be compensated for the holidays specified in the agreement, a logical consequence of the holiday recognition and compensation being recognized as an earned right and integral component of the parties' wage package. If the holiday compensation is to be considered as part of the employee's overall compensation, it follows that the employee should be given full compensation for those holidays, regardless of the vagaries of the annual calendar and the employee's schedule, so that absent language to the contrary, all employees would be entitled to compensation for all the holidays, whether or not they fall on the employee's normal workday.

Disputes sometimes arise over the amount of compensation to be paid for the day. The problem is less acute in the case of employees on hourly rates with compensation paid for the number of hours normally worked per day. It may become more troublesome in the case of employees on piecework or incentive pay. In recognition of the potential for conflict over this issue, most collective agreements covering piecework or incentive-paid employees will set forth formulas for such compensation. These formulas are usually tied to a daily average compensation received over a comparable time span, such as the average of compensation per day that week or the preceding week, or the actual compensation received on a comparable day, such as the prior day's pay or the pay for the same day in the preceding week.

The realities of the workplace sometime require that employees be required to work on holidays, either because of rotating schedules, the essential nature of their routine work function, or the pressures of work during the holiday in question. Because employees are to be paid for the holidays on which they do not work, it follows that their compensation when they do work on the holiday reflects that fact. Some collective bargaining agreements provide that the employee be provided a substitute day off of the employee's choice, with pay for the missed holiday. This is particularly common in rotating schedules, when employees are scheduled routinely to work on holidays. A more frequent likelihood, particularly for those cases in which holiday work is an exception, is for the negotiation of premium pay for those employees who are required to forego the opportunity of free time with their families on a holiday in order to meet the employer's demand that they work on the holiday. The rate of premium pay for such worked holidays, if a matter of negotiation between the parties, may be in addition to straight-time pay for the holiday worked, resulting in as much as triple pay for work on that particular day.

CASE: THE PYRAMIDING PREMIUM PAY

Mark Goldweitz was scheduled to work on Saturday, November 11 which was Veterans Day, a legal holiday in the state and a day recognized as a paid holiday under the parties' agreement. For a number of years, the contract had provided for double time to be paid in addition to holiday pay for work on a holiday. In their last negotiations, the parties agreed to pay double time for Saturday work. The company paid Goldweitz straight time for the holiday plus double time for working that day. Goldweitz filed a grievance claiming entitlement to quintuple pay: double pay for the Saturday work, double pay for the holiday work, and straight pay for the holiday itself. The grievance was denied and appealed to arbitration.

At the hearing, the union argued that each of the three pay demands was justified under the contract and that each was a separate claim for compensation. When Goldweitz was asked to work that day, he was entitled to all the benefits for that work, particularly as there was no contractual language banning the pyramiding of premium pay.

The employer argued that the pay demand for quintuple compensation was excessive and that the parties never intended such high payments. The double pay for the Saturday on which Goldweitz worked was all that was required for working on a holiday, the company stated, and a prohibition of pyramiding premium pay must be read into the agreement to limit the compensation to triple pay for that day.

The arbitrator held that the parties were free to negotiate any premium payment for holidays worked, for Saturdays worked, and for the holiday itself. It was incumbent on the parties to insert a contract provision precluding the pyramiding of premium pay if that was their intent. Absent such a prohibition, the grievant was entitled to each one of the premiums applicable to the day on which he worked, including the holiday pay, the holiday worked, and the Saturday pay. To hold otherwise, the arbitrator concluded, would be to ignore and indeed to cancel one of the double payments, by holding that a holiday worked would be paid the same on a Saturday as on Monday through Friday regardless of whether an employee was working a regular workday or a weekend day. But the parties negotiated separate provision for work performed on Saturday paying more than Monday to Friday work. Neither the holiday pay premium nor the Saturday premium could be waived or ignored. The grievance for quintuple pay was sustained.

Discussion Question 1: What might the union have presented?
The union could have shown any discussions during negotiations concerning the pyramiding of overtime, particularly in the most recent negotiations in which the Saturday premium was introduced. It could have argued that it was the employer's obligation to insert a cap on the multiple premium payment if that had been its intent, and that because no such pyramiding ban had been proposed, all premium payments were required. The union could have researched the practice concerning other premium payments, such as overtime on holidays worked or call-in pay benefits on holidays worked to ascertain prior instances in which double premiums had been paid by the employer.

Discussion Question 2: What might the employer have presented?
The employer, too, could have examined the notes of the negotiations and its prior premium practices. It might have cited cases in which arbitrators had implied a pyramiding prohibition, even if one had not been specifically negotiated. It might also have presented a cost argument if a large number of employees so worked.

Discussion Question 3: What would have been the result if the grievant had been required to work overtime on Saturday with a time-and-a-half overtime clause?
If the grievant had been required to work overtime, the time-and-a-half payment would have applied to those overtime hours. Assuming he received double time for what would have been straight time, it might follow that time-and-a-half would be required for any overtime hours, or triple pay beyond the double time for the holiday-worked pay. A similar argument could have been made for overtime on the Saturday pay. The resolution of this issue would have depended on the contract wording for the work.
    If the contract had read, "Employees working on Saturdays will be paid

double time," the time-and-a-half normally due those working more than eight hours would be subsumed by the double time for Saturday pay. If the holiday worked provision had read," Employees working on a holiday will be paid double time," the same theory would limit the overtime pay to the continuation of double time for hours worked beyond eight hours. Unless the Saturday or holiday-worked provisions referred to a restriction of the double-pay benefits to the normal workday, most arbitrators would find that the greater benefit (the double pay) had precedence over the lesser pay (time-and-a-half) for overtime. Thus, they would not provide time-and-a-half of either of the double-time benefits, as the time-and-a-half provision was based on the assumption of a employee working at straight time throughout that day. Since the grievant was already benefiting from double-time entitlement for all hours worked during the day, there probably would be an implied ban on pyramiding the overtime pay on top of those double-time payments.

Holiday Eligibility

In addition to the foregoing issues, there are frequent concerns over the eligibility of employees to holiday pay. Are employees entitled to holiday pay when on layoff, on sick leave, or on vacation? Frequently, the parties negotiate specific language to cover these issues. Some arbitrators have held that employees are entitled to holiday pay while on layoff, but not while on sick leave. Other arbitrators, following the theory that a paid holiday is a negotiated part of the wage package, have granted the holiday pay to employees when a holiday falls during their vacation.

An added rationale for such payment is that because the holiday is paid for when it occurs on a nonwork day, it also should be paid when an employee is on vacation. To deny the holiday pay during vacation is to penalize those who opt for those vacation periods in which a holiday falls. This might lead to avoidance of such vacation periods, thereby reducing the periods during which vacations may be chosen or penalizing junior employees who may be forced to take vacations during such periods.

A more common problem arises from efforts to control absenteeism by attempting to avoid employees extending the holiday by taking off the day before or the day after the holiday. To avoid such expansions of the holiday, the parties frequently negotiate a requirement that the employee work the day before and the day following the holiday. The wording of such restrictions gives rise to frequent disputes. Is the employee required to work the full shift or only part of the shift on the day before and the day after in order to be entitled to the holiday pay? What if the employee comes to work for an hour, gets sick, and then leaves with the foreman's permission? The parties frequently ignore that possibility when they negotiate the restrictions. Sometimes they rely on the word *or* instead of *and*, so that an employee who worked the day before *or* the day after may receive holiday pay, although the parties may have intended work before *and* after the holiday.

A similar problem arises over what is meant by the requirement of work the day before and the day after the holiday. Must the employee work that workday or forfeit holiday pay, even if his or her personal work schedule has that employee off that day? To so hold would deprive an employee not scheduled for work on the day immediately preceding and following the holiday of holiday pay. Frequently, the parties negotiate restrictions in terms of a requirement of working "the regularly scheduled" last day before and first day after the holiday, or the "employee's personally scheduled" last day before and first day after the holiday. Arbitrators may assume what the parties meant, but more often they will find themselves bound by the words the parties agreed to in their contracts.

CASE: THE STRETCHED HOLIDAY

The parties' agreement specified that an employee was required to work the last regularly scheduled day before the holiday and the first regularly scheduled day after the holiday. The holiday in question was Labor Day, falling on the first Monday in September. Jim Powers, a maintenance employee, was advised on the previous Wednesday that he was to report for work the Saturday before Labor Day. He worked the regularly scheduled shift on Friday, but declined the opportunity to work on Saturday, as was his entitlement under the parties' agreement. Only maintenance employees were scheduled for Saturday work on the day in question. Powers worked the Tuesday after Labor Day but was advised that he was not entitled to the holiday pay for Labor Day because he had failed to report as scheduled on the preceding Saturday. Powers filed a grievance, which was appealed to arbitration.

At the hearing, the union argued that the last scheduled workday for the enterprise was on Friday; that Powers had worked that day, that the Saturday assignment was a specialized assignment affecting only a few employees; and that since under the agreement such overtime was voluntary, the grievant had the option of declining the overtime work. It argued that Saturday should not have been considered a scheduled workday, referred to as the controlling entitlement to the Labor Day pay.

The employer argued that the parties had negotiated the phrase *last regularly scheduled day* and that Powers indeed was scheduled to work on the Saturday in question. As a shop steward, he was aware of the requirement of fulfilling his employment obligation on that last day, and when he exercised his option to refrain from working, he also forfeited his entitlement to pay for Labor Day.

The arbitrator ruled that Powers was entitled to pay for Labor Day. The parties negotiated the term *last regularly scheduled day* and that term must be interpreted to apply to the regular schedule of the facility as a whole. The Saturday assignment was not a regular schedule but a limited schedule for maintenance workers, and Powers was a maintenance worker with the option of working on that Saturday. The arbitrator asserted that Powers should not have been held to a higher standard of precondition for holiday pay than other employees in the enterprise who were not scheduled to work on the Saturday in question if his working was optional. The arbitrator further argued that the employer had the option of insisting on different contract language, and the language might have read "on the *employee's* last scheduled work day." Nevertheless, the language agreed upon was sufficient to entitle Powers to the holiday in question. The arbitrator sustained the grievance and granted Power's request for a full day's holiday pay.

Discussion Question 1: What evidence might the union have produced?
The union might have produced evidence of the negotiating history to show whether the discussions had contained restrictive language that would have applied to Powers' personal work schedule. It also might have produced evidence of past practice on other holidays to show that employees who had been paid for holidays had been absent on the day preceding or the day following the holiday under similar circumstances. It might have produced evidence to show that employees who failed to work a voluntary overtime assignment on the last day before a holiday had not been denied holiday pay in the past.

Discussion Question 2: What arguments might the employer have raised?
The employer likewise might have examined the negotiating history of the parties to ascertain the terminology they used in establishing eligibility for holiday pay. It could have reviewed the experience of the holiday-pay entitlement to ascertain if employees in similiar situations had been denied holiday pay.

Discussion Question 3: What standards should an arbitrator apply in determining eligibility for holiday pay?
Although the holiday-pay entitlement should be adequate to provide that benefit to all employees who are on the work force during the holiday, the history of extended days off before and after the holiday and the parties' consequent negotiation of prerequisites of work on the last day before and the first day after the holiday have shifted the burden from an employee's automatic entitlement to the employee's need to demonstrate entitlement. Thus, if an employee is absent on the day before or after the holiday, it constitutes a prima facie case of nonentitlement. That may be overcome by

evidence of legitimate illness with medical documentation or other evidence to show that the absence indeed was beyond the employees' control. Most arbitrators accept the negotiations of such restrictive language as justifying strict construction of the contract on the issue of holiday-pay entitlement.

Discussion Question 4: What if the grievant had come in to work on the day before, had become sick after a few hours, and had been sent home by his supervisor?

The purpose of the requirement of working the scheduled day before and after the holiday is to prevent deliberate holiday stretching. If an employee had come to work able and intending to work the full shift, the goal of the provision would have been met. Thereafter if he became legitimately ill, it was a condition beyond his control and would be viewed by most arbitrators as fulfilling the requirements of the clause. If, however, the illness was feigned, if the grievant left early without permission, or if he returned to work late on the day after the holiday, such deliberate acts would be viewed as contrary to the intent of the provision, with the employee's not having met the conditions for entitlement to the holiday pay.

Vacations

Vacations and vacation pay have been negotiated by the parties as benefits that are of mutual advantage to the employer and the employee. For the employer, they constitute an opportunity for providing rest and rehabilitation time for employees in the expectation that they will be more productive on return to work. Additionally, these benefits provide a vehicle for rewarding senior employees by escalating the benefits to which they are entitled by virtue of longer years of service. For the employees, vacation is likewise an opportunity to secure some relaxation, rest, and rehabilitation as well as an opportunity to separate from the work area. Although vacation was at one time considered to be a bonus gratuity, the more prevalent view is that vacation is an earned benefit or a deferred compensation, as demonstrated by the fact that both the vacation duration and the vacation compensation are matters of frequent contract negotiation as elements of the employee's wage package.

Negotiations of wages frequently focus on choosing whether to put more money into increases in direct wages or into increases in vacation benefits. By negotiating longer periods of paid vacation, the parties also increase the cost thereof to the employer. Additional costs may also result from the necessity of providing replacements for vacationing personnel. Negotiated compensation for those who work in lieu of their vacation-time payment further tends to increase the financial impact of the benefit.

Selection of Vacation Time

Vacation-time selection may be determined by the fact that the company shuts down for a vacation period, during which all employees are forced to take the same vacation period. Because vacation shutdowns are usually for only one or two weeks, senior employees with entitlement to longer vacation periods may choose to take additional time pursuant to the contract provisions for vacation-period selection.

Agreements vary as to the period during which vacation may be taken. Some agreements require the vacations be taken between fixed dates, such as between May 1 and September 30. Other agreements offer employees the option of taking vacations anytime during the calendar year, perhaps with a restriction that a portion of the vacation be taken during the summer vacation season.

Vacation Eligibility

In order to qualify for vacations, employees usually are required to have worked a certain number of hours during the preceding year. Sometimes disputes arise over whether time spent on strike, on sick leave, or on layoff is to be considered as time worked for purposes of vacation entitlement. Those who are out on strike during the buildup time generally are denied credit for such time unless the strike-settlement agreement specifies that their seniority and other rights, including vacation entitlement, will not be diminished by the strike period.

In the case of absence due to sickness or short-term layoff, arbitrators tend to view such incidents as beyond the employee's control and are often unwilling to deduct sick time or short-term layoff. However, when sick leave or the layoff is of long duration, so that little of the eligibility period is worked, then arbitrators would tend to hold that the eligibility requirements have not been met. The same result would probably obtain in the case of an employee out of work for several months on maternity leave, on the theory that with such long periods of leave anticipated when the maternity-leave provision was adopted, the union was alert to the fact that the extended absence of the employee would have interferred with her accumulation of the requisite months of active employment necessary to entitle the employee to vacation time. With that attributed awareness, it would be the union's responsibility to secure management's agreement to a waiver of the eligibility period for any employees on maternity leave.

CASE: THE VACATION ENTITLEMENT

John Edward began work for the company six years ago. He became active in the union and took a two-year leave of absence to be on the staff of the international branch of the union. He then returned to work as a bargaining unit employee. The parties' agreement provided that "employees with more than five years seniority will be eligible for three weeks of vacation." The grievant requested a three-week vacation, which the company denied, stating that his two years out of the bargaining unit left him with only four years of service. Edwards filed a grievance, and the case was appealed to arbitration. The pertinent provision of the parties' agreement read, "Employees will be given leaves of absence for up to two years for union, Peace Corps, and Vista work."

The union contended that the vacation clause required five years of seniority for a three-week vacation and that the two years of union service was not an interruption in seniority, but an authorized leave. Edwards' seniority was not readjusted on his return to the bargaining unit, the union argued, and his seniority had remained intact and had been relied on for transfers and promotions throughout that time.

The company argued that Edwards had accumulated no seniority while working for the union for two years and that the leave of absence protected his job but did not assure continuing accumulation of seniority. It argued that the vacation clause requirement of five years' seniority was to reward those who had worked for the company throughout that period and that the grievance should be denied.

The arbitrator noted the distinction between the eight months of service required per year as a prerequisite for eligibility for annual vacation and the five years of seniority required for three weeks of vacation. The former was a requirement of actual work performance, while the latter was a listing, on the employer's roster, as an employee for five years. The evidence showed that Edwards was listed on that roster and that his original seniority date was retained even after the two-year leave of absence and was used to determine shift assignment and promotions after his return. Because the grievant had retained his seniority during his leave of absence and because seniority was the standard for determining eligibility for the three-week vacation, the arbitrator sustained the grievance.

Discussion Question 1: What position could the union have taken?
The union could have produced the documents covering Edward's shift changes, moves, transfers, and promotions as well as the seniority lists in effect at each move. It could have provided evidence of Peace Corps volunteers whose seniority was unimpaired after their return or evidence of the negotiations, if they showed that seniority was to be retained during periods of leave.

Discussion Question 2: What position could the company have taken?
The company could have shown that the negotiating history of the layoff clause anticipated a break in seniority during leaves. It could have researched

records to ascertain if seniority had remained intact for the other employees, and it could have investigated the grievant's shift changes, transfers, and promotions to see if the moves were dependent on the extra two years of seniority he claimed he had acquired while on leave of absence.

Discussion Question 3: What remedy would have been in order?
Edwards presumably took the two-week vacation the employer agreed was due him. Once he won the grievance, he would have been entitled to an additional week of vacation. The remedy would have been for an additional week off rather than any money payment because the issue was time, and time was still available. Even though the case in arbitration may have proceeded into the winter, the week's vacation was still his due. Whether or not it could be taken as a fourth week the next summer would have been dependent on the availability of vacation slots and the willingness of the grievant and the employer to wait that long for implementation of the remedy.

Vacation Compensation

Even though employees may have met all the qualifications for securing their vacation periods and thus their vacation pay and may have selected their choices of vacation periods as justified by their seniority, the entitlement to take that time on schedule is still not absolute. As in the case of holidays, the agreement may have a provision to combat absenteeism by requiring attendance at the "regularly scheduled" or the "employee's last scheduled" workday before *and* after the vacation period.

The needs of the employer might have changed at the last minute to require that the employees who were anticipating vacation remain at work for a few more days. The employer reserves the right to cancel or postpone vacation on the grounds of legitimate business need.

CASE: THE FOREGONE VACATION DEPOSIT

Abe Zuman, a senior employee, had the entire vacation period from which to choose his vacation. He opted for vacation during the first three weeks of August. In anticipation of his vacation, Zuman arranged for a rental of a house by the seashore and invited friends and family to share the house for the first two weeks of that three-week period. On July 25, the company experienced a breakdown of its boiler system, depriving it of the water necessary for the continuance of its operation. The company shut down while Zuman was sent to make arrangements for the purchase of a substitute boiler. The boiler was delivered on July 31. Zuman, who was packed and prepared to drive the 700 miles to the shore, was told that his vacation would have to be postponed and that he was required to remain at the plant to supervise the installation of the new boiler. Zuman remained as ordered, called the resort facility to cancel the rental, and advised family and friends that the vacation rendezvous had been canceled. Zuman was given a postponed vacation commencing September 1. But he was unable to secure a reimbursement of the $500 deposit he had made on the summer house. He filed a grievance requesting the reimbursement of the deposit.

At the arbitration hearing, the union argued that the grievant was entitled to the vacation at the time he had bid for; that he had acted in reliance on his access to vacation at that time; that the deposit payment was an essential prerequisite to his being able to take the vacation at the place and time he wanted; and that when the employer ordered him to remain at work, it resulted in his loss of the $500. It argued that the proximate cause of this loss was due to the employer's actions and that the employee was entitled to the money lost. It concluded that the employer should bear the cost.

The employer argued that it had the right to postpone the grievant's vacation because of an emergency that only Zuman was compentent to handle and that the commitment to pay the $500 for the rental was the grievant's responsibility and not the employer's. It argued that had it acted within its authority in declining to provide the agreed-upon vacation time; its action was a legitimate exercise of management's right to provide work for everyone else in the plant. The company stated that the grievance should therefore be denied.

The arbitrator acknowledged that Zuman was entitled to the vacation at the time he requested and had the right to make whatever arrangements he deemed appropriate for the time and place where he wished to vacation. However, the arbitrator further held that the right to vacation was not absolute. Because Zuman continued to be an employee of the company and because there was demonstrable need for the services of which he was in unique possession, the employer had the right to cancel the vacation, particularly in light of the fact that the enterprise could not be in operation until Zuman was able to supervise the installation of the new boiler. As the employer had the right have Zuman remain at work as a business necessity, it had the right to postpone the grievant's vacation. The arbitrator noted that the employer's obligation was to provide the grievant with the time and the compensation for the time spent on vacation, but that it had no obligation to pay for consequent damages undertaken as a result of the grievant's personal desires to vacation at the beach. Accordingly, the arbitrator found that the grievance lacked merit.

Discussion Question 1: What arguments might the union have provided?
The union could have investigated prior grievances to determine if the employer had ever paid a comparable cost beyond the actual vacation pay in similar emergencies.

Discussion Question 2: What arguments might the employer have made?
The employer also could have researched prior practice of pay in the event of a vacation cancellation. The company also might have investigated the cost of the deposit, any forfeiture clause, and whether the grievant had made any effort to mitigate damages by trying to get one of his relatives or friends to assume the lease or by advertising to find a replacement for himself.

Discussion Question 3: What would have been the consequences if Zuman had taken his vacation contrary to employer's orders and had been terminated?
There is no question that if Zuman had contradicted the employer's order to remain at work and to handle the installation of new boiler, he would have been subject to discipline. The degree of that discipline would have been dependent on the grievant's record. Because Zuman was a senior employee and because the company was relying on his skills in starting the boiler, it is clear that the grievant had a particularly heavy responsibility to complete the task to which he had been assigned. Nonetheless, unless the grievant had extensive elements of discipline in his record, it is unlikely that termination would have been imposed for that offense, as refusal of employer orders to remain at work would not constitute a capital offense and would not justify termination on first instance.

Discussion Question 4: What if Zuman had warned the employer of the potential for a $500 claim through the grievance procedure when told to work that period?
Although notification might have made the employer think twice about the assignment or might even have elicited an offer to pay the employee the $500, the ultimate decision still would have been based on the employer's right to make such an assignment. Because the employer did have that right without liability for the $500, the result unquestionably would have been the same.

Discussion Question 5: What if the grievant had been paid for the vacation in August and had agreed to the postponement until September, and a wage increase had gone into effect on September 1?
The employer would argue that the grievant had been paid for the vacation requested, while the union would agree that the employee would be entitled to the rate in effect when he took the vacation. Most arbitrators would hold that the vacation pay was to reflect the wages the grievant would have received had he been at work at the time. Because the company was unwilling to let Zuman have his vacation at the wage rates in effect in August, he was deprived of the chance to vacation then and work in September at the higher rates. Inasmusch as the vacation was taken in September, his

vacation check should have reflected the salary rates then in effect, for to hold otherwise would have cost him the difference between his August vacation check and the salary he would have earned if he had been allowed to work those weeks in September at the new higher rates.

8
Layoff

C onsistent with the employer's inherent right to direct the work force and determine the nature of operations is its right to decide the number of employees to be utilized in those operations. As long as the employer expands the work force, there are few problems. The problems arise when the employer decides to reduce the work force because it is excessive for the company's present work demands and forecast level of operations. There is no question over the employer's right to reduce the work force, provided it is done subject to the parties' negotiated contract language. Handling the reduction of what the employer deems to be excess personnel may be done in several fashions.

Reduction of the Workweek

If an employer is faced with the need to reduce weekly work hours by 20 percent, one way of accomplishing this is by reducing the number of personnel by 20 percent, utilizing the parties' layoff procedure. Another way of accomplishing the 20 percent drop in work hours is by imposing a 20 percent cut in the workweek of all employees. Thus, if employees worked a forty-hour, five-day week, a reduction to a four-day week for that same number of employees would accomplish the desired reduction.

However, most collective bargaining provisions dealing with reductions in the work force are geared to the preservation of full-time jobs for the benefit of senior employees at the expense of junior employees. Senior employees under such provisions are recognized as entitled to retain their full-time jobs, while junior employees are the ones subject to the layoff. A commitment to maintain continued full employment for all employees at a reduced workweek runs contrary to that traditional concept of seniority protection against layoff. But the parties could, of course, negotiate for such a special arrangement of a reduced workweek for all employees. More often, the change occurs when the employer unilaterally reduces the workweek as an exercise of managerial authority in an effort to avoid the procedures calling for reduction in force. The advantage to the employer of such a reduction in workweek is the sharing of the loss equitably by all employees without the risk that the laid-off personnel might seek work elsewhere during layoff and not return when full work load resumes. Grievances may arise when senior employees object to their hours of work being reduced in violation of their seniority entitlements under the parties' layoff procedures.

CASE: THE REDUCED WORKWEEK

The employer learned that a supplier had gone out of business and was no longer able to supply product. A meeting was called among management officials to determine what course of action to take. It was decided that the current inventory was sufficient for one month's production but that it would take close to six weeks to arrange for a resumption of supplies from another supplier. Management decided that it would be less harmful to the work force if the company was to reduce its production to a four-day week for the six weeks until the supply returned to normal, rather than work for the month and then shut down the plant for the intervening two-week period. The company posted a notice saying that "due to economic conditions confronting the employer, the operation will be reduced to a four-day basis for the next six weeks." The union president filed a grievance alleging that the company's action violated the parties' layoff provision.

At the arbitration hearing, the union argued that the contract called for a forty-hour work-week and that the company's predicament constituted no more than a need for a reduction in employees. Such a reduction was contemplated by the parties' layoff provision. The union argued that the employer should have instituted the layoff procedure by providing continued full employment for senior employees while laying off junior employees to the extent necessary to meet its desired level of output.

The employer argued that the change was not a matter subject to the layoff procedure, but rather a reduction in hours consistent with the employer's authority to determine the hours of work. According to the employer, the options open consisted of continuing the work force in full operation for a month and then laying off the entire work force or reducing the work hours for all employees on a weekly basis during the period. There was no requirement for laying off junior employees for the six week period so that senior employees would be entitled to continue working full hours, the employer argued.

The arbitrator held that the company's efforts to cushion the loss of earnings by reducing the workweek for all employees was perhaps, laudable but that its action was, indeed, an effort to deal with a problem that the parties had identified and dealt with in their negotiation of the reduction-in-force provision. She found that the six-week problem was indeed precipitated by a reduced need for man-hours; that such was the anticipation of the parties' negotiated layoff clause; and that unless the company was able to negotiate a variation in that procedure to provide for a reduced workweek for all employees, the layoff clause of the agreement would take precedent. Under that provision, the arbitrator noted, the junior employees would be placed in the position of layoff prior to senior employees. Although the employer could have continued full operations for a month and then laid off all employees, if it opted to continue operations for the six-week period it was required to comply with the layoff procedure, with its initial impact being placed on the junior, rather than the senior, employees. As the remedy, the arbitrator ordered that those employees who would have been retained throughout that period had normal layoff procedure been implemented be paid the difference between the thirty-two hours they did work and the forty hours they should have worked.

Discussion Question 1: What arguments could the union have used?
The union could have cited the negotiating history of the layoff clause to note that the parties had discussed reduction in hours as the basis thereof and that there was no discussion of reduction in workweek. It could have cited the negotiating history of the workweek clause to show that there had been no discussion of the employer's unilateral right to reduce that workweek.

Discussion Question 2: What arguments might the employer have raised?
The employer likewise might have cited evidence of the negotiating history or provided evidence of the need to maintain the operations for the plant throughout that six-week period at a reduced basis. It could have cited the need for the unique skills of junior employees and the disruptive effect that a reduction in force of all employees would have had. It could have provided evidence of the history of negotiating the forty-hour workweek provision to show a forty-hour week was to be a normal rather than a guaranteed workweek. The employer also could have shown that its action was justified by a legitimate business need to retain the skills of all employees to keep the plant open for the entire period and thus avoid the loss of skilled junior employees to other enterprises and to provide the work force mix necessary for producing the product.

Discussion Question 3: Could the employer have avoided the invocation of the layoff language by relying on emergency language in the parties' agreement?
Many collective bargaining agreements contain emergency clauses that allow the employer to bypass other contractual commitments in the event of an emergency. If the emergency clause were sufficiently broad to cover a loss of supplier or if it were specifically related to the employer's right to schedule work, then it might have some applicability. Such an emergency clause might excuse a schedule change of a day or two, but when the change would continue for a six-week period, arbitrators would be more skeptical about

finding that an emergency existed, particularly if the parties had negotiated a layoff procedure that could have been invoked during that period.

Discussion Question 4: What if the employer had foreseen the break in supply but continued to operate with full staff and then shut down for two weeks on the grounds of an emergency?

If the employer felt that the emergency clause was sufficiently strong, it might have undertaken the tactical approach of waiting until the supplies ran out at the end of four weeks and invoking the emergency clause at the two-week hiatus. Of course, at that point it probably would have been discovered that the company had known for a four-week period that the break in supply was anticipated, thus overcoming its assertion of an emergency. In that case, the arbitrator would have had to decide if the employer's action was a deliberate device to avoid resorting to the layoff obligations. If so found, the remedy would have been to reimburse the senior employees for the wages they would have received had the proper layoff procedure been followed.

Discussion Question 5: What if the contract had specified that the regular workweek would remain at five days per week?

The arbitrator in that case might have decided that because the contract provided for a regular workweek of five days, the employer could reduce it to a nonregular workweek of four days when such a decision was not arbitrary or capricious and was for a period of reduced production. That might have overcome the layoff provision.

Conditions for Layoff

Short-term Shutdowns

The parties to a collective bargaining agreement often make distinctions between short-term or temporary layoffs and long-term regular layoffs. They negotiate differing procedures for handling reductions in work demand that are expected to last for a long or an unanticipated duration. In such short-term situations, the employer reserves the right to lay off without being bound by the negotiated layoff procedure.

The short-term layoff grants the employer full discretion concerning who is to be retained for work, while similarly limiting the employees' opportunity to invoke seniority in order to avoid layoff. In some agreements, the parties merely negotiate language referring to "short-term reduction in work" or "long-term layoff" without specifying the dividing line between the two. Such vague standards open the door to grievances and the arbitrator's eventual determination of how long a layoff may proceed before the employer is obligated to adhere to the negotiated layoff procedures. In other agreements, the employer specifically is granted discretion concerning who may be laid off or retained without regard to seniority, provided the temporary layoff lasts no longer than, for example, two working days or perhaps five working days. If a reduction of the work crew is to exceed that negotiated period, then the contract layoff procedures are to be followed.

Notice Requirements

Once the layoff procedures are triggered, the negotiated prerequisites fall into place. Many agreements require that employers provide employees with advance notice of layoff, not only to provide senior employees an opportunity to claim other jobs, but also to provide junior employees an opportunity to prepare for layoff. For both senior and junior employees, the advance notification provides for their layoff. For other senior and junior employees, the advance notification provides an opportunity to verify the accuracy of their seniority listing and to verify the prospects of a layoff or bumping based thereon. Sometimes the layoff occurs so suddenly, as in the case of a machine breakdown or cancellation of orders or supplies, that there may be no time for the employer to provide the contractually required advance notice of layoff. If the parties' agreement excuses advance notice under such exigencies, the employer would have no liability, but if the contract is explicit in requiring a specified number of days of advance notice, the employer would be expected to keep the employees at work until the permitted layoff date or else to pay the employees for the number of days notice thus denied them.

CASE: THE INADEQUATE NOTICE

The superintendent received a telephone call that the order that was to be shipped out the following week was suddenly being canceled. As a consequence, the company had an overextended inventory of product, no immediate customers, and a need to cut back its operation. It posted a notice that a layoff was going into effect that evening for all production workers. Maintenance employees were unaffected by the layoff. The parties' agreement provided the following:

> In the event of a layoff, the company will provide the union with a list of those employees affected at least five workdays before the effective date of their layoff. In the event the company does not provide such a list within five days, each laid-off employee will receive three days' pay except where the layoff is due to strikes, work stoppages, or acts of God.

The union filed a grievance over the sudden closing without the five-day notice, and the case was appealed to arbitration.

At the hearing, the company argued that the cancellation of the order was unexpected and similar to an act of God. The loss of work had placed the employer in great financial peril and it would have been even more economically painful if the company had been required to pay employees three days' pay when there was no work for them to perform. Because the cancellation was beyond the company's control and deprived it of any opportunity to comply with the contract clause, the company argued the grievance should be denied.

The union argued that the company had a contractual commitment to provide five days' notice or three days' pay and that it did neither. Because the shortage of work was due neither to a strike, a work stoppage, or an act of God, the grievance should be sustained, the union stated.

The arbitrator ruled that the parties had anticipated layoffs in their negotiations, and had agreed to a five-day notice and a three-day penalty for failure to provide such notice. The parties further agreed to three exculpatory situations for which the employer would be relieved of both notice and penalty-pay obligations: strikes, work stoppages, and acts of God. As the cancellation of a work order was not a strike, a work stoppage, or a natural phenomenon anticipated as an act of God, the company was not relieved of its notification or pay responsibility. Accordingly, the arbitrator found that the three-day payment in lieu of the five-day notice was justified and thus sustained the grievance.

Discussion Question 1: What could the union have presented?
The union could have produced evidence of the negotiations over the notice or penalty provision, and in particular the discussions that led to agreement on the three exceptions. It could have secured evidence to show that the company had known, could have known, or should have known of the order cancellation prior to the day it occurred.

Discussion Question 2: What could the company have shown?
The company could have shown its efforts to get the supplier to provide advance notice of any change in orders or evidence to bolster its claim that the notification of cancellation was unexpected, that its decision to layoff employees was an instantaneous and necessary response, and that it had notified the union and the employees immediately thereafter. This good-faith effort, the company could argue, was consistent with the parties' intent to prevent surprises when they negotiated the clause. The company also could have provided evidence of discussion over the three exceptions to show that *work stoppage* was intended to mean cessation of work, rather than union-

inspired work stoppage, and *that act of God* was meant to apply to conditions beyond the control of the employer.

Discussion Question 3: Would the result have been different if only the first sentence of the clause had been included and there had been no agreement to a three-day pay penalty or to the exceptions?

The arbitrator had found that the second sentence showed an intent to provide a penalty with three restricted exceptions. If that second sentence had not been negotiated, an arbitrator might have concluded either that a five-day payment was due or that no financial penalty was contemplated as a remedy for failure to provide the five-day notice. If the latter were the case, the arbitrator might have found the employer in error and warned against repetition, on the theory that if the parties had intended a penalty, it was incumbent on them to have included it in the agreement.

The absence of the second sentence would also have excluded reference to the three exceptions. Is it reasonable to conclude that the five-day payment would be ordered as a penalty for failure to provide five-day notice in all cases? Arbitrators tend to invoke the standard of reasonableness. Thus, if the employer argued that the failure to provide five-day notice was due to strike, work stoppage, or act of God, as in the negotiated language, the arbitrator might have withheld a penalty payment. Indeed, the arbitrator may even have implied a broader exception of a condition beyond the control of the company. Under that reasoning, the employer might have received a broader grant of exception than it received in the actual negotiated language.

Discussion Question 4: What if the order cancellation was due to a strike or work stoppage in the facilities of the supplier or buyer, rather than in the employer's enterprise?

Under the second sentence of the clause, there is reference to a strike or work stoppage. While it is reasonable to conclude that those references are to layoffs resulting from a strike or work stoppage in the relationship between the contracting parties, it could be argued that the intent of the provision was to relieve the employer from liability for events beyond its control. Certainly, a strike or work stoppage in a supplier's or a buyer's facility would be beyond the employer's control and could arguably protect the employer against the penalty. This is the type of conflict over intent in which testimony of the negotiating history would be relevant or perhaps determinative, particularly if the goal of the discussion was to relieve the employer of liability for emergency conditions for which it was not responsible.

Superseniority

As noted in chapter 2, the right of entitlement to union representation in the event of layoff has resulted in negotiated provisions assuring the retention, during layoffs, of union representatives whose normal seniority would not otherwise protect them from being laid off. Such provisions are to assure that remaining employees are provided with effective union representation. That protection generally is limited to employees exercising a shop-steward type of function.

A comparable invocation of protection against layoff for junior employees may be exercised by the employer. Just as the union negotiates exceptions to layoff to assure that its members have adequate representation in presenting and processing grievances, the employer negotiates exceptions to layoff to assure the retention of certain employees whom it deems essential to the continued functioning of the enterprise during layoff. Frequently, the parties' agreement will set forth certain employee categories that the company will have the right to retain by providing superseniority. These categories are often described as maintenance employees, employees with specialized knowledge of a particular job, and employees whose skills are essential to continued operation of the enterprise during the layoff.

Sometimes employers also seek language to protect employees with exceptional promise to prevent them from seeking alternate employment during layoffs. A particular problem exists in the case of handicapped employees, whose physical limitations enable them to do the work of their normal assignment, but who may not be able to do the job into which they might bump in avoidance of layoff.

CASE: THE DISABLED VETERAN

Waldo Johnson was a black Vietnam veteran who had lost his legs during the war. He had been hired by the company as part of its community outreach program to provide work for disabled veterans who were former drug users. A job had been created that enabled him to tighten nuts on the company product by having the product roll by his workstation on a special conveyor and turntable, obviating any need for him to move his wheelchair to perform the work. After six years of exemplary service, Johnson was caught in a long-term layoff. Several employees signed a petition urging the company to retain Johnson. The company sought union agreement to exempt the veteran from the layoff on the grounds that it would be demoralizing to Johnson and to others who had supported the program and on the grounds that a long-term layoff might result in his return to drugs and vitiate his years spent in rehabilitation.

The union, as cosponsor of the community outreach program, was sympathetic but pointed out that the retention of Johnson would force the layoff of another employee whose seniority would otherwise protect him from layoff. The union noted that the company had failed in its effort to negotiate the right to exempt a number of special employees from layoff. The veteran was retained in a bargaining-unit clerical position and continued to work in his wheelchair. The union filed a grievance on behalf of the next senior employee who was laid off and the case was appealed to arbitration.

At the arbitration hearing, the union argued that the grievant's seniority was insufficient to avoid a layoff. It argued that there were no negotiated exceptions for the employer to invoke to exclude Johnson from that layoff grouping, that the layoff language contained no exception for handicapped personnel, and that its duty-of-fair-representation obligations forced it to require adherence to the layoff procedures in order to protect the next senior employee, who had been laid off in lieu of Johnson when the latter had been reassigned to the clerical position.

The company argued that the veteran had been recruited and hired under a joint labor-management program and that his continued presence had made a positive contribution to improving morale at the plant. According to the company, Johnson's layoff would have had a disastrous impact on him as well as morale among all the employees; in addition, it risked being sued by Johnson for violating Title VII of the Civil Rights Act. The company argued that it retained the right to place Johnson in a clerical position in lieu of layoff on humanitarian grounds as well as on grounds of managerial prerogative.

The arbitrator recognized the good-faith efforts of the company and other employees to continue Johnson in its employ. The arbitrator also noted that imposition of the layoff might have subjected the employer to legal action by Johnson for discriminatory treatment both as a black and as a disabled veteran. However, the arbitrator continued, the issue in dispute was confined to the application of the layoff procedures, not whether the procedures as applied to Johnson constituted a violation of external law. Those issues were the responsibility of other fora.

On the basis of the contract, the arbitrator continued, Johnson lacked the requisite seniority to insulate him from layoff. When the company placed him in a clerical position within the bargaining unit while laying off a more senior employee, it violated the parties' layoff procedures. Inasmuch as there was no contract language permitting exemptions for handicapped or otherwise special employees and inasmuch as the petition did not constitute an official waiver by the union of its right to invoke the seniority provisions of the layoff clause, the arbitrator found the grievance had merit and that the retention of Johnson had been improper. The most senior employee who was laid off in lieu of Johnson and who would have otherwise been retained was reimbursed for earnings lost for the period of time that Johnson was exempted from the layoff.

Discussion Question 1: What position might the union have taken?
The union might have shown its internal efforts to seek agreement exempting Johnson from layoff in view of the petition and its obligation to the grievant, who was laid off in place of Johnson. It could have presented testimony and evidence of the company's unsuccessful effort to create an exception to the layoff clause, and it could have cited a list of positions outside the bargaining unit or in management to which the company might have moved Johnson without interfering with the layoff procedures. It also could have shown its liability to lawsuit by failing to assert its claim on behalf of the employee who was laid off in lieu of Johnson.

Discussion Question 2: What position might the company have taken?
The company could have sought any available testimony of the union's commitment to continue Johnson's employment as a negotiated exemption from the layoff procedure; it could have provided evidence of employees in the past being exempted with the union's acquiescence and nonprotest. It could have brought in legal opinions to show that the union as well as the employer might have been subject to external legal action after laying off Johnson.

Discussion Question 3: What if the employees' petition had represented a majority of bargaining-unit employees objecting to Johnson's layoff?
The union as a party to the layoff procedure did have the right to agree to exempt Johnson from the layoff. But a petition from a majority of the bargaining-unit employees was not sufficient to bind the union to that view, as the claimant who was laid off in lieu of Johnson still had individual rights under the agreement, rights that the union was obligated to enforce. A different result might have obtained if the grievant himself had signed the petition and then filed the grievance. Although the arbitrator might have found that such action constituted an individual willingness to support Johnson's retention, it did not override the union's right to insist on compliance with the layoff procedure or the affected employee's rights under the contract. A petition to retain Johnson could have been interpreted as supporting his retention in a nonbargaining-unit position and need not have been construed as a surrender of the affected employee's right to insist on his protection under the bargaining agreement.

Discussion Question 4: Could the company have had the union grant Johnson shop-steward status to avoid his layoff?
The union retains the right to determine who will serve as shop steward and receive superseniority protection against layoff. But because such positions are widely held to be effective insulation against layoff, they are eagerly sought and competed for by union members. Whether or not Johnson would have been designated for such a position would have been within the union's

purview and presumably would have been subject to its own internal procedures and controls. Any such designation might have deprived another union member of the right to serve as shop steward, which would have created an internal political question for the union to resolve.

Accuracy of Seniority Listings

As noted in chapter 2, the company is considered as having the responsibility for preparing an accurate seniority roster. The periodic posting of the roster provides the union and the bargaining-unit members with the opportunity to advise the employer of any perceived errors and the opportunity for corrections therein. Failure to catch or correct errors within the specified time are generally viewed as confirmation of the accuracy of the list.

Downgrade Or Layoff

An essential element of a layoff is the right of employees to invoke seniority and move into positions, held by junior employees, that are uneffected by such layoffs. Bumping into such positions is an essential element of the layoff right. It generally is held that the employer is obligated to notify senior employees in the enterprise of the layoff action and of the availability of alternatives in the form of positions into which the senior employee could move to displace junior employees.

Consistent with the employer's right to operate the enterprise is the condition that the senior employees must be capable of fulfilling the tasks of the position into which they bump. Some collective bargaining agreements, in detailing the requirements for bumping, may specify that employees are entitled to bump only into a position that they previously had held. Agreements may also specify that the employee doing the bumping must be able to perform the full range of tasks required by that position immediately on entering it, without any of the traditional opportunities for breaking in that often accompany other transfers or promotions.

Usually the choice of downgrading into an open position through a bump or the choice of taking a layoff is left to the employee. In some cases, the availability of substantial layoff benefits, the desire for a break in work, a feeling of discomfort over the prospect of working in lower-paid or unfamiliar positions, and perhaps the prospect of early recall to one's former position may all influence the employee's choice of whether to bump or to take a layoff.

CASE: THE CHOSEN LAYOFF

Paco Juarez was a ten-year employee in the machining department when he received word that the company was going to lay off all the employees in his department. He was told that he had sufficient seniority to bump into the storeroom, where he could work handling supplies. Juarez declined the demotion, stating that he preferred to take the layoff. The company ordered him to accept the junior position. Juarez declined the work opportunity, left the plant, and applied for state unemployment insurance. The company notified the state of his refusal of the available position, and Juarez was denied unemployment insurance. He filed a grievance against the company's action, and the case was appealed to arbitration. The contract did not specify whether an employee had any right to choose layoff or demotion.

At the arbitration hearing, the union argued that absent any contractual restriction, the grievant had the right to choose layoff instead of a demotion; that Juarez was fearful that his weak command of English would place him at a disadvantage in the clerical position; and that by accepting it, he feared he might be disciplined or possibly discharged for misunderstanding orders. It argued that he had the right to accept the layoff and have access to unemployment insurance and that the employer had acted unfairly in opposing his claim. It sought to have Juarez restored to the unemployment insurance roster, with reimbursement of the money he would have received had there been no opposition to his claim.

The company asserted the Juarez was fully qualified to fill the clerical position. It argued that the contract gave him no right to reject that assignment and choose instead to receive unemployment insurance; that the company risked increasing unemployment insurance costs from employees seeking Juarez's route instead of continuing at work, albeit at lower-paying jobs; and that it acted properly in opposing the grievant's petition for unemployment insurance.

The arbitrator held that the grievance lacked merit. According to the arbitrator, there was no contractual provision granting an employee the option of choosing between being laid off and bumping into a lower-paying job. Absent such an option, assignment to the lower-paying position was a legitimate exercise of the employer's right of assignment and transfer and was done consistently with the layoff provisions of the parties' agreement.

The arbitrator recognized the grievant's fear that he might be subject to disciplinary action for inadequate performance in the lower-paid position, but noted that the employer deemed him qualified and concluded that he would have had the right to protest any discipline through the grievance procedure, during which he could raise as a defense his assertion that he had been placed into a position for which he lacked the requisite qualifications. Because the employer had acted within its authority in assigning him to the lower-rated position and because it had a vested economic interest in discouraging unwarranted claims for unemployment insurance, which might have adversely affected its insurance rating, the arbitrator denied the grievance. The arbitrator noted there was no contractual authority to alter the ruling of the office of unemployment insurance.

Discussion Question 1: What position could the union have taken?
The union could have provided evidence of disciplinary and discharge actions taken against other employees who had accepted offers of demotion in lieu of layoff. It could have cited cases in which employees had been permitted to exercise the option of layoff or shown a negotiating history in which that right of layoff had been assured. In this respect, a withdrawn company negotiation proposal prohibiting the option of layoff might have bolstered the union's position that contractual silence on the issue implied the right to choose layoff. It could further have argued that the company's failure to discipline or terminate Juarez when he refused the demotion showed acquiescence to his actions, with the company's objection being limited to the grievant's application for unemployment insurance, rather than to his exercising the layoff option.

Discussion Question 2: What position could the company have taken?
The company could have provided evidence of all employees having conformed to the demotion order without any having taken the course that Juarez did. It could have cited evidence from negotiations that the union proposed, or at least spoke in behalf of, that option but withdrew that request. It could have offered evidence of the success of other employees in fulfilling the requirements of the new positions to which assigned or evidence of their having been given a break-in period or an option to move if troubled in the new position. The company could have offered evidence of the relative cost of unemployment insurance contrasted with the savings of employees accepting the demotion assignments. It could have noted the arbitrator's lack of jurisdiction over unemployment insurance findings.

Discussion Question 3: What if the company had disciplined Juarez for absenting himself from the assigned position?
If the company had imposed discipline for Juarez's action, the focus of the case would have shifted to his undertaking self-help in lieu of taking the demotion and then filing a grievance over the propriety of the assignment or over his deprivation of the layoff option. If the company had terminated Juarez, the arbitrator would have had to confront the issue of whether Juarez had acted in the honest belief that he had the option and whether he fully knew the consequences of his refusal to accept the assignment and then to determine whether Juarez had intended to abandon his employment. If the

arbitrator found that Juarez had acted in good faith, reinstatement would probably have been in order, although because his loss of earnings was of his own doing, there would not likely have been any provision of back pay.

Discussion Question 4: What if the contract provided for a breaking-in period for the demotion?
If the contract so provided, the arbitrator might have reasoned that once Juarez tried the position chosen by the company and established by objective evidence that he was unable to do the job, then there might be an implied alternative to have the company either provide another job or provide him with layoff and access to unemployment insurance.

Upward Bumping

Bumping is a function of layoff. An employee cannot use a layoff to bump into any filled position that he or she prefers. Such moves, even if downward, may better position an employee for promotion in another department, may be preferred by an employee because of better hours, or may be preferred because of a superior work environment or the relative ease of the job. In the absence of layoff, senior employees have no right to pick and choose positions to which their seniority or the layoff clause entitles them. If a layoff does occur, the accommodation of opening up other jobs in lieu of layoff is not a formula for permitting free movement between jobs.

Sometimes the advent of layoff in a department results in the senior employees looking to positions held by junior employees, positions that the employer, absent layoff, could have filled only by resorting to the bidding and promotion procedures. In other words, the junior positions may be in higher-rated classifications. Generally the assumption is that an employee faced with layoff has the option of bumping into a lower position on the same ladder that that employee had traveled up to get to his or her present slot. However, the question sometimes arises of whether an employee facing a layoff can bump to a higher-paying position vacated by a junior employee on layoff.

Unless the parties' past practice has been to permit such upward bumping, unless the contract is construed to permit it because of silence on that issue, or unless the contract language is broad enough to state, for example, "The laid-off employee may bump into any position of his or her choosing," most arbitrators would view the upward bump as contrary to the purpose of the layoff procedure. To permit an upward move would be to employ a procedure for protecting employees against layoff as a tool for securing a promotion that would otherwise be attainable only through the promotion clause and that presumably would authorize promotion only if there was a vacancy.

Additionally, the ability of an employee to perform fully the tasks of the position into which he or she bumps could be problematic, as the employee on an upward bump would not have occupied such a position and might invoke the option of requiring a break-in period. Finally, such an upward move would create questions regarding qualifications and the need for increased supervision at a time when the economic pressures on the employer should relieve it of such additional problems.

CASE: THE UPWARD BUMP

John Thompson had been working as a senior tool operator for several years and had been seeking to move into a more sedentary, clerical position. When the company notified Thompson that it was forced to lay off employees in his department, it advised him of his right to bump into a position held by a junior employee. The parties' agreement provided that employees faced with layoff had the right to bump into positions for which they were qualified.

Thompson opted to move to an open clerical position in the next higher labor grade, a position that had been vacated by a laid-off junior employee. The employer rejected his proposed move on the grounds that the work involved typing and other skills not in Thompson's record. Thompson testified that he had taken typing courses and had operated his own business, which had involved complex record keeping. Thompson filed a grievance, which was appealed to arbitration.

At the arbitration hearing, the union argued that the layoff was not of Thompson's creation. It stated that the new position constituted a substantial drop in his earnings, that the contract language was broad in its grant of right to bump into any positions for which qualified, that Thompson had the requisite qualifications, that Thompson was within his rights in opting for the job, and that he had the right to fill that job.

The employer took the position that the clerical position was one to which Thompson would not have been entitled to move because of his work experience and record. A position not otherwise available to him without layoff should not be one into which he should be permitted to move during the layoff, it argued. It noted that particularly in the time of layoff, the employer must be certain that the employees fulfill the full obligations and responsibilities of the jobs into which they bump and thus increase the efficiency of the operation, with the goal of working toward recall. Breaking in Thompson would impose too great a burden on supervising personnel.

The arbitrator took the position that the purpose of the job move during layoff was to protect against layoff, that there was an established system of filling promotional vacancies, that Thompson could not invoke seniority during a layoff to move into a higher position for which numerous other employees were also entitled to bid, and that the proper procedure for filling that higher position would have been through posting it for bid. The arbitrator reasoned that the primary objective of the bumping procedure was to provide employees with an opportunity to remain at work rather than face layoff and was not to provide promotions; that the goal was avoidance of layoff, which was achieved in this case by Thompson's being offered a number of other lower vacant positions; and that the employer had no obligation to provide an employee with a position into which he would normally not have been able to move. To hold otherwise, the arbitrator concluded, would have vitiated the promotion procedures by providing an open shopping forum for promotions whenever there was a layoff.

Discussion Question 1: What arguments might the union have raised?
The union might have cited the negotiating history to show that the employer had agreed to very broad language without any restrictions on upward moves and that there had been employees in the past who had been moved into other similar positions without employer objection. It might have provided testimony from other employees who had taken part in similar moves. It could have offered evidence of Thompson's outside clerical work and expert testimony concerning his typing skills and scores.

Discussion Question 2: What position might the employer have taken?
The employer likewise could have scrutinized negotiating history records to determine if there had ever been discussion of limitations on job moves. It could have examined evidence of prior layoffs and the cost of breaking someone into a new job. It could have offered evidence of the number of employees who had bid for the disputed position when it had been posted in the past. Evidence of Thompson's limited clerical experience outside of work and of his failure to advise the employer of those skills and evidence that he had not used these skills in his previous job would have been relevant.

Discussion Question 3: What would have been the result if Thompson had opted for the job?
The employer presumably would have offered testimony of a number of other jobs into which Thompson could have moved, consistent with his work experience. If none of these was suitable, the only reasonable conclusion would have been that the employee was not qualified for retention. Most arbitrators would be forced to the conclusion that the grievant would have had to take a layoff in lieu of bumping into a junior position until such time as a job reopened that was within his abilities.

9
Seniority

One of the most notable impacts of collective bargaining on management's authority to direct its work force is in the concept of seniority. Before collective bargaining, the employer could freely move its employees (promote them, demote them, lay them off, or transfer them). The decision of who was to be moved was entirely within the employer's discretion. As a means of introducing a rational alternative to management's unilateral and arbitrary placement of the work force, unions adopted seniority. In the unions view, those employees who have worked the longest for the employer are entitled to first priority in the sharing of any beneficial consequences of that employment relationship, particularly access to a better job. The greater experience of the most senior employee provides him or her with necessary credentials for any move into a new situation.

Clearly, seniority brings with it experience in numerous jobs within the enterprise, so that the average senior employee has amassed considerable experience in a variety of jobs into which he or she may be moved by promotion, bumping, transfer, or shift change. Even in cases of moves into positions never before held, unions assert that the experience that comes with seniority facilitates quick learning of any new skills necessary in a newly assigned, upgraded position.

Seniority Determination

The concept of seniority certainly means determination based on length of service. But in negotiating a seniority clause, the parties are faced with formulating various components of that seniority concept: When does seniority commence? With what will that service be compared? Do all employees accumulate seniority equally? May seniority be suspended or interrupted? How is seniority lost? The answers to these questions depend on the strength of the union, the power of the employer in restricting reliance on seniority, and the political skills of both parties in ironing out language that respects the needs of both sides.

Commencement of Seniority

Logic suggests that seniority should commence with an employee's initial date of hire. But what if two employees are hired to begin work on the same day? Two employees commencing work on the same day may share a common seniority date, but one employee must have precedence over the other if the seniority clause is to have any effectiveness.

One device to differentiate between the two employees is to accord seniority on the basis of alphabetical listing. Thus, employee A would be listed as being of higher seniority then employee B. Another device is to base seniority on the time when the employees were hired. If employee C is hired at 10:30 A.M. and employee D is hired at 2:00 P.M., employee C would prevail in terms of seniority. A third device is to use the filing date of the employment application, while a fourth device resorted to by some parties is to have the two employees toss a coin to determine which of the two is to be granted the higher seniority.

Even when there is agreement on the commencement date for purposes of seniority, every employee does not at once become a regular employee. To provide seniority at the time of hire would entitle new workers to all the contractual protections of the parties' collective bargaining agreement, including the right to file grievances over discipline and discharge. Such a right is in direct opposition to the concept of probationary employment and the employer's right to hire employees on a test basis with the right to cancel that hiring by summary termination without recourse by the employee. The probationary period is so instilled in our industrial relations that both parties accept the employer's right to weed out new workers whom it deems unsuitable for regular, continued employment. Thus, employees who satisfactorily complete their probationary periods usually are credited with seniority retroactive to their date of hire.

CASE: THE PROBATIONARY BIDDER

Marge Hiatt, a three-week employee of the company, noticed a posting of a vacancy for the position of wrapper. The bid posting specified that the bids had to be filed on a date that was one day prior to the completion of her probationary period. The position would be awarded one week later. Hiatt filed a grievance claiming her right to file a bid. The employer denied the grievance on the grounds that her probationary status meant that she lacked the standing to invoke the contract bidding procedure. Her claim was subsequently appealed to arbitration.

At the arbitration hearing, the employer asserted that Hiatt was a probationary employee and that her effort to seek the open position occurred through a bidding process that was put into motion during her probationary period. She had no access to that procedure because of her probationary status, the company asserted, and thus the grievance was not arbitrable.

The union took the position that the grievant was entitled to take advantage of the benefits provided by the contract if those benefits were to go into effect after her probationary period. Although the bidding occurred during the probationary period, it was a prerequisite to an award that was to be made thereafter and to which the grievant was entitled to partake. Thus, the union argued, the case was one in which the grievant should prevail.

The arbitrator asserted that the issue focused on the grievant's rights at the time of her probation and that she was seeking to rely on an employee's access to bidding rights under the contract. The arbitrator acknowledged that the employer could at any time sever that probationary period by removing the employee from its roster, but that while the employer tolerated her employment, she was entitled to utilize whatever benefits come with that employment under the parties' collective bargaining agreement.

The arbitrator concluded that because the employer had the right to sever the grievant's employment relationship at any time prior to the end of probation, the employee should have the right to rely on the contract entitlements until the employer exercised its termination authority. To hold otherwise, the arbitrator continued, would place the grievant at a disadvantage for employment advancement by denying her contractual rights until the end of her first month of employment, rather than giving her retroactive seniority standing on the completion of her probationary period.

Discussion Question 1: What evidence might the union have presented?
The union might have presented evidence of negotiating history to show how the parties had dealt with prior instances of employee assertion of rights during the probationary period. It might have produced evidence of the extent to which employees were given the benefit of holiday pay, sick days, overtime, and other contractual benefits including, perhaps, a recognition of seniority among probationary employees and the granting of overtime.

Discussion Question 2: What position might the employer have taken?
The employer might have sought evidence of a prior practice of denying probationary employees access to certain benefits. It also might have gone along with the idea that it could have extended such benefits as a unilateral grant without the employee's right to challenge such grants under the grievance procedure of the contract. It, too, could have investigated the negotiating history, particularly any language dealing with seniority standing and seniority dates.

Discussion Question 3: What rights, if any, would a probationary employee have on disciplinary matters?
The purpose of probation is to grant authority to the employer to determine whether or not it wishes to continue to employ an individual after it has

observed that individual's performance. That inherent right leaves to the employer the discretion of determining the grounds for removal. The employer could, therefore, terminate an employee without expressing any reasons. The question arises whether an employee could utilize the disciplinary procedure and challenge a discipline short of discharge during that probationary period. If an employee has the right to enjoy the benefits of the contract, it follows that the employee also should have the right to challenge disciplinary actions short of termination. The employer has the option of either imposing that discipline or terminating the employee. Having exercised the option of imposing a penalty, should the employer be held accountable under the theory of just cause? Or should the employer be relieved of that accountability to protect against probationary employees' being terminated for what would have been minor infractions for those employees past the probationary period?

To hold that an employee has no right to enforce contractual rights during the probationary period would grant the employer complete freedom to impose on probationary employees whatever wages, hours, or working conditions it wished, irrespective of the contract, until the probationary period was concluded. This would be a contradiction of the concept of seniority standing commencing at the time of hire except for the employer's right to terminate probationary employees prior to the end of the probationary period.

The Seniority Unit

One would expect that seniority should be related to the hiring dates of other employees, or in other words, that seniority should be companywide. Although companywide seniority is usually the basis of invoking most seniority rights, the parties may negotiate for seniority based on the date of entry into a subdivision of the company. Thus, seniority may be by date of commencement of work in a particular plant, department, or shift. It is not uncommon for the parties to negotiate different seniority bases for different purposes. Thus, company seniority might be the basis for entitlement to vacation selection, while access to job openings on promotion may be based on seniority in the department in which the vacancy occurred. In this context, it is possible for one employee to have concurrent seniority in several departments if he or she has been transferred to different jobs in different departments. It likewise is possible to have seniority based on shift used to determine access to overtime hours or preferred work stations on that shift. Such categorization and delineation of seniority groupings is a function of the parties' efforts in collective bargaining negotiations.

CASE: THE BYPASSED BIDDER

Jaime Summ applied to work for the company in 1979. In her employment application, she noted that she had worked as a garage attendant and automotive mechanic and that she also had certifications in diesel motor overhaul. The company had no openings in its automotive repair department and offered Summ a position in the clerical support department, where she handled paperwork involving parts requisitions and invoices. She was promoted to higher positions in that department and was chief of her unit seven years later when the company was in need of a new automotive-repair person.

The employer posted a bidding notice on all the bulletin boards of the automotive repair department, consistent with its practice of posting vacancies in the department in which they occurred. The notice was not posted on any of the bulletin boards in the clerical department. One car washer and two mechanic's aides submitted bids, and the position was awarded to the senior mechanic's aide, who had been in the same position with the company since 1983.

Summ learned of the vacancy after it had been awarded and filed a grievance protesting her exclusion from the bidding process. The grievance was denied and appealed to arbitration. The parties' agreement stated that "promotion shall be based on seniority of the bidders for a vacancy, provided the winning bidder has the requisite skill and ability."

At the arbitration hearing, the union argued that there was no contract language limiting promotions in the automotive repair department to incumbents in that department, that the proper seniority for such promotions should have been companywide rather than departmentwide, and that the company violated the parties' agreement by failing to post the vacancy throughout the plant where Summ would have seen it and been permitted to bid for it. The union requested that Summ, who had held a comparable job before coming to the company and who had obvious qualifications for the position, be granted the position with reimbursement for earnings lost.

The company argued that there had been a consistent practice of posting vacancies only within the department where the vacancy arose, that the practice was followed in every department and had never been challenged by the union, that the grievant had never performed any jobs on permanent or even temporary transfer to the automotive repair department, and that it had no way of determining that she was a contender for the vacancy if she did not bid for it. The company argued that the burden was on Summ to find available postings in the departments where posted and then to bid on them if interested. In this case, the company concluded, its actions were proper, and the grievance should be denied.

The arbitrator recognized that there had been a consistent practice of posting vacancies within the department and of considering for promotion only those employees who had been assigned to and accumulated seniority within that department. The arbitrator noted that the failure of the union to challenge the practice in negotiations did not constitute endorsement of the departmental seniority for bidding because there was no evidence that any employee from another department had ever bid for a job in a different department and because the company had never put the union on notice that it would exclude bidders from other departments. The arbitrator continued that there was no evidence that any employee had ever bid for a vacancy in another department, let alone filed a grievance over exclusion from the bidding or denial of the vacancy.

The arbitrator ruled that for a past practice to prevail, the party against whom it was being established must have had knowledge of the practice and have acquiesced in its continuance. The arbitrator held that because the union was never put on notice in negotiations, by memo from the company, or even by its role in processing a grievance protesting the company's assertion of departmental seniority, the company's claim of past practice establishing such departmental seniority was inadequate to prove the existence of such seniority.

Instead, the arbitrator held any claim of departmental seniority must be founded on the contract language. The agreement made no reference to departmental seniority, so the arbitrator concluded that there was no departmental restriction on the posting of or the bidding for vacancies and that the grievant was entitled to have partaken in that bidding process. The arbitrator noted that there was no contract language confining bids to the department where the vacancy occurred and that the company's action in restricting postings to the automotive repair department deprived the grievant of knowledge of the vacancy. Although she could have sought out the postings in that department if she had known the postings were confined thereto, she had no reason to know the postings were so confined and had reason to believe that when a vacancy became open in that department, a posting would be made at a bulletin board to which she had normal access. Thus, the proximate cause for Summ's not bidding was held to have been the company's failure to post the vacancy on a bulletin board within her normal purview or to advise her when such postings would be made. Because Summ had a bulletin board in her work area where vacancies were routinely posted, it was reasonable for her to look at that board for all postings for which she would be eligible.

Summ's grievance was sustained. The arbitrator reasoned that there was no certainty she would have been selected if she had bid for the job and that the wrong in her case was her being denied the opportunity to bid. Accordingly, the arbitrator held that the vacancy should be reposted plantwide and the grievant be permitted to bid.

Discussion Question 1: What position could the union have taken?

The union should have examined its negotiating notes and its records of prior grievances in bidding to make certain that the company had never been granted departmental seniority for promotions and that the union had never known of the company's assertion of departmental seniority. The union also could have asserted the company's obligation to examine its records to learn which employees might be suited for promotion to any vacancy. From such examination, the company could have ascertained Summ's qualifications from its employment applications, and even under its narrow view of seniority, it should have been held to the obligation of finding qualified employees for vacancies. The union also could have argued against reposting of the vacancy as being an unfair remedy because by the case's notoriety the bidding had been opened to other employees who might have had no earlier interest in the position. Thus the status quo to which the grievant was entitled would have been disrupted.

Discussion Question 2: What position could the company have taken?

The company should have examined its notices to the union, its negotiating history, and its handling of grievances to find some language that could have been interpreted as notice to the union that it was relying on departmental seniority for vacancy bidding. It could have questioned the grievant and all other union witnesses about their observations of the bulletin boards in their departments to establish that they had never seen postings from other departments. In this, the company might have been able to establish union awareness of department-only postings and thus shift to the union the burden of questioning the practice. Since the union did not do that, it would strengthen the company's case that the union knew, or should have known, of the departmental posting practice and that by doing nothing to challenge it, must be held to have accepted it.

Discussion Question 3: Was the company obligated to seek out Summ's bid because of her prior experience in automotive repair?

The advent of computers makes it a relatively simple matter for the employer to file information on prior employment experience as set forth in employment applications, but such information neither establishes prior qualifications nor potential in a new vacancy. The bidding procedure is intended to place on employees the burden of undertaking to express their interest in upgrading themselves. The fact that an employee may have claimed to have done the same work for an earlier employer demonstrates neither ability nor interest to do the work called for in the bid for the posted vacancy.

Discussion Question 4: What would it have taken to establish departmental seniority for bidding?

The most effective means of establishing seniority is by negotiating for it. If the parties' contract had referred to seniority without any reference to a unit smaller than the company, the reasonable inference is that the parties had assumed seniority to be on a companywide basis. Thus, if there was an intent to establish a more restrictive seniority unit, the burden would have been on the party seeking to establish it. If not done by direct negotiations, the restrictive seniority base could have been established by the company's writing to the union of its intent and thus shifting to the union the burden of objecting to that action or of having its silence be interpreted as acquiescence. Merely proceeding, as here, as if the departmental seniority was a fact ran the risk of challenge and economic loss if overturned.

Discussion Question 5: Was the employee truly made whole in the remedy in this case?

The grievant's claim was that she was entitled to have bid and that if she had bid, she would have been selected for the promotion; thus, she was entitled to reimbursement of the money she had lost by the company's failure to promote her to the open position when it made its selection. The "loss" was compounded by the length of time it look to process the case to arbitration, and the remedy Summ sought included the lost earnings throughout that period.

However, to grant the remedy as requested would have required the arbitrator to rule that Summ was the one to whom the job should have been granted. Yet her grievance was based on the company's failure to consider her bid. The remedy fashioned by the arbitrator was to correct that deficiency by reopening the bidding. Although that created a new universe for the company to promote from and disadvantaged the person already selected, it was the most reasonable way of turning back the clock. But that remedy could not mandate that Summ would be chosen as the successful bidder, for to so rule would take from the company the right to make its own choice among the bidders. The goal of the remedy was to assure that the company had Summ's bid among those it reviewed in making its choice for the promotion. For the arbitrator to find that Summ should have been chosen would have made the rebidding procedure a nullity. Likewise, to promise Summ back pay if selected would certainly have tilted the selection away from her.

Seniority on Union Work

Seniority may provide more than the simple rights occasioned by length of time since date of hire. Most collective bargaining agreements provide for seniority for union officials or for shop stewards to protect their employment while on union work.

CASE: THE OVERDUE RETURN

Beverly Smith was a bargaining-unit member with ten years' seniority and had been active in the union. Representatives of the international union approached her about attending a three-month training program in union finance. Smith was granted a three-month leave of absence for attendance at the training program. The parties' agreement protected the seniority of employees who opted to go on leaves of absence of various types.

On February 1, Smith began her training program, which ran until April 1. One week before the end of the program, the international union arranged for all course participants to journey to its headquarters for one week's on-the-job training on union finances. Smith knew of the week's additional time but made no effort to inform the company of the delay in her return. On April 1 the grievant did not return to work nor did she or the union call in to advise the employer of the reason for her absence. Smith finally returned to the plant on April 10, when she was advised that she had overstayed her leave and thus had forfeited her seniority. She filed a grievance over the company's action, and the case was taken to arbitration.

The company argued that Smith had been given a three-month leave of absence, that that leave placed the company at a disadvantage in terms of manpower, and that the employee had an obligation to resume her job responsibilities on the day agreed upon for her return to work. When she failed to return on that day or even to call in, she had violated the terms of her leave of absence and had in effect waived her right to return to work. It concluded she had given up her job.

The union argued that Smith was improperly deprived of her seniority, that she had taken the three-month leave by agreement with the company, and that she simply forgot to call in about the extra week of study. According to the union, the infraction was similar to being out ill and deserved a minimal disciplinary penalty, if any. It urged the grievance be sustained.

The arbitrator held that the three-month leave of absence was an explicit agreement for Smith to be out for that duration and to return promptly thereafter. Her failure to return was a direct violation of her commitment and was quite distinct from being taken ill without warning. But even in an unforeseen illness situation, the employee is obligated to call in to report her inability to work. In the present case, the arbitrator asserted, there was no illness and no report to work. The grievant as a union official should have been particularly mindful of the risk she ran by failing to return on time from her leave of absence. Her grievance was denied.

Discussion Question 1: What position could the company have taken?
The company could have researched prior cases of leave to verify that severance of seniority was the consequence of failure to return from leave on time. It could have examined the negotiating history to determine if there had been any discussion of the consequences of failure to return from leave on time. The company also could have researched the grievant's role in securing other leaves or in disciplinary infractions for being AWOL and not reporting in to establish that she knew the rules. It could have argued that the reason for her tardiness was not at issue; the reason for severance of seniority was her failure to return from leave as scheduled.

Discussion Question 2: What position could the union have taken?
The union also could have examined the incidence of tardiness in returning from leave and the negotiating history to determine if there had ever been discussion about termination for tardiness on return from leave. The union could have examined the history of AWOL and absenteeism and sought to establish an analogy between the grievant's forgetting to call in and the absences of other employees of similar duration, citing the difference in penalty imposed. The union could have strengthened its case by citing examples of other employees returning from leaves taken with management and then returned to the bargaining unit who had not been similarly penalized. The union might have suggested that the disparity in treatment was a consequence of anti-union animus.

Discussion Question 3: Would the result have been different if Smith had called in?
Although the employer asserted that Smith might have been separated even if she had called in at the end of her scheduled three-month leave, such a call would have clarified the situation for the grievant. Either she would have been granted an extension of the leave, or she would have been told of the penalty for the tardiness. At that point, she would have had permission to take the extra week or been ordered to return to work immediately. If the employer had told her that she would lose her job by not returning as scheduled, she undoubtedly would have returned on time and thus saved her job.

Interruption of Seniority

Seniority is assumed to continued to accrue throughout employment from the date of hire. Thus, if there is to be any deviation from the accrual of seniority as long as the employee is at work, it is incumbent on the party seeking to alter that concept to secure the accord of the other party. Seniority is a valuable commodity because with it comes priority access to better position, better hours, better choice of vacation period, and longer vacation periods.

Employers are loathe to dispense the seniority benefit when there is no employment service provided in return. Thus, if the parties negotiate arrangements for employees to take leaves of absence away from the enterprise, it is only reasonable for the employer to seek to have accrual of seniority suspended for the period of leave. The nature of the leave may determine whether or not seniority is accrued or held in abeyance. Leaves of absence for community service, such as the Peace Corps, military service, and the like, generally permit the employee to continue to accrue seniority even though absent from work for as long as one or two years. Leaves of absence for work outside the bargaining unit, either in management or for the union, are more likely to be treated as not justifying seniority accrual for such periods, with seniority already accrued being frozen or held in escrow until the employee returns to work.

Seniority so preserved is naturally a matter of negotiated agreement between the parties. Absent such agreement, a departure to work in another enterprise, even for a few months, may more likely result in loss of seniority and of employment as well. The negotiation of seniority provisions for union business usually involve the union seeking seniority protection for as large a union contingent as possible, while the employer seeks to restrict access to that status, as it often entails retaining union officers at work who are less skilled and proficient than the employees they replace during leaves.

The determination of whether seniority continues to accrue during such leaves of absence or periods of work for the company or union is a function of what the parties have negotiated. In some agreements, departing to work for the union or for the company in a nonbargaining-unit position may even result in forfeiture of seniority and thus severance of the bargaining-unit position and relationship.

Severance of Seniority

Seniority is a necessary concomitant to continued employment. When that seniority is severed, employment is terminated. The methods of terminating employment are, therefore, an important matter of negotiation between the parties.

Termination may occur in several ways agreed to by the parties and incorporated into their agreement as the means by which seniority is severed. The first may be termination by the employer on just cause grounds. Thus, when an employee is fired for just cause and fails to file a grievance over the removal or when an arbitrator endorses the employer's action, it constitutes a severance of the employment relationship as well as of seniority.

A second way is through failure to respond to an order to return to work within the contractually mandated number of days following a recall from layoff. Usually three to five days is allowed for a positive response to the request to return to employment. The employee may not be required to return to work within the three to five days, but must advise the employer of the intent to return to work once he or she has left any current employment.

A third method for losing seniority often is through failure to provide medical verification following an absence when the employer had determined the employee to have abandoned his or her job. A fourth way may be through an excessive period of layoff. The parties frequently agree that an employee who has been on layoff for two or three years and has not been recalled during that time has lost seniority and has severed his or her employment relationship with the employer. Fifth, the employee who has resigned his or her employment likewise may have severed seniority. Finally, an employee who fails to return to work as scheduled following completion of a leave of absence likewise is considered to have lost seniority.

CASE: THE SUDDEN RESIGNATION

Joel Bell was a telephone reservationist for a transportation company. As such, he answered customer questions about transportation schedules and had the authority to call customers on the company's telephone lines. A periodic review of Bell's outgoing calls disclosed a series of calls lasting more than the customary two minutes to locations outside the company's normal geographical range of business. Bell was called into the office by the management and was shown the company telephone records. The manager advised Bell that the company would terminate him and take legal action against him to recoup the cost of the telephone calls unless he resigned. The manager supplied Bell with a pretyped letter of resignation. Bell signed it and left the office. When he went back to his switchboard to collect his things prior to leaving, he met the shop steward and explained the situation. The shop steward suggested he file a grievance alleging improper removal. He did so, and the case was appealed to arbitration.

At the arbitration hearing, the union argued that Bell was the victim of constructive termination, that he did not resign of his own volition, and that the company's action was a threat against him to deter him from utilizing the grievance procedure. The union stated that he had not severed his seniority tie by his action because there had been pressure on him to resign to avoid termination and because Bell was not cognizant of his rights under the collective bargaining agreement at the time of the employer's action. The union asserted it had not been involved in the termination process and that Bell had a right to arbitrate the propriety of the company's action.

The company took the position that Bell was competent to make a choice

about whether or not to resign, that he was given the alternative of resignation to avoid legal action; that he made that decision in a calm manner,
and that there was no pressure brought against him and no threat more than
what the company deemed sufficient to persuade him to resign to avoid the
risks of legal action. It asserted that its prime goal of voluntary resignation
had been achieved, that Bell had taken that course of action and was bound
by it, and that the case was not appealable to arbitration because Bell's
voluntary resignation severed his employment and thus he lacked access to
the contract's grievance procedure.

The arbitrator held that the initial question for resolution was whether
or not there had been a resignation by Bell. If Bell had resigned, he had
severed his seniority and was not entitled to access to the grievance procedure. If, on the other hand, Bell had been forced into the resignation, then
it would have constituted a constructive termination, entitling him to arbitrate the issue of whether there was just cause for his removal.

The arbitrator found that Bell had been aware of the choice open to him
and of the option of challenging a company termination action and even a
legal action; that he opted voluntarily to avoid the termination and the legal
action by resorting to his right of resignation; that he voluntarily signed the
document; and that it was not until he was advised by a fellow employee to
file a grievance that he apparently even thought about recanting his voluntary resignation. At that point, the arbitrator found, Bell's action had been
voluntarily taken. He had, in fact, severed his seniority under the parties'
seniority clause, and having voluntarily taken that action, he could not then
unilaterally place himself back on the company's roster to be in a position
to invoke the challenge to the termination on just cause grounds.

Discussion Question 1: What evidence might the union have presented?
The union might have presented evidence of a history of antagonism between
the supervisor and Bell, of Bell's being harassed by the supervisor, or of
Bell's reporting the incident to the shop steward as one in which he had felt
the threat and been intimidated into the action. It might have researched
union records to determine if there had been any other instances of such
recanting of resignations. It also might have tried to establish that Bell did
not know the meaning of his acts, that he was confused by the pressure of
the situation, that he was uninformed of the collective bargaining agreement,
or that he was unaware that any resignation could have precluded his right
to invoke the grievance procedure.

Discussion Question 2: What position might the employer have taken?
The employer might have produced evidence to show that Bell had made
the phone calls in question, that they were to relatives or to friends, that he
acknowledged either in word or in action that he was responsible for those

improper calls, and that he even was aware of other employees' having resigned under similar circumstances. The objective would have been to show that Bell had acted of his own volition, that the exchange had been a tranquil one, and that it was not until the shop steward suggested that Bell might have had a chance to fight the issue that Bell even thought about altering his position on the voluntary resignation.

Discussion Question 3: Would it have made a difference if the confrontation between the supervisor and Bell had been hostile?

The environment of the confrontation was crucial to the arbitrator's decision. If the evidence had shown that Bell was intimidated or that he was being subjected to pressure to a degree that would have deprived him of the right to make a calm judgment, then the arbitrator might have ruled that the decision was not a voluntary decision and that Bell had, in fact, not resigned but had acted to avoid the threat of harsher action. The arbitrator's ruling was based on the conclusion that Bell had acted on his own volition without pressure and that he was given an option between resignation and administrative and legal action.

Discussion Question 4: Would it have made any difference if the union had shown that Bell was not intelligent and did not understand his rights under the collective bargaining agreement?

Arbitrators generally hold that employees are responsible for knowledge of the collective bargaining agreement and that claimed ignorance of contract entitlement is not grounds for failure to act to enforce the rights contained therein. A different result might occur if there was evidence that the company had been aware of Bell's limited intelligence and at other times had asked the union representative to explain things to him. Even if Bell was of less-than-average intelligence he still had the option of resigning to avoid other problems. His discussions with his shop steward may have given him second thoughts about resigning, and encouraged him to bring the case to arbitration. But the arbitrator's role was limited to determining the bona fides and perhaps Bell's competence in deciding to resign.

Discussion Question 5: What if the evidence had shown that immediately after signing the resignation, Bell had sought out the shop steward to protest the action, rather than the shop steward's having initiated the idea of protest?

Such a postresignation response from Bell would have constituted strong evidence that he had acted under pressure when he signed the resignation and that his immediate reaction had been to find a way to challenge the resignation. If such evidence had been introduced, the arbitrator might have concluded that Bell had not acted entirely voluntarily when he signed the resignation and that the signing was done with intention to protest it thereafter.

If the latter had been the case, the arbitrator might have reasoned that the resignation was not voluntary and that there was indeed a constructive termination. The controlling standard in such cases is the determination of whether the employee had voluntarily severed his employment relationship. When an employee has terminated that relationship of his or her own volition, the action is permanent and the employee has taken himself or herself out of the relationship. There is no contractual provision for recision of that decision nor timetable for any reconsideration. The act, once taken, is controlling.

Seniority Verification

The employer is considered to be custodian of the records necessary to ascertain employee seniority and correct placement on the seniority roster. The employer enforces the contract provisions that rely on seniority. But seniority dates may not be scrutinized until years later, when neither the employee nor the union are in a position to ascertain the accuracy of the employer's records.

Accordingly, contracts often provide an opportunity for employees or the union to verify the accuracy of the employment roster and the seniority dates therein. Such verification opportunities occur periodically when the employment list is posted, giving employees the opportunity to verify the accuracy of the dates of hire or seniority and giving the union the opportunity to verify the accuracy of the dates from its own records and to correct records in anticipation of the need to verify such data in the event of layoffs, job bids, and so on.

Once the seniority roster is posted and is unchallenged and the closing period for such the challenges has passed, all employees and the union have waived their right to challenge the accuracy of the data. The seniority roster is then considered to be an accurate record of employment and seniority dates.

CASE: THE LOST SENIORITY

Dan Bernard had a seniority date of October 7, 1980. The company followed the contractual requirement of posting seniority lists every six months, with employees and the union having ten days to provide corrections thereto. Bernard had checked his listing over the years and had found it to be accurate. In January 1983, Bernard took a six-month leave of absence to go to work for the union. The parties' agreement read as follows: "Any bargaining-unit member who opts to serve up to six months on leave of absence with the union will retain his seniority during that period."

Bernard decided to return to work early, coming back in March. The July 1983 seniority listing showed Bernard as having three years and three months of seniority, reflecting the anticipated six months' leave without seniority accumulation, rather than the three months' time he actually spent out of the bargaining unit. The grievant was on vacation on July 1 when the July listing was first posted, and the union did not catch the error. Bernard returned to work on July 7. In January 1984, Bernard noticed the inaccuracy in the listing and asked his supervisor to correct it by adding the three months attributable to the time he returned early from leave. The supervisor responded that it was too late and that job changes had been made based on the July 1 listing.

At the arbitration hearing, the union argued that the three-month error was not the grievant's. He had told the supervisor, on his return, that he assumed the six-month leave had been adjusted to reflect the three months he was away. Because he was away on vacation on the date of the July 1 posting, his record should be corrected to reflect his true seniority date. It argued that the consequences of the company's action in perpetuating the error would place Bernard at a permanent disadvantage in any future job moves, a penalty not of his making and one that could best be corrected when first discovered.

The company acknowledged that it had been negligent in entering the six-month leave rather than the three-month leave. Nevertheless, the error was not intentional, and it was incumbent on the grievant and the union to make the requisite corrections within the contractually provided time. It noted that the list became official when no protest was entered, and that job assignments, transfers, promotions, and demotions had been made based on the posted dates, changes that would be impossible to unscramble after the fact.

The arbitrator expressed concern over the adverse consequences that could befall an employee who was denied the full credit of his legitimate seniority, particularly in areas of jobs, promotions, shift preferences, layoffs, and so on. The arbitrator identified seniority rights as among the most important achievements of unions in collective bargaining specifically because of the preciseness and fairness the seniority system provided in allocating benefits and handicaps among competing employees. That equity also assisted employers in avoiding charges of favoritism by relying on the preciseness of seniority in rendering assignments, particularly in a large enterprise.

But, the arbitrator continued, for the seniority system to have its full impact as a reliable gauge of comparative length of employee service it must be mutually accepted as the final decider of seniority dates. Although the employer had greater control over the files and records that contained the seniority dates than the union or the employees, management's record keeping was not infallible. But because seniority is by its nature a comparative standard, the arbitrator stated, there must be recognition and acceptability of a fixed, finite list of these comparative dates, as any change in an employee's seniority date will impact on all other employees as well. To move one employee three months up the seniority list would deprive those employees who had moved from above to below that employee of rights to future moves and might result in their loss of promotion, shift preference, or other benefits that may already have been granted without awareness of an error in the seniority list.

For that reason, the arbitrator continued, the parties negotiated for the posting of the seniority lists on a periodic basis to permit the union and individual employees to examine the dates for accuracy. The parties also agreed that there had to be a statute of limitations on making adjustments to the posted list. Otherwise, its value would be lost in that personnel moves based on a changeable list would always be in jeopardy.

In this case, the parties had agreed on a ten-day posting period, during which changes in seniority dates could be made. That list, including the acknowledged three-month error in Bernard's case, was posted on July 1. Bernard returned to work on July 7, but did not examine the list or discover the error. The contract provision called for the list to be posted until July 10. Bernard was aware of the seniority list's being posted semiannually, and he was aware that his leave would have triggered an adjustment in his seniority rights. Although he was absent when the list was first posted, he was in the plant July 7–10 and was working in areas where bulletin boards containing the listing were in sight. It was his responsibility to observe and examine the list during that time. Having had that opportunity and having failed to exercise it, he must be held bound by the seniority date as posted. To hold otherwise would run contrary to the intent of the parties in negotiating the provision and would disrupt and negate a whole series of moves, transfers, and shift changes made from July 10 to January 1 and based on the error in the seniority listing. The grievance was denied.

Discussion Question 1: What position could the union have taken?
The union could have examined all the personnel moves that had occurred from July 10 to January 1 to see how many were a direct consequence of the three-month error and perhaps could have secured the acquiescence of those involved to moving back to where they would have been had the error not been made. It could have offered to waive any claim for changing people back where they should have been in exchange for a January 1 correction in the listing. The union could have explored the possibility that the error was deliberate and based on the anti-union animus of someone who had

intentionally failed to correct the six-month leave to three months. If that could have been established, Bernard probably would have prevailed because of fraud on the company's part.

The union also could have examined prior instances of error discovery to determine whether the ten-day deadline had always been strictly adhered to or whether there had been tardy exceptions. The negotiating history also might have shown how the parties intended to deal with tardily discovered errors.

Discussion Question 2: What position could the company have taken?
The company could have examined the negotiating history and past practice to determine if a similar situation had been anticipated or had ever occurred. It, too, could have assessed the number and type of personnel moves that had been made as a result of the error and perhaps have developed similar data about earlier changes that had remained in effect despite other tardily discovered errors.

The company could have shown that it provided the list to the union and that the union brought to its attention other errors. It also could have shown that Bernard worked in close proximity to the posted lists.

Discussion Question 3: What was the union's responsibility in not detecting the error?
Although the arbitrator confined the opinion to Bernard's responsibility, the union too, shared culpability in the matter. The contract granted the union the right to correct errors and with that right came the responsibility to do so. If, as would have probably been the case, a copy of the list was sent to the union, it was obligated to check for accuracy. In this case, it would not have been liable if it had not known of Bernard's return from leave. But if the company could show that the union had been sent either the notice of Bernard's going on leave or the notice of return or that the union had been notified that Bernard had returned early, it could have been liable.

The arbitrator's opinion focused on Bernard because he was personally liable, but it was possible the union was also at fault. The arbitrator was perhaps sensitive to the prospects of Bernard's suing the union for not having found the error. Even if the union had responsibility to review the record, Bernard certainly had an equal or greater obligation to discover the error.

Discussion Question 4: What if Bernard had not known of the error until January 1?
Again, the question arises of whether the union knew or should have known of the leave-of-absence error. If it knew of the error, it might have been bound by the listing when it failed to protest it. If it did not know of the error, it might not have been liable for failure to discover it on the listing.

As for Bernard, if he had been absent during the entire July posting period, he would honestly not have known, nor could he have been expected to know of the error. Thus, if he had not discovered the error until January, he might have prevailed. What might have been the crucial determinant was whether the contract held the union *and* the employee or the union *or* the employee responsible for discovering the error. If the contract said the union *or* the employee was bound by the deadline, then Bernard would have been bound by the union's failure to catch the error. If the contract said the union *and* the employee were bound, then even if the union had not found the error, Bernard's not having had the opportunity to check the list until January might have given him an opportunity to upset the listing.

Transfers

In enterprises with multiple site locations under a single collective bargaining agreement, the issue of transfer between locations is a normal subject of collective bargaining negotiations. The problem may be complicated by different production operations entailing different skills in different locations. Seniority clauses are thus tailored to provide employees the right to transfer among facilities while assuring the employer that those who elect to transfer will have the requisite skills to enable them to serve as productive employees at their new locations.

This may be accomplished by a number of procedures. One approach is to require that any employees who seek to transfer possess the requisite skills to enable them to fit into a vacancy and perform acceptably therein. Under that arrangement, there must be a vacancy as well as a qualified bidder seeking to move from another facility. The vacancy and bidding arrangement would, in effect, be no different than the routine bidding within a department or between departments of a single-facility employer.

Another procedure would grant freer movement between facilities based on company seniority but ceding to the employer the right to assign employees who opt to transfer to positions of the employer's choice. But even under this free movement, there must be a recognized protection against wholesale transfer to avoid disequilibrium in the work forces of two locations or to avoid transfer to locations where no work is available.

Even within a single plant, arrangements must be negotiated to provide for smooth right of transfer. Whether the transfer be to an identical job in another department or from one shift to another that the employee finds preferable, the seniority provisions prevail. In personnel movements between shifts, the contract may permit transfers by seniority as long as there is a vacancy within the employee's skill range into which he or she may move.

Successor Contracts

Employers are confronted on occasion with the need to sell the enterprise. The National Labor Relations Board has established rules governing the continuation of a collective bargaining agreement. Under such circumstances, the employer sells to a successor employer and employees continue to work in that company under a continuing collective bargaining agreement. The prevailing rule is that seniority will continue to be based on date of original hire even though there has been a transfer of the ownership and management. The contract continues in effect, as do the seniority rights agreed to under the prior employer's control.

If and when the parties negotiate a successor agreement with the new employer, the question of seniority, seniority standing, and seniority rights become matters for negotiation with the new employer. A similar result occurs in the case of an employer transferring its operation to a different location with the same union. Employees may be given the option of moving and continuing under that employer's collective bargaining agreement. Those employees who have opted to move usually continue to accrue seniority from the date of their hire at the prior location.

10
Promotion

Employers who prior to collective bargaining had the right to move employees to upward, downward, and lateral job classifications were faced with restrictions on that freedom of movement by the advent of collective bargaining. Collective bargaining agreements continue to recognize the employer's right to determine if there is or if there will be a vacancy and grant to the employer the authority to determine when and if that vacancy is to be filled.

Collective bargaining agreements also identify a promotion as distinguished from a transfer. Probably the most important impact of collective bargaining on the employer's right to promote comes in the qualification imposed as a prerequisite to promotion: the balancing of seniority with skill and ability to perform the new job. Collective bargaining agreements also encompass the rights of the employee and the employer in establishing the duration of the promoted employee's tenure in the position and of the break-in period, if any, and in establishing the employer's right to demote an unqualified employee. Improved access to promotional opportunities through collective bargaining is a vital accomplishment for employees and frequently comes in conflict with the employer's need to assure that those promoted are the best suited to protect the prosperity and efficient operations of the enterprise.

Management's Right to Fill Vacancies

Management's right to direct the operation of the enterprise and its work force grants to the employer the right to determine the size of its work force as well as the personnel to be assigned to various classifications. Only when the parties negotiate fixed crew sizes does management surrender this right.

CASE: THE DISAPPEARING CRANE OPERATOR

For the past ten years, the company had functioned with five crane operators. When the senior crane operator retired, the employer posted the position for bids. Several employees applied, and the company announced that none of the applicants would be granted the position and that the position would not be filled. The company announced it would continue to operate with four crane operators. The union filed a grievance alleging a contract violation. The case was appealed to arbitration.

At the arbitration hearing, the union argued that the company had always had five crane operators; that the crane operator classification was referred to in the collective bargaining agreement; and that the company was obligated to fill that fifth position when it became vacant. It also argued that the company's action in posting the vacancy indicated a recognition of that commitment and that the company was obligated to fill the position once it had posted it and accepted the bids.

The employer argued that it had no contractual obligation to have five crane operators and that it had never contracted to have five crane operators. According to the company, the listing of the classification in the job description did not necessitate the position's being filled. It argued that it had the discretion to determine that the applicants were not acceptable, that it did not wish to hire outside personnel to reach the former complement of five operators, and that the grievance must be denied.

The arbitrator held that management had the right to determine whether or not to fill a vacant position, that the listing of a classification in the collective bargaining agreement did not mandate that there be five crane operators, and that the company did not waive its right to retain only four crane operators when it posted the vacancy for the fifth crane operator. The arbitrator stated that the employer was within its rights in examining all the applicants in order to determine if it would continue the five positions, but that when it exercised its right to decline the bids, it acted within its authority to declare that the vacant position would not be filled. Accordingly, the arbitrator denied the grievance.

Discussion Question 1: What position might the union have taken?
The union might have shown a negotiating history in which the employer assured the union that there would always be five crane operators. It might have secured evidence of prior cases in which vacancies in other classifications had always been filled and shown instances in which the employer had, after union protests, filled a vacancy that it had declared it would not fill. The union could have shown that the bidders were qualified and that the company was discriminating among the qualified bidders by refusing to fill the crane operator's position.

Discussion Question 2: What position might the employer have taken?
The employer likewise might have looked at prior practice to show other positions that had been vacated, that had been left unfilled, and that had been posted and bid for and had not been filled. The question of whether comparable information in this case was binding on the union was depend-

ent on whether the union had received notice of the company's action in not filling the position. Either prior notification from the company to the union or constructive notice through having had a union officer bid for a position that was later not filled could establish the union's acquiescence to the company's right not to fill a position. By this latter action, the employer could claim that the union was on notice of the employer's action in not filling a vacancy and that the union, by not having filed a grievance over that action, must be considered to have waived its right to dispute the nonfilling of a vacancy.

Discussion Question 3: What would have been the result if there had been only one crane-operator position listed in the parties' rate schedule, with the crane operator being among the skills covered by the recognition clause?
Does such identification of a classification require that it always be filled?
Most arbitrators would agree that the company still has the right to decide to fill all positions and that the listing of a classification in the recognition clause merely constitutes recognition that the classification is to be within the bargaining unit, although it might constitute a restriction against the employer's subcontracting that task to a nonbargaining-unit member. Because the union had jurisdiction over the classification, it would not permit that classification to be staffed by nonbargaining-unit personnel.

Concerning the listing of the classification in the wage-rate section of the parties' agreement, that listing constitutes recognition that the parties have negotiated a specified rate for that task when performed. It does not dictate and require that the classification always will be filled. It generally is held that the listing of the classification in the parties' agreement may be a protection against that work being contracted out to nonbargaining-unit personnel, but unless the parties specify that there shall be a specific number of employees filling each classification during the life of the contract, there is no assumed obligation to fully staff to fill the schedule. Some industries do negotiate specific work-crew sizes and for specific numbers of employees to be assigned to various classifications. The evidence in this contract did not show any such commitment to fill a specific number of vacancies or, indeed, to keep vacancies filled.

Promotion or Transfer

Collective bargaining agreements usually discriminate between transfers and promotions. The company maintains its right in most cases to make transfers on a temporary basis, and the parties may negotiate restrictions on such temporary transfers as well as on the duration of such transfers before they are considered to be permanent transfers. The dispute arises in the definition of what constitutes a promotion. It is assumed that a promotion is an upward move, rather than a lateral move. Most people opt to take advantage of openings in higher-paying positions. But there are moves that employees may consider to be promotions although they are lateral, rather than upward, moves. Indeed transfers may be used to enhance qualifications for future promotions.

Should the promotion clause apply to such moves? Such is a matter for the parties to negotiate in their contract. But if the arbitrator were to interpret the contract as defining a promotion as being in the eyes of the bidder, then the promotion clause might be expanded to include positions perhaps of a lateral direction but with better hours, greater promotion potential, and better working conditions, even though paid at the same compensation rate.

CASE: THE NEPOTISTIC TRANSFER

The son of the company's president applied for a job as a machine operator, but because there was no opening in that position, he was hired as a shipper's helper. After eight months in that position, one of the machine operators retired, and the superintendent assigned the son to the open higher-paying position as a temporary transfer. The parties' agreement specified that the employer could make temporary transfers at its discretion to fill a vacant position for three weeks. By that time, the position must be posted for filling pursuant to the terms of the promotion clause. At the end of the third week, the son returned to his former position for one day and was then again transferred to the machine operator's position. The union filed a grievance, stating the assignment violated the company's obligation to post the vacancy.

At the arbitration hearing, the union argued that the company's action was an improper exercise of nepotism. It argued that the son lacked the qualifications to work as a machine operator; that the contract required the posting of the position within three weeks; and that the employer had no right to reassign the son for a second three-week stint, as it was merely an underhanded effort to build up his experience as a machine operator so that he could be given the assignment on a permanent basis through future bidding.

The company argued that the supervisor had sole discretion over who was to be assigned to a vacancy for a three-week period, that the son returned to his prior position at the end of that period, and that the company was not restricted from making another temporary assignment if the son had returned to his regular job as shipper's helper. It argued further that there was no requirement that the company post the machine operator's position if it decided to leave it empty and that the two temporary assignments were made during a period when the company was deciding whether to continue that position. It noted that the position ultimately was not filled after the son returned from his second stint as a temporary transfer and urged the grievance be denied.

The arbitrator held that there was no restriction in the contract against nepotism or against the sons of owners being employed or used by the employer as long as the contract provisions were observed. The arbitrator ruled that the employer had the right to transfer the son for the first three-week period because the agreement granted it sole discretion in such a transfer.

But by the end of that three-week period, the employer was obligated under the agreement to remove the temporary transfer and either to choose to fill the position by posting it or to declare it closed. Although the son did return to his shipper's helper's job, it was only for one day, making the reassignment to the machine operator's position a transparent violation of the prohibition against temporary assignments of more than three weeks, as well as a violation of the requirement of posting a position after three weeks of temporary transfer.

Although the employer had the option of closing the position, as it apparently did at a later date, there was no question that at the time of the grievance the position was still being filled, to the deprivation of those who would have bid for it if it had been posted. The arbitrator ruled that the position be posted and that the successful bidder be assigned the position or, in the absence of its being reopened, be reimbursed for the earnings that would have been lost by that successful bidder until the date the position was closed.

Discussion Question 1: What position could the union have taken?
The union could have researched the son's background to show his lack of experience for the position of machine operator. Such evidence, if put into the record, might have precluded the employer from awarding the position to him when the job was posted. As a further protection in this regard, the union could have asked the arbitrator to retain jurisdiction to assure that the remedy was properly and fairly implemented without it becoming a device for permanently placing the son into the position. The union also could have presented evidence of prior temporary transfers to show that none had been reassigned, as in this case, as well as evidence from the negotiating history to show that the temporary transfer clause was formulated to assure the position remained filled until a permanent replacement was designated, pursuant to the bidding procedure.

Discussion Question 2: What position could the employer have taken?
The company could have demonstrated that the son had the qualification to be machine operator to diffuse the claim that the transfer was a nepotistic assignment. It could have produced evidence of its continuing uncertainty over whether to post and continue the position, and it could have shown

that the repeated transfer was an interim device until the job was closed and thus was not a temporary assignment until the job was posted for permanent assignment.

The company also might have challenged the right of the union, rather than an individual employee, to file the grievance. The union's rights in that regard would need to have been established either by the definition of the grievance under the contract or by contractual authorization to file a complaint. In this case, no particular employee had a right to claim he or she was injured or aggrieved because there had been no posting, bidding, or deprivation. The union could have made a reasonable case that it was protecting union rights of access to the bidding procedure so that individual bargaining-unit members would have the right to bid for the prospective opening.

Discussion Question 3: Is nepotism ever violative of the collective bargaining agreement?

There may be collective bargaining agreements that preclude employees from reaping certain benefits if related to other employees or to members of management. Indeed, there are enterprises that will not employ relatives at the same facility. But the controlling document in determining employee and management rights is the collective bargaining agreement, and unless there is a specific restriction against nepotism agreed to by the parties, the rights and benefits and obligations are to be shared by all.

Limitations on Seniority in Promotions

Although the inclusion of seniority rights in a collective bargaining agreement would appear to pave the way to promotions based on length of service, most employers have been successful in negotiating into contracts as ancillary to seniority rights the retention of some authority in the selection of who is to be granted a promotion opportunity. Thus, seniority alone is not enough to justify promotion unless there is some recognition of the bidder's ability to perform the work to which he or she is otherwise entitled by seniority. Collective bargaining agreements therefore usually provide for a blend of seniority and ability as requirements for promotion.

There are numerous variations that have been negotiated to accommodate these potentially contradictory priorities. One example is the phrase, "Seniority and ability shall be considered as equal factors in the granting of promotions." That language raises the vision of a balance, with seniority on one end and ability on the other and with greater seniority and lesser ability being balanced with lesser seniority and greater ability.

Although apparently symmetrical, that concept could virtually eradicate either seniority or skill and ability if the other element in either case were sufficiently strong. Under this theory, an employee of forty years' service effectively could command entry into any position in the enterprise, even though lacking any qualifications to perform the work. Similarly, the concept would permit a new employee with widespread experience and expertise to gain access to any position, with priority over even the most senior employee of the enterprise.

A second standard calls for seniority to be the determining factor, provided the applicant has minimal or threshold skill and ability to perform the work of the position in consideration. Under that standard, the senior employee need only establish ability to perform the task. Thus, even if the next-senior employee had far greater qualifications and had held the disputed job for years, if both could do the work the senior employee would prevail, as there is no standard of relative comparability or relevance to the fact that some bidders may be more qualified for the job than others.

Under this concept, what steps must be followed to determine if an employee has the qualifications necessary for selection for promotion? First, the employee claiming promotion must be senior to other applicants. Second, he or she must have the necessary qualifications with reference only to the job as it will be performed, without comparison to how other applicants would perform the job, because relative and comparative ability are not relevant. The qualifications in terms of both mental and physical capacity can be shown through the applicant's having enough training and experience to be suitable for the breaking-in period. Those qualifications may be ascertained by offering the employee the routine orientation and instruction generally offered to an employee new to that classification on the expectation that once offered the position and given the normal break-in and orientation, the employee should be able to stay on top of the job.

In order to avoid unnecessary disputes arising from the employer's insistence on its choice of preferred bidder, it is prudent for the employer to interview the senior employee as well as the selected bidder to avoid a charge of being arbitrary or capricious. Such an interview would also serve to help the employer avoid overlooking crucial qualifications possessed by the senior employee; would test the necessary qualifications of the senior employees through examination via the interview; and would ascertain whether prior education, previous work record, or prior job assignment within the plant have provided an opportunity to develop the requisite skill and ability to handle the job.

A third standard and one that is more common grants even greater relevance to skill and ability by providing that "in the event of equal skill and ability among applicants, the senior applicant shall be granted the bid." Sometimes the phrase, "in the event of relatively equal skill and ability," is inserted as a variant in the standard. Under that variant, the senior employee is not required to show that "he or she is equal to the most qualified, but only that he or she is relatively equal to the most qualified bidder."

Although this latter phrase offers a somewhat less stringent standard for the union to enable seniority to prevail, the thrust of both standards permits the employer the preferential reliance on skill and ability. Thus, if an employee can be shown to have superior skill and ability even if junior in seniority, there is no need to turn to the seniority standard. By the terms of the agreement, seniority becomes relevant only as a tiebreaker in cases of equal or relatively equal skill and ability. Although there are no clear distinctions over the definitions of skill and ability to perform a job not yet undertaken, the general view is that skill refers to the competence to perform relevant tasks in previously held jobs, while ability is related to the competence to use those skills in such a way that the employee has a reasonable prospect of the ability to perform adequately in the sought-after position. Generally, the terms are used together with little effort at separate definitions, except that together they are taken to mean a level of previously proven competence and future potential that will enable the selected employee to perform successfully in the new position.

Such superior skill and ability may be established in a number of ways. The employee may have done the same work during schooling, during prior employment, during prior transfer to the open position, or as part of the job currently held. Skill and ability may have been established by job testing or by careful questioning during interviews.

The mere fact that the employer deems an employee to have the requisite skill and ability does not constitute proof thereof. If the union challenges the assertion of superior skill and ability through the grievance procedure, then evidence must be presented to an arbitrator to persuade that arbitrator that the company-selected employee does not possess superior skill and ability and that the grievant has equal or relatively equal skill and ability—the standard for invoking reliance on seniority.

CASE: THE RELATIVELY EQUAL BIDDER

Jim Murphy was a machine operator, class 3. Upon seeing a posted notice for promotion to the position of machine operator, class 2, Murphy filed a bid. He was one of three employees in the labor grade 3 classification to bid for the job. Employee A was junior to Murphy. He had been trained at a technical school, where he had learned machining, and had filled in on the machine operator, class 2 job when the regular operator was on vacation. Employee B, also junior to Murphy, in an earlier employment had held a job that the company asserted was equal to that of the machine operator, class 2 position. Murphy himself, the third applicant, had served longer than either employee A or employee B in the machine operator 3 classification, but had only had one three-day temporary assignment on an upgrade to the machine operator, class 2 position. Employee A had filled the machine operator 2 classification on three occasions during the two-week vacations of the machine operator, class 2. The company interviewed the three applicants and selected employee A, the least senior of the applicants. Murphy filed a grievance, and the case was appealed to arbitration. The contract language in dispute read as follows: "Promotion shall be on the basis of seniority provided skill and ability of the bidders is 'relatively equal.' "

The union argued that Murphy had the requisite experience in the labor grade 2 position to match the vacation upgrades of employer A. Although employee A had served longer during such upgrades, there had been no protest over Murphy's performance, which therefore must have been determined to have been relatively equal. Accordingly, it urged the grievance be sustained.

The employer argued that Murphy had only a passing experience in the labor grade 2 position and that he did not have the length of service or variety of tasks thrust upon him as had employee A during the three sessions of vacation upgrade. Murphy's skill and ability might have been deemed relatively equal if he had a few days' less experience than employee A, but that the disparity was so great that employee A was far superior to employee B and Murphy, thus justifying the denial of the grievance.

The arbitrator held that the objective of the skill-and-ability clause was to determine if the applicant had the competence to commence work on the job for which he was bidding. Murphy had, in fact, been assigned to that task and had performed the job without challenge over his competence, and although employee A had served in the position for a longer period of time, there was no showing that the diversity of tasks was any different during those periods than was performed by Murphy during his short upgrade. Employee A's service in the class 2 job might have made him somewhat more competent than Murphy, but the arbitrator found that the parties' insertion of the term "relatively equal," if to be accorded weight, should result in Murphy's being granted the upgrade on the basis of his seniority.

Discussion Question 1: What position might the union have taken?
The union might have detailed the types of work that had been done by Murphy on his upgrade in anticipation of the company's showing that employee A had done the wide variety of skills demanded of the higher-level job. It might have examined other promotion cases in which the company had granted the position to senior employees based on their having done the work of an upgraded job for shorter periods of time than had junior employees. The union also might have been able to show disparate treatment in the interviewing process if the evidence showed that the interviewer had

not asked Murphy about his prior work or what he had done during his upgrades.

Discussion Question 2: What questions might the employer have asked?
The employer could have gone through a detailed examination of the work performed by grade 2 machinists, describing the tasks therein that had been performed by employee A but not by Murphy. It might have introduced evidence to show that even the outside-trained employee B had sufficient qualifications to fill the job in preference to Murphy and that its choice of employee A was based on its belief that he had, by far, the best qualifications.

Discussion Question 3: What if the employer had shown that it had interviewed employee A and employee B, but not Murphy?
Most arbitrators would take the view that the employees were all entitled to equal access to the opportunity to prove their qualifications. The interview was an essential element of the employer's decision process, and by denying it to one or more of the applicants, the company placed that applicant at a disadvantage if the selection were based on the employees who were interviewed. In such a situation, the arbitrator might have ruled that the selection process was flawed and that although employee B or Murphy might not have been entitled to the position, they were entitled to fair consideration. The arbitrator therefore would have ordered a reexamination of the job-filling process. Generally, such a reopening would be limited to interviews of those who had been bidders.

Discussion Question 4: What would have been the result if the contract language had called for equal qualifications, rather than for relatively equal qualifications?
Although employee A may have spent more time on the job, that would not necessarily have established that he had greater potential to perform the tasks necessary to the new position. Clearly, he did have more experience on the job. Indeed, he may have acquired more skill on the job by virtue of his longer tenure there than Murphy had the opportunity to acquire during his short upgrade. In the case of equal showing of skill and ability, employee A presumably would have prevailed.

Discussion Question 5: Who would have the burden of proof in such a case?
If the issue agreed upon by the parties had been whether the company had violated the parties' agreement by promoting employee A to the position of machine operator, class 2, most arbitrators presumably would conclude that because the standard was seniority prevailing over relative ability, the union, by proving employee Murphy had a greater seniority and had some experience on the upgraded level, had shifted the burden of proof to the company

to establish that employee A had the requisite qualifications and that Murphy did not. If the arbitrator found that the company had not proven its case and that the company had violated the contract by promoting employee A, that would not establish that Murphy was indeed the appropriate recipient of the job. Indeed, it could be argued that the only issue resolved was that employee A was not sufficiently better qualified than Murphy, leaving open the question of employee B's qualifications compared with Murphy's. In most cases, the arbitrator would seek the stipulation that employee B was not a contender in the bidding for the position awarded to employee A or that the parties should reword the grievance to ask whether Murphy rather than employee A should have been assigned the promotion.

Discussion Question 6: What standards are used to prove ability?
Unions and management embrace several criteria to establish proof or to challenge proof of an employee's ability. Among them are written tests; experience, including duration of experience in either prior jobs or the new position; and training, either academic or on-the-job training at the plant or elsewhere. Production records to show the employee's competence in the incumbent position and the testimony of supervisors who have observed the various applicants at their regular tasks or on their temporary assignments also would be relevant.

Break-in Periods

Many collective bargaining agreements make contractual arrangements for employees who are the successful bidders into upgraded positions to test their abilities to meet the requirements of a position or their willingness to remain in a position. Such trial periods are not training periods. They are not viewed as the opportunity for the employee who is not qualified and who does not have the skill or the ability to make the upward move to acquire the skills necessary to fill the position. Instead, the assumption is that the employee can perform the task. The employee is then given an additional period of either fixed duration, for time established by past practice, or for time viewed as reasonable by the employer and the arbitrator reviewing the matter as an opportunity to establish competence in the task and remain in the position.

Even though the parties' agreement may specify a break-in period of perhaps ten days, that is not an automatic entitlement for the employee to remain in the position for that period of time if that employee has demonstrated an inability to meet the requirements of the new position. Thus, if an employee who is a successful bidder is guilty of repeated substantial nonfeasance or malfeasance in the new position, most arbitrators would say that the employer, having given him or her an opportunity to become accustomed to the job, need not suffer additional damage or loss while the employee tries to recoup from such adverse performance by insisting on remaining throughout the break-in period. Other arbitrators hold the employee is entitled to the full period to show his competence.

Employees utilize the break-in period as an opportunity to test themselves in the positions, with the right to return to their former positions if persuaded that the task to which assigned is beyond their competence or beyond their liking. Employees who are unsure of their performance may opt to return to their former positions rather than complete a break-in period and then find themselves being disciplined for poor workmanship in a task that may be beyond their competence.

CASE: THE UNFULFILLED PROMOTION

Rebecca Widom had worked as a computer analyst for several years before bidding for the bargaining-unit position of lead computer analyst. She was selected from four bidders because of her superior accuracy and programming skills. The promotion involved a change of starting times from 10:00 A.M. to 8:00 A.M. because one of the requirements of the new job was to prepare work for the other analysts prior to their coming to work. The parties' agreement provided for a two-week break-in period following any promotion.

Once she started in her new position, Widom performed well in the substantive aspects, but she apparently had difficulty in adjusting to her new starting time. On the second day she was thirty-five minutes late. On the subsequent days she reported fifteen, twenty, and ten minutes late. During the second week she was late three times, until on the last day of the break-in period the manager told her that she had not qualified for the promotion and was being returned to her former classification. She filed a grievance, and the action was denied and appealed to arbitration.

At the arbitration hearing, the union argued that Widom was improperly removed from the position, that she had demonstrated her job proficiency in her prior position, that the management had recognized her skill and ability by offering her the promotion, and that her job performance since her promotion showed that she was qualified to retain that promotion. It asserted that the problem with her attendance was unrelated to her work, that it resulted from the sudden change in her starting time, that it was readily overcome by giving her time to adjust to the new hours, and that it was more properly a matter for corrective disciplinary treatment than removal from a job for which she was obviously qualified. It urged the grievance be sustained.

The company argued that the grievant had not adequately fulfilled the job requirements of the position and that it had acted properly in returning Widom to her former position. The company asserted that the 8:00 A.M. starting time was a known requirement of the new position, that the grievant was aware from her former work that the lead computer analyst had to report two hours earlier than other analysts, and that tardiness cut into that preparation time to the detriment of departmental production.

The arbitrator held that the parties had negotiated a break-in period in recognition that anyone deemed qualified for promotion would lack the on-the-job exposure to that new position, exposure that would be essential to determine if the employee's potential for competence would be borne out by the reality of working in the position. The break-in period thus would provide either the employer or the employee the opportunity to cancel the promotion as not suitable.

In this case, the arbitrator continued, it was clear that Widom did possess the skill and ability to work as a lead computer analyst. But an added element of that job, one that had not been inherent in her former position, was a requirement of reporting to work promptly at 8:00 A.M. Only by so doing would Widom be able to adequately arrange assignments for the computer analysts due in at 10:00 A.M. The evidence showed that Widom was unable to report at the prerequisite starting time. Even if one or two unavoidable obstacles had impeded her on a few of the ten days, it might have been excusable or chargeable to conditions beyond her control. But Widom was tardy seven of the ten days of the break-in period. She was advised of the necessity of prompt reporting and of the consequences of continued tardiness, yet she continued in the same pattern. To have continued her in that position would have increased the risk of her being subject to discipline, possibly including termination, for what appeared to be an inability to respond to the demands of her job. Under the circumstances, the arbitrator concluded, the grievant had not fulfilled the expectations of full competence, that she lacked the requisite skill and ability required to meet the requirements of the job and the cancellation of her promotion was appropriate. She was properly returned to her former position.

Discussion Question 1: What position could the union have taken?
The union could have researched prior promotions and break-in periods to determine whether similar tardiness after shift changes had similar results. It could have analyzed the reasons for the individual instances of tardiness and how they had been addressed. It could have argued that the change in shift-starting time was a particularly heavy burden that was secondary to Widom's obvious competence in the new position, and it could have argued for an extension of the break-in period to overcome the tardiness problem. It could have argued that the tardiness was independent of her work per-

formance, that she was willing to continue in the position while being sub-jected to progressive discipline for any future tardiness, and that she recognized the ultimate result might be her termination from employment.

Discussion Question 2: What position could the company have taken?
The company could have shown that it had told Widom in advance of the requirement for prompt reporting for work as an essential element of the new position and that failure to meet that requirement would be grounds for canceling the promotion. It could have researched prior promotions to show that others who had been unable to meet all the requirements of the upgrade had been similarly returned to their former positions. It also could have demonstrated how the seven instances of tardiness would have resulted in escalating discipline if considered independently from the break-in period and could have resulted in her immediate termination had she not been returned to her former position. Finally, the company could have examined her work assignments during the break-in period and compared them with her predecessor to demonstrate the adverse consequence of her tardiness on the computer analysts whose assignments for the day were less than they should have been.

Discussion Question 3: For whose benefit is a break-in period designed?
The general view is that a break-in period is designed to provide both the company and the employee with (1) the opportunity to test the employee in the actual working conditions of a new position to see if the employee fulfills the promise of job performance and (2) to see if the position meets the expectations of the employee. The expectation is that the break-in period is offered as a good-faith test, with either the company or the employee having the option of canceling the promotion and returning to the status quo with-out ill will and without adverse inference or consequence.

Discussion Question 4: What would have been the appropriate procedure for refilling that position once Widom had been returned to her former job?
Unless there is specific contract language to the contrary, the general view is that the employer may reassign someone else to the open position. The employer would presumably have had the right to select a new winner from among the bidders, consistent with the parties' promotion clause. Absent any acceptable candidate among the remainder, the company would presum-ably have had the option to repost the positions. An argument might have been made for the latter by the union on the grounds that the prior posting with Widom's name as a bidder might have deterred other potential bidders who felt they could not match her qualifications or seniority. Thus the union

would have argued that a new posting would call for a new universe of bidders who felt an earlier bid against Widom would have been futile.

Discussion Question 5: As Widom had been removed and replaced during the pendency of her appeal to arbitration, what was the union's obligations to her successor while processing Widom's appeal?

The responsibility of the union is to protect the rights of the individual employee when there is evidence of a contract violation. Although Widom's successor was also a bargaining-unit member and entitled to the union's protection, her advancement into the position came only as a consequence of the company's alleged improper action. The successor thus would have been told that the union would have done the same for her if she had been in Widom's position and that it would similarly protect her against improper company actions in the future.

Demotion

Unlike promotion or even some types of permanent transfers, demotion is not an action that usually is triggered at the initiation of an employee. Indeed, the concept of demotion implies that it is action taken against an employee's interest in retaining his or her position and thus is an action taken by the employer.

Demotion generally is viewed as an action based on an employer's desire to remove an employee from a position for which he or she lacks competence. It thus is an effort to place the employee in a position where he or she will be more suited to meet the requirements of the job rather than run the risk of discipline for nonperformance of a job that the employer believes to be beyond the employee's capabilities. Demotion under such circumstances is not disciplinary in nature; indeed, it is an avoidance of discipline.

The alternative of demotion is an option entitling the employer to return the employee to a position at a lower grade where job competence would be less in question. In cases in which the employee challenges the demotion, the union claims the burden is on the employer to show that the employee is not qualified for the position to which he or she had been promoted, that the employee had been given a reasonable time in which to perform the tasks of the higher position, and that he or she had failed to do so and was thus properly being returned to a lower-graded job. The employer tends to take the position that the burden is on the union in challenging the employer's action, particularly as the employer's action is not disciplinary and is taken specifically to avoid disciplinary action against the incumbent.

CASE: THE DELICENSED TRUCK DRIVER

Barry Hayes was a truck driver who made deliveries from the company warehouse to its customer's stores. He had held the job since he had been hired to that position ten years earlier and had an excellent work record. While driving his family car on vacation, Hayes had an accident that resulted in a six-month suspension of his driver's license. Hayes dutifully reported this to his supervisor. He was advised that he was being demoted to the position of shipper with a $1.50 per hour pay loss. Hayes filed a grievance over the demotion, and the case was appealed to arbitration.

At the arbitration hearing, the union argued that Hayes's personal life outside the plant was separate from his work; that the loss of his driver's license was unrelated to his job duties; that the loss was only temporary; and that because the grievant had such an exemplary work record, it was improper for the employer to remove him from his classification and pay rate, particularly as the demotion was to be permanent. It urged that he be returned to his former job classification while being reassigned to work in the warehouse at his former rate until the license suspension had run its course and that he then be reassigned to his driver's position.

The company argued that possession of a valid driver's license was an essential element of Hayes's job qualification; that the suspension of his license deprived the company of its legal right to utilize Hayes for the reason he was hired; that the company needed to replace Hayes with another driver capable of performing the full requirements of the position, including driving; and that it was acting within its contractual authority and with compassion in offering Hayes a job he could perform in the warehouse, albeit at a lesser rate, in lieu of terminating his employment. It acknowledged that the license suspension was only for six months and assured Hayes that thereafter he would be given every consideration should another driver's position become open for bidding.

The arbitrator held that Hayes had been hired as a truck driver; that possession of a valid driver's license had been an essential element of his qualification for the position; and that when he had lost the driver's license, even though for personal driving, it had a direct impact on his job qualification and rendered him unsuited for continued service as a truck driver. The arbitrator ruled that there was no need to deal with the question of whether the employer had the authority to terminate Hayes's employment, as he had been demoted to a warehouse position, but that there was still the question of whether the change was appropriate as a permanent, rather than six-month, move and whether the reduction in compensation was proper.

The arbitrator reasoned that there was nothing in the contract that required the employer to continue the grievant at the truck driver's rate for six months when he was performing warehouse rather than truck-driving duties. The demotion to the warehouse man's classification at the warehouse man's rate was within the employer's authority since Hayes no longer met the requirements of the position and not violative of the parties' agreement.

Similarly as to the demotion being permanent rather than temporary, the arbitrator held that there was no contractual requirement that Hayes be retained in his truckdriver's classification if he had lost one of its essential qualifications and that it was within the authority of the employer to determine that there was need to replace Hayes as a truck driver. Its move of Hayes to the warehouse man's position was also a legitimate exercise of the managerial authority of job assignment and one that justified a demotion of Hayes on a permanent basis. Because his truck driver's position had been properly filled, there was no guarantee that at the end of the six months he would be able to return to it. Accordingly, the grievance was denied.

Discussion Question 1: What position could the union have taken?
The union could have presented evidence of prior license revocations or other impediments to employees' meeting the full requirements of a job classification. It could have endeavored to establish an analogy to a medical restriction, under which an employee would have been unable to perform the full range of duties for six months. The union could have sought evidence of how the employer had treated medically imposed work restrictions that impeded performance of the full range of duties. It could have argued that the move to warehouse man was required to be treated as a temporary transfer rather than as a demotion, stressing the interim nature of the move and citing any pertinent provisions covering temporary assignments, restricted work loads, and the like.

Discussion Question 2: What position could the company have taken?
The company could have set forth any prior instances of employees taken off jobs for lack of a license or for loss of other qualifications. It could have demonstrated its financial inability to carry two employees on the payroll as truck drivers for the six months. It could have relied on contract provisions restricting the duration of transfers of this length, both for the new replacement driver and for the grievant. It could have taken the position that the suspension of the driver's license constituted a permanent impairment of the grievant's driving qualifications because of the extra insurance costs it would impose on the employer as a consequence of the suspension.

Discussion Question 3: Which party would have had the burden of proof in this case?
Although the union brought the grievance protesting the employer's action as a violation of the employee's right to retain the truck driver's classification, most arbitrators would probably hold that the employer had the burden

of proving that the removal from the truck driver's classification was proper. The employer disrupted the status quo by its action, and the burden of proving it was correct in doing so would probably have fallen on its shoulders.

Discussion Question 4: What if the grievant had suffered a heart attack out of work and the insurance company had notified the company? Would that have been grounds for removing Hayes from the truck driver's classification?

In such a case, both parties would have had to provide the arbitrator with evidence of the grievant's physical condition and of prognosis for future truck driving without reoccurrence of the heart attack. Such conflicting evidence would be largely medical, and the arbitrator presumably would permit the grievant to continue driving unless persuaded that there was a reasonable risk of reoccurrence. If the company had said it was taking him off the truck driver's assignment because it could not secure continued insurance coverage for the grievant, that would be grounds for demotion, but if the consequence was merely a modest increase in insurance costs, that would probably not be sufficient to sustain a demotion.

11
Through the Grievance Procedure to Arbitration

T he previous chapters have examined the various substantive issues confronted by unions and management during the life of their collective bargaining agreements. For each of the issues, there has been repeated emphasis on the research that the parties should undertake to strengthen their respective cases. The discussions of the issues also have included some theorizing as to how arbitrators might decide the various issues. The preparation of the case, the presentation of the argument and of the evidence, and the postulation of how the arbitrator would or should rule all have their testing at the arbitration step. It is, therefore, important to understand the process and the structure of the arbitration procedure in order to optimize preparations for the hearing.

The Grievance Procedure

Arbitration is the last step of a complicated and sometimes arduous and exhausting grievance procedure, usually consisting of three or four steps. Arbitration is the failure of the grievance process, not its goal.

Grievance Steps

The parties developed the multi-stepped grievance process as a vehicle for encouraging resolution at the lowest possible step, at the occurrence of the dispute. It is then that the grievant, shop steward, and foreman have the best chance of resolving the dispute. They strive for settlement and recognize that a failure of resolution will lead to higher levels of the union and the management becoming involved and second-guessing their judgments. The very structure of the grievance system endeavors to introduce into the dispute partisans of higher authority at each step in order to increase the chances of resolution. Thus, at the first step, the foreman and the employee with the shop steward seek to resolve the dispute. If they are unsuccessful, then the employee has the right to appeal the adverse ruling of the foreman to the second step, where the general foreman and the business agent, for example, will enter the case and meet with the grievant, the foreman, and the shop steward in an effort to resolve the dispute at that second level.

If that level of discussion is unsuccessful, then the employee has the right to appeal the case to a higher level, with the infusion of more expert involvement on the union's side and on the management's side. At the third step, the general manager, the plant manager, or the industrial-relations vice president may join the employer's side, with the union's international representative or international vice president entering the scene on the union's side. Again, the introduction of new union and management executives with higher authority is expected to shed new light on the dispute and its resolution and to avoid the need to proceed to arbitration.

If at the end of the usual three-step grievance procedure the parties are unable to resolve the dispute, it becomes ripe for arbitration. At each level of the grievance procedure, the participants reexamine the facts and the collective bargaining agreement; examine past practice, letters of understanding, and available and pertinent witnesses; and seek to assess the prospects for settlement. The grievance may be granted, it may be denied, or the parties may seek to develop a compromise to avoid the appeal to arbitration.

Throughout the grievance appeal process, the parties are not only seeking to resolve the dispute, but they also are considering the prospect of the case's going to arbitration. Thus, they make continual assessments of how they perceive the arbitrator would rule on the case, should it get to that step. The parties, although in an adversarial situation, generally are sufficiently sophisticated to recognize the potential for a win or a loss in arbitration. For the union that has a strong case with substantial precedents and contract language in its favor, there is less inclination on its part to compromise on what it views as a case potentially winning in the arbitration forum. On the employer's side, a recognition of the same prospects may encourage the employer to be more generous in its settlement offer, if only to avoid taking the case to arbitration and risking the loss of an important position, the establishment of an adverse precedent, and a potential financial disbursement to fulfill its obligations under the contract.

If arbitrators were universally alike in their rulings, there would be little incentive for a potentially losing client to be willing to submit that case to arbitration. However, the reality is that with a marketplace of hundreds of arbitrators, there is always the possibility that even the party with the weaker case might be persuasive and win in arbitration. Arbitration is not guaranteed to produce the same results on the same facts before different arbitrators, although it is likely. Indeed, it is one of the attributes of the system that the parties are able to select their own arbitrators and that the arbitrators function independently, basing their decisions on their judgments in each particular case.

Union Grievances

Most collective bargaining agreements recognize that employees have the right to file and process a grievance up to the step prior to arbitration, with their union thereafter having the right to determine whether the case should proceed to the arbitration step. Unions, too, have the right to file grievances if so agreed-upon by the parties, but such union grievances generally are confined to issues that uniquely affect the union, rather than the individual employees.

Thus, an individual employee may file a grievance on the issues of wages, hours, working conditions, or discipline that affect that employee. The union may file grievances on matters such as its entitlement to dues payments, the failure of the employer to terminate an employee under a union shop when that employee fails to join the union, the right of the union to certain union leave, or the issue of superseniority. Those union entitlements or union-based grievances may also include complaints involving a large number of employees on the theory that if numerous employees wish to process a complaint, it would be more economical and expeditious if the grievance were filed and processed on behalf of many employees by their representative, the union.

In view of the fact that many union-based grievances arise from a broader base than a particular incident or may involve a contractual issue for the enterprise as a whole, the parties frequently permit such grievances to be filed by the union on its own behalf at the second step of the process. Nevertheless, whether a grievance is an individual grievance or is a union grievance processed through this appeal procedure, the parties generally seek to resolve the disputes at the lowest possible step.

Grievance Settlements

There are numerous incentives for resolving a grievance at the lowest possible step prior to arbitration. First, the parties avoid the time and cost of the appeal procedure. The loss of time to witnesses and the loss of time to supervisors conducting the investigations and hearings usually constitute a reasonable economic incentive for the parties to resolve the grievances as early as possible. A second financial motivation is the desire to avoid the cost of going to arbitration. There, the additional cost of bringing in an arbitrator, who charges for days of the hearings as well for study time, the cost of expenses in coming to a hearing, the cost of bringing in outside lawyers to serve as advocates (if that is the parties' practice), the potential cost of a transcript, the cost of the time spent and lost opportunity cost of supervisory personnel and union executives, and the cost of witnesses' attending the hearing all constitute positive incentives for settling.

The cost factor may be even greater if the case involves the potential of back pay, as in a discharge case in which the time taken in getting to arbitration may result in an award of many months of back pay. Such extra costs could readily be avoided by resolving the dispute at an earlier step.

An added stimulus to settlement is the uncertainty and the risk entailed in presenting the case to arbitration. Although this book is filled with assertions of how the majority of arbitrators would rule, there is no certainty over an arbitrator's judgment, and the parties potentially run the risk that the arbitrator will do them more harm by the imposition of an award that one or neither of the parties can abide. A potentially disruptive decision by an arbitrator would constitute an unalterable precedent for the duration of the contract and potentially even beyond that contract.

An additional stimulus to settlement is the fact that the parties can readily agree on a compromise in a dispute that might be beyond the arbitrator's reach. For instance, if a discharge case is appealed to arbitration, the arbitrator traditionally would have the responsibility to determine whether or not the removal was for just cause. If it was found to be for unjust cause, the arbitrator would impose a remedy. The parties on their own, prior to arbitration, may resolve the dispute not only along those lines, but in addition might be successful in compromising in the potential remedy or in agreeing to pay the grievant, to encourage that employee's resignation, the amount of money that might otherwise go to the arbitrator. The parties may fashion an individual contract with the grievant, whereby as a condition for reinstatement on a last-chance basis the employee surrenders certain additional benefits or commits himself or herself to participate in an employee's assistance program or the like.

Such agreements are exclusively within the authority of the parties, and opportunities for such resolutions may be, and usually are, lost when the case is appealed to the more rigid arbitration forum. The authority of the parties to settle is, of course, absolute, and an arbitrator is unlikely to reopen a case if the parties have settled the case.

CASE: THE UNSETTLED SETTLEMENT

Edward Egan was issued a letter of removal on the grounds that he had been involved in a fight with his supervisor at a local tavern after a day of hostility at the plant. Egan filed a grievance, which was appealed to the second and later to the third step of the process. At the third hearing, the union pointed out that it had numerous witnesses to testify at the arbitration that the supervisor had harassed Egan and forced him into a fight; that the conflict was totally unrelated to workplace activities; and that Egan had sought to walk away from the conflict when the supervisor went after him and reopened the matter, resulting in a substantial fistfight. The employer, lacking witnesses other than the supervisor, was planning to rely on Egan's record of having had some fights with other employees and on the foreman's clean record in terms of his relations with other employees. The employer was endeavoring to use the supervisor's testimony to tie the fight to Egan's refusal to follow a legitimate order on the shop floor. During the third step of the grievance procedure, the employer's representative said to the union's business agent, "This case could go either way. Why don't we settle it?"

The union representative agreed, and the parties worked out a compromise that called for Egan to be returned to work but to a different department, where he was to be placed under a new supervisor with whom he previously had enjoyed excellent relations. The reinstatement was to be forthwith, and there was no reference to back pay. By this time, Egan had been out of work for two months. The union and management representatives signed the settlement agreement. Egan signed it, saying, "I don't like it, but I'll sign it." Egan was returned to the workplace the following Monday, when he submitted a grievance seeking reinstatement for the amount of money lost during the two-month suspension. The union tried to point out to Egan that he had signed a settlement and that he was bound by it, as was the union. Egan then threatened to sue the union for breach of the duty of fair representation if it failed to process the case. The case was appealed to the arbitration step.

At the hearing, the union argued that Egan had signed the settlement agreement under duress. It argued that it had been an agreement to put him back to work without any reference to the back-pay issue, that that back-pay issue was unresolved and unaddressed, and that Egan had the right to have that part of the case resolved by the arbitrator.

The employer took the position that there had been a final and binding settlement of the dispute. According to the employer, Egan had signed the settlement even though he initially had objected to it and thus was bound by it. The case had been resolved at the third step and thus was not properly appealed to arbitration and could not be resolved by the arbitrator, the employer argued.

The arbitrator held that the grievance lacked merit; that Egan had been a party to the settlement discussion; that the purpose of the meeting had not been to prepare for arbitration but to resolve the dispute; that the supervisor present had suggested that the case be settled; and that after some discussion, the parties had agreed to the resolution of the case by returning Egan to a different department forthwith without back pay. The arbitrator reasoned that if the union had intended that Egan receive back pay, it was incumbent upon it to raise that issue in the settlement discussions. The arbitrator recognized that Egan had objected to the settlement and noted that Egan had the right to agree to it in terms of his reinstatement while retaining the right to proceed to arbitration on the issue of back pay. The arbitrator held, however, that after his initial misgivings, Egan had agreed to the settlement and had signed it. He thus was bound by it and lacked any authority to reopen his grievance and appeal his case to arbitration. Accordingly, the arbitrator held that the case lacked merit.

Discussion Question 1: What position might the union have taken?
The union might have produced witnesses from the third-step meeting to testify that there had been no discussion of dropping its demand for back pay. It might have investigated records to ascertain if there had ever been a return to work with the issue of back pay left for resolution by an arbitrator. It might have researched arbitration hearings to show that the parties in this case or elsewhere had agreed to a bifurcated settlement reinstating the employee while the issue of back pay or wage-loss penalty was submitted to the arbitration forum.

Discussion Question 2: What position might the employer have taken?
The employer certainly would have introduced the settlement agreement with the grievant's signature on it. It would have produced witnesses at the third-step meeting who could testify to the union's having explained the settlement to Egan and witnesses to testify about Egan's resistance and ultimate acquiescence and signature. It might have introduced arbitration awards to show that absent an agreement between the parties to take the case of back pay to arbitration, the issue was resolved as part of the settlement agreement.

Discussion Question 3: Is it feasible to bifurcate a settlement by permitting an employee to go back to work while arbitrating a remedy question?
An increasing number of parties take this option as a means of reducing their liability. If the employer has recognized during the processing of the grievance or thereafter that it runs the risk of the employee's being reinstated with back pay, the employer may be increasingly willing to acknowledge that the termination was in error and to reinstate the employee while leaving to the grievance and arbitration steps the determination of the amount, if any, of back pay. This effort to mitigate damages is beneficial to both parties and can avoid back pay accumulating for several months or years.

Discussion Question 4: If the parties had agreed to a reinstatement on a last-chance basis, would that have precluded a grievant who was again terminated from taking his or her case to arbitration?
The settlement of a case on a last-chance basis does not preclude an employee from exercising the contractual rights to challenge the propriety of that removal action. Even though the employee may agree to reinstatement on a last-chance basis, that stipulation does not deprive that employee of contractual entitlement.

In some settlement agreements, the parties specify that the employee will waive any right to arbitrate subsequent removals. Some arbitrators would say that the employee has surrendered the right to challenge any subsequent removal through the grievance procedure. Other arbitrators would take the position that the deprivation of the right to invoke the grievance and arbitration procedure is improper pressure on the employee. The employee may not know the consequences of this action at the time, and the action could be challenged as being arbitrary and capricious if a subsequent removal is taken without any justification. Most arbitrators would seek to have that second removal processed through the arbitration forum, if only to endorse the propriety of the employer's action and to remove from the employee any doubt of having been capriciously treated by a second removal.

The Arbitration Hearing

If parties have processed the case through the grievance procedure without any resolution of the dispute, the case proceeds to the arbitration step. The parties must thereupon determine their choice of arbitrator, after which the arbitration hearing commences.

The Selection of the Arbitrator

There are several ways in which an arbitrator can be selected pursuant to the parties' agreement. The parties may agree on a single arbitrator who has jurisdiction over all cases that may arise over the duration of the collective bargaining agreement or until either or both of the parties request the arbitrator to leave.

A second method of selecting an arbitrator is for the parties to contractually agree on a panel of arbitrators, with the decisions being rotated among panel members. Under that arrangement, the parties may agree to the hearing of a case in the order of the panel members, going from one arbitrator to the next. The parties also may grant to one party the choice of the arbitrator from the panel on a rotating basis, with unions choosing one arbitrator for one case and management choosing the arbitrator for the next case. They also may agree on a selection process from the panel, with the parties alternately removing the names of panel members until the last mutual choice becomes the arbitrator of the case in question.

A third procedure is for the parties to endeavor to agree on an arbitrator when a dispute arises, and if unable to do so, to refer to the American Arbitration Association or the Federal Mediation and Conciliation Service for the provision of a list pursuant to the rules of the respective organizations. The parties would then designate by alternately deleting from the lists supplied by the designating agency those arbitrators who are unacceptable for that particular case. The surviving name becomes the designated arbitrator. Under this procedure, if the parties were unable to agree on an arbitrator on their own, they would be required to return to the designating agency each time for the provision of the list from which they could designate the highest mutual choice of arbitrator. A final method, which stems from the failure of the parties to agree on an arbitrator through the agency's process, would be to designate either of those agencies to appoint the arbitrator for a particular case.

There are benefits to be gained from any one of the foregoing procedures. Certainly, to have a regular single arbitrator permits the parties to alert that arbitrator to their particular needs, and through continued exposure to the parties, the arbitrator is able to understand the parties' relationship, process, and method of resolving disputes. This understanding may be able to contribute to a more meaningful decision geared to the needs of the parties than might be the case when the arbitrator is new to the parties and who will depart and not return after hearing a particular case.

The panel selection process has the benefits of both granting the arbitrator experience with the parties and providing a fresh view of the parties' particular dispute, thus freeing them from reliance on one particular arbitrator for the life of a contract. The parties with such panels do, in fact, continue to rotate arbitrators to live up to the contractual arrangements for selecting from the panel. But in other relationships, the parties tend to tire of the arbitrators on their panel, and in one instance where there were thirty arbitrators on the panel, only five or six were used with any regularity. Indeed, some panel relationships become so closely knit that the parties decline to tell an arbitrator when he or she has been relieved of his or her duties just to avoid embarrassing that arbitrator, and thus the arbitrator's name may be kept on the panel roster even though the arbitrator is by mutual agreement not to serve again.

The Role of the Arbitrator

The arbitrator, once selected, has the responsibility for establishing the hearing; for gaining a stipulation on the issue to be decided; and for conducting the hearing in a reasonable manner calculated to provide both parties with a full opportunity to present their cases, their witnesses and their arguments. The arbitrator also rules on questions of admissibility of evidence, and when the evidence is in and the witnesses have testified, the arbitrator has the responsibility of weighing the evidence and providing the parties with a decision and opinion explaining his or her rationale.

Arbitrability

The Supreme Court in *United Steelworkers v. Warrior and Gulf Navigation Co.* 363 U S at 584–5(1960) granted to arbitrators the authority to make binding rulings on issues of procedural arbitrability. The Court held that an arbitrator does not have the authority to determine if he or she has the jurisdiction to hear the case unless the parties so grant it. Thus, matters of jurisdictional arbitrability are ultimately for the courts to decide, and there is no deference to the arbitrator on that issue.

If the parties have not agreed to submit an issue to arbitration, the arbitrator has no authority to rule on the matter. Thus, for example, if the parties agree that issues of discipline shall not be subject to arbitration, a grievance filed by a terminated employee, even though it comes to the arbitration step, is not necessarily arbitrable. If the employer fails to challenge the issue of arbitrability, the arbitrator would be within his or her authority in continuing the case and deciding the issue of termination on its merits. But if the employer raises the issue of arbitrability on the grounds that the contract grants the employer, rather than union, the authority to determine the appropriate discipline, then the arbitrator would lack any authority to hear that case and to alter the employer's disciplinary ruling. Furthermore, if the arbitrator lacks the jurisdiction over a case, any improper assertion of authority is unauthorized and may be challenged at any time. Thus, an improper assertion of jurisdiction is subject to challenge before, during, or after the arbitrator has conducted the hearing or issued an award, because if the arbitrator lacks the jurisdiction to hear the case, he or she obviously lacks the jurisdiction to issue an award.

In procedural arbitrability, on the other hand, the arbitrator does have the right to render interpretations of whether a case is arbitrable. The theory is that the interpretation requires substantive expertise of the nature that the parties hope to invoke by having agreed to arbitration by an expert.

Procedural arbitrability, unlike jurisdictional arbitrability, is expected to be raised at the outset of the hearing. If the party believes that a case is not arbitrable (for example, if a grievance was filed on the eighth day after an incident when the contract calls for the filing of the grievance within five days), then it would be a matter of procedural arbitrability of whether a grievance is viable. The accepted theory is that the party challenging the arbitrability of a case has a responsibility to do so at the earliest possible step. The rationale for that position is that if a party believes a case is not arbitrable, it is incumbent upon that party to so advise as rapidly as possible so that the other party can prepare and investigate relevant evidence while the information is still available in order to challenge that position. In addition, an early challenge of arbitrability would ensure that the party is not misled or led astray financially by investing substantial time and money in processing a case that the other party would then have held not arbitrable on a procedural basis. The prevailing rule is that if the party with the arbitrability challenge does not raise it promptly at the start of the grievance process, then that party would be held to have waived the right to do so by going forward with the case on its merits.

Procedural arbitrability may come in many forms. There are many areas of procedure set forth in the parties' collective bargaining agreement that, if not followed, give rise to legitimate challenges to the arbitrability of the grievance. Some of these are considered below.

Timeliness. The parties' collective bargaining agreement specifies certain times as maximum periods that are permitted to lapse between the incident and the filing of the grievance, between the grievance filing and the employer's answer, between the grievance answer and the appeal, and so on. The arbitrator whose obligation is to interpret and apply the collective bargaining agreement is just as much bound by the time-limit provisions of the parties' agreement as by the more substantive language that may be the grounds of the merits of the grievance. Arbitrators are prone to have a dispute resolved on the merits if it is at all justified, but if necessary will deal with and be limited by the time-limit issue in determining arbitrability.

To aid in determining whether a grievance has been filed in a timely fashion, most collective bargaining agreements provide a fixed number of days from the disputed event for the filing of a grievance. Often the collective bargaining agreement will call for the grievance being filed within a certain number of days after the incident or within a certain number of days from the time the grievant knew or should have known of the incident.

Thus, in the case of an incorrect payment, an employee who was paid improperly for overtime work performed on a Thursday would probably not have been aware of that improper payment on Thursday if he was not paid until the following Monday. Even if the employee was paid on the Monday following the incident, there may have been no clear indication at the time that the overtime pay was improper. Indeed, the employee might not have discovered the impropriety until two or more weeks later during a discussion with his supervisor or another employee or while reading the contract. The employee would thus be able to file the grievance even weeks after the event if he grieves when he first learned of the impropriety, unless it could be shown that he had an obligation or knew how to learn of the improper payment by simply reading the pay stub.

The issue of whether an employee knew or should have known of a matter subject to grievance is a frequent matter for resolution by arbitrators. Similarly in cases being appealed, the contract language may be specific, but the parties may not have been as exacting in processing the grievances. Thus, it may turn out that the contract calls for a ten-day appeal period from a second-step denial to the filing of a grievance at the third step, but the evidence of past practice may show that there has been a tradition of filing that third-step appeal not within the contractual ten-day period, but fifteen or twenty days later. Even though the union may assert employer laxity in adherence to the strict time limits, the employer may effectively counter such an assertion by evidence that the only time there has been an extension beyond ten days was when the union had been granted a specific oral and/ or written request for an extension. Evidence of such requested and granted extensions would buttress the employer's position that there has been an understanding of strict adherence to the time limits in processing the grievances, except where agreed to the contrary.

An additional element of the processing of grievances that is related to time limits is the consequences of delay in appeals. Some collective bargaining agreements are explicit in providing that if either party exceeds the time limit, that constitutes an automatic acquiescence to the other side's position. Thus, if the union fails to meet the time limit for appeal, the employer may prevail on the argument that the union's failure to meet the time limit constitutes an acquiescence to the last-step answer and precludes filing the appeal.

There are some collective bargaining agreements that place a similar burden on the employer, providing that if the employer does not respond within a fixed number of days, that triggers an automatic granting of the grievance and the resolution thereof. However, the more prevalent view is that the failure of the employer to adhere to the time limits for providing a response to a grievance results in the grievance being considered a denial, and thus it is automatically appealed to the next step.

In cases involving appeal to the arbitration step, the prevailing view is that the union has the burden of filing the appeal in timely fashion. If the grievance is not filed within the appeal time, that constitutes an acquiescence to the employer's last-step answer, and the grievance is therefore resolved and is not arbitrable.

Definition of a Grievance. When the parties negotiate the grievance procedure, it is a prerequisite to the effective utilization of that procedure for the parties to define a grievance. The most common definition of a grievance and the standard that is used in most appeals is to define the grievance as any question concerning the "interpretation or the application of the parties' agreement."

The term *interpretation* permits a challenge by the grievant to the employer's action based on the meaning of the words of the provision. Thus, if the contract says that an employee must file a bid for a position within ten days and the employer withdraws the notice after ten calendar days, the employee might protest that action on the grounds that the notice was not posted for ten working days. Thus, the dispute between the parties is the interpretation of the word *day* in the parties' agreement. If the parties are unable to resolve that issue in interpreting what the word *day* means in their agreement, it would be a proper matter for appeal to arbitration.

The term *application* involves resolving whether the employer's authority to apply the contract should include the particular situation confronting the grievant. If the contract specifies that a promotion shall be granted to the senior employee, and if the grievant maintains that his seniority is higher than that of the employee selected for promotion, it is a matter of dispute over not what the term *seniority* means, but over which of the employees has the senior date and therefore whether the employer properly applied the seniority language of the parties' agreement.

The most frequent dispute over application of the contract is in the area of the application of a standard of just cause for discipline. Although the parties may not have negotiated a specific just cause clause, disciplinary and discharge cases are usually considered to be based on the employer's right to apply a standard of just cause as an element of its right to hire and fire. In other words, did the employer act with just cause in taking disciplinary action against an employee?

The parties agreed-upon definition of a grievance may encompass the interpretation or application not only of the parties' agreement, but also of applicable rules and regulations. That broader definition may be more often found in public-sector collective bargaining, where parties recognize the employer's obligations under certain rules and regulations and expand the grievant's access to challenges of those rules and regulations that may take the place of the collective bargaining agreement at the workplace. Even broader definitions of the grievance may extend to any employee's complaint that may not necessarily be based on the contract language or on any rules and regulations, but that may go beyond that and be based on any aspect of the employment relationship that the employee believes has been injurious to him or her.

Sometimes the parties develop combined language that will permit some protests to rise to certain levels, while confining appeal to the arbitration step more narrowly. Thus, a grievance definition may reads as follows: "A grievance is any dispute or complaint that arises out of the workplace, but only questions of interpretation or application of the parties' agreement may be appealed to arbitration." Under that language, any complaint might be processed through the last step of the grievance procedure, but a more narrow definition is applied to the grievances permitted appeal to arbitration.

Under the standard definition, the grievant has the right to challenge the employer's action, with the traditional burden of proof being on the employee in challenging contract matters and on the employer in proving its right to impose discipline and discharge. But in some elements of the contract, the burden on the employee in challenging the employer's proper interpretation or the application of the contract may not be an equal weighing of one side's interpretation versus the other. In some provisions of collective bargaining agreements, the parties negotiate that the employer shall have a higher standard of authority and that the employee filing a grievance over that interpretation or application would therefore have a higher burden of proof.

For example, the contract may state the following: "The employee is entitled to leave for personal use of five days per year, and the employer shall grant such leave on showing of reasonable use therefor. The employer shall be the final authority in determining whether such leave is to be granted." Under that provision, the parties have granted to the employer the authority that one would think would be given to the arbitrator to be the final determinant of whether the employer's denial of leave was proper or improper. With such language, a grievance definition might not grant the employee the right to challenge the employer's denial of such a leave. There is still a grievance, but the defense on the employer's side would be that the employee cannot challenge the employer's action. The grievance' of course, would still prevail if the employee, despite the language, was able to show that the employer was arbitrary or capricious in withholding the grant of leave, as even the retention of final authority to the employer could not be used to rebut a challenge to irrational, arbitrary, or capricious behavior.

Signatures. In many contracts, the parties' definition of a grievance may include detailed specifications of what is to be submitted with the grievance. That may include a requirement that the employee sign the grievance. If there is also an opportunity for the union to file a grievance, there may be, in addition, a requirement that the union president or the union officer sign the union's grievance. The purpose for such requirements is to assure that there is a justiciable issue raised by a particular employee. The argument against such signature requirements is that the employee may feel pressure against filing a grievance and would prefer the anonymity of an unsigned grievance or the union's filing a grievance on that employee's behalf.

The rebuttal to that argument is that the right of an employee to file a grievance and invoke the procedures of the collective bargaining agreement is well protected under the National Labor Relations Act. The employee has the obligation to stand up and identify what the charge is against the employer. This is particularly important because at the earlier steps of the grievance procedure, it is crucial for the involved employee to testify about the reason for the grievance. That, of course, also would be the case if the claim comes to arbitration.

The motivation of most employers in seeking the employee's signature is to protect themselves against cases in which only the union seeks to enforce the contract or in which the employee concerned is not interested in so doing. Such a signature protects against anonymous grievances and against the union's protesting conditions that are acceptable to the respective employees.

Specificity in the Grievance. In addition to requiring signatures, many collective bargaining agreements call for the employee to be specific in framing the grievance, including perhaps the citation of the relevant provisions of the parties' agreement being allegedly violated. It is certainly desirable to have specificity in the grievance, not only to alert the employer about the provision of the contract that is being challenged, but more important to protect against the grievances subsequently being expanded into unrelated areas during the appeals process.

The question arises over the extent of specificity required in filling out the grievance form. Most arbitrators would hold that the purpose of such specificity is fulfilled when the grievance cites the contract article that is in dispute or perhaps the article and section in dispute. The degree of specificity required may depend on the parties' prior practice and on whether the employee was aware of that extent of specificity.

In many cases, arbitrators are faced with the issue of whether the union can raise an uncited contract proviso in defense of its position at the arbitration step. The general view is that the goal of specificity required in the grievance forum is to alert the employer of the nature of the charges based on the facts. But that requirement does not preclude the union from relying in later steps on the more expert counsel and advice of its higher officials or outside consultants, even if they raise other arguments based on the facts alleged in the grievance itself.

At the higher steps, those who may peruse the contract may find other contract clauses allegedly violated as well. The test is whether those other contract clauses create a new issue or whether they are merely supplemental to the charge originally filed by the grievant. The governing standard is the recognition that the employee cannot be conversant with the entire contract and his or her rights. That is the reason for bringing in the higher level of expertise. The employee who files the grievance should not be victimized by his or her lack of legal expertise. To hold otherwise would deprive employees of their inherent right to file grievances and would place a requirement of having to check with lawyers each time a grievance was filed. As long as the goal of notification to the employer of the general issue in dispute is achieved, most arbitrators will hold that the requirements of specificity have been met.

Probationary Employees Clause. The employer's right to hire an employee usually carries with it the right to try out an employee before determining whether that employee is to be retained as a permanent member of the work force. The unions are interested in the point at which an individual becomes an employee for purposes of dues collection and union membership.

The point when an individual becomes an employee is accepted generally to be at the conclusion of the probationary period, with the date of seniority adjusted to reflect the date of hire. As discussed in chapter 9, the question arises over the right of a probationary employee to a file a grievance under the parties' contract. If the employer has the authority to remove an employee prior to the conclusion of the probationary period and the employee has not yet been granted the status of union protection, it follows that the employee should not have the right to file a grievance over his or her removal prior to the completion of the probationary period. That is consistent with the understanding between the parties as to the nature of the probationary period. It is totally within the employer's discretion to determine whether the individual will be permitted to complete the probationary period before being granted employee (and union membership) status and contractual protections. Because the probationary period is geared to the employer's satisfaction with the employee's work performance, the denial of contractual rights is confined to the area of discipline and performance, matters that might affect the employee's retention.

A probationary employee generally would be viewed as having the right to challenge the employer's failure to provide the contractual rate of pay during that probationary period, although the parties could have agreed that the probationary employee would have no access to the grievance procedure. Most arbitrators would say that the employee on probation has the right to protection of the collective bargaining provisions. This avoids the employer's utilizing such probationary employees at reduced wage rates or for improper assignments. The union has a stake in enforcing the contract even for the probationary employee who may not yet be a union member because of the impact of its failure to enforce the agreement. For example, the impact of an unchallenged underpayment could become a precedent that might subsequently be used to the disadvantage of bargaining-unit members. Therefore, the employee is viewed as having the right to seek enforcement of contract clauses other than in the workmanship area, and the union is viewed as having the right to process such protests.

CASE: THE PROBATIONARY EMPLOYEE

Keith Hunter was a probationary employee who was issued a letter of warning, a two-day suspension, and a ten-day suspension for repeated absenteeism during the first two months of his three-month probationary period. In the issuance of its ten-day suspension, the employer stated that if the grievant was tardy or absent one more time, he would be subject to removal. He completed his probationary period, was granted status as a regular employee, and in the following week was absent for a two-day unexcused absence. He was terminated by the employer. He filed a grievance challenging the termination as unjust, and the case was appealed to arbitration.

At the arbitration hearing, the employer argued that although it had the right to terminate Hunter at any point during the probationary period, it had been trying to instill a sense of job pride in Hunter and wanted to keep him as a regular employee if he could overcome his attendance problem. It argued that it therefore volunteered to give Hunter progressive discipline, which it need not have done under its inherent management rights, and that the employee was placed on proper notice that any unexcused absences after the ten-day suspension would result in his removal. The incident in the week following his securing tenure justified the imposition of discipline. The employer held that the grievant had been held to a higher standard by the prior warnings, and that determination should be upheld.

The union argued that although the employer had the right to impose the discharge penalty during the probationary period, it did not choose to do so. Thus, the employee must be held as having satisfactorily completed that probationary period. Once that probationary period had been completed, the employee's record was wiped clean and he started from scratch in accumulating discipline. It noted that Hunter had been given lesser disciplinary penalties during the probationary period, and that there had been no opportunity for the union to challenge such disciplinary penalties because the employee had lacked union standing. The union argued that for it to undertake the practice of defending employees charged with lesser disciplinary penalties during probation would run the risk that the employer would not impose such minor penalties, which could be subject to challenge, when it could instead remove the employees without running the risk of challenge by the union.

The arbitrator took the position that the employer had the right to terminate an employee during the probationary period, that it was encouraging the employee to better behavior by imposing lesser penalties as a means of corrective discipline, and that it had acted properly in hoping that that progressive discipline would lead to improved attendance habits. The arbitrator also noted the union's prohibition from processing such cases and, in addition, the inability of the union to go back to challenge those disciplinary penalties as a part of Hunter's case because the penalties had occurred so long ago and investigation of them would place the union at a disadvantage.

Accordingly, the arbitrator took the position that the employer had the right to remove the employee up to the final date of the probationary period and that after having reviewed the employee's record at that time, had deemed the employee suitable for retention as a regular employee. Thus, prior disciplinary penalties that indeed had been within the authority of the employer were expunged, and the employee started his regular employment with a clean slate. However, the arbitrator held that the employee was on particular notice of the necessity for improved attendance and that his unwarranted absence in the week following his securing of regular employment was deserving of a disciplinary penalty. Hunter was reinstated with a two-day disciplinary layoff.

Discussion Question 1: What position might the company have taken?
The company could have taken the position that the union had the right to file a grievance over the earlier disciplinary penalties; that there was no restriction to its doing so under the collective bargaining agreement; and that having failed to do so, the union must be viewed as having accepted the penalties imposed by the employer. It could have cited negotiating history concerning the probationary period or the prior practice of the parties in handling probationary employees, including evidence that the union had filed grievances on behalf of probationary employees and involving contract interpretation questions.

Discussion Question 2: What position might the union have taken?
The union might have shown that it was deterred from filing grievances because of statements by the employer that it was easier to fire an employee than to give him a lesser penalty. It might have brought in testimony to show that the employer had reviewed Hunter's entire record at the end of the probationary period before determining that he should become a regular employee. It also could have cited the contract clauses that stated that a grievance must be filed within a certain number of days of the event to show that the union did not have the standing after Hunter became a regular employee to go back and reconsider the earlier disciplinary penalties.

Discussion Question 3: If the arbitrator held that Hunter's record was clean, what was that arbitrator's grounds for imposing a disciplinary layoff rather than a letter of warning?
Consistency would have dictated that because Hunter had been granted the status of a regular employee and because his prior record had been cleared, he should have been subject to a first-step penalty (a letter of warning). That would have justified reinstatement with full back pay without a disciplinary suspension. The arbitrator in this case was trying to hold the grievant to a higher standard of performance and understanding of the consequences of unwarranted absence and did bypass the earlier steps of the grievance procedure.

If Hunter's record was cleared, he was entitled to the initial warnings that would have been granted to any employee with a clean record. Arbitrators run the risk of affronting the winning party by such efforts to placate the losing party. This is an example of a case in which a minor penalty would not have placated the employer, as the cost of the penalty saved it only the two days of back pay. Instead, the arbitrator in this case might have wound up antagonizing the union for not being consistent with his holding of the clean record while antagonizing the employer by offering a two-day suspension but still requiring the employer to pick up the total costs of the reinstatement. Arbitrators do better when they seek consistency within their awards, which the parties are more likely to accept, than when they try to water down decisions to maintain acceptability.

Discussion Question 4: Should the end of the probationary period have given the union the right to go back and file grievances over the earlier disciplinary penalties?

If the purpose of a prompt filing of the grievance is to resolve the dispute at the lowest possible level, that purpose is defeated if the union is to be required to file a grievance over an incident that may have occurred three months earlier and that, because of the inability of the union to intervene at that stage, may have become more firmly entrenched. When examined later, each grievance already has become a crucial element in the imposition of any subsequent removal action and is not likely to be subject to any reduction by the employer. Additionally, the information is old, and the union should not be placed at the disadvantage of having to investigate an incident so long after the fact when the employer already had reviewed its facts promptly and taken action without the union's participation in that action. The persuasive view is that the end of the probationary period precludes any independent evaluation of the propriety of the earlier discipline. The record is, indeed, clean.

The Departed Employee. It would appear that a terminated employee lacks the standing to file a grievance, yet it is well understood that the employee has the right to invoke the contract on issues of termination. The termination is a separation of the employment relationship only upon the completion of the grievance and arbitration steps of the parties' agreement.

Clearly, an employee who files a grievance over contract interpretation, such as entitlement to holiday pay, would have the right to process that grievance even though he or she is subsequently removed from the employment roster either by termination or by resignation. It generally is held that an employee who voluntarily resigns from employment has sacrificed any rights to protest the interpretation or application of the contract after that resignation. However, any grievance submitted prior to that resignation may continue to be processed, even through the arbitration step, because it entails an employee's entitlement while that employee was on the work force. The arbitration step may even require that the former employee testify to an entitlement that he or she had while a member of the work force. The union's processing of such cases is an integral protection for other members of the work force; and although that employee may no longer have any role in the union or in the employment relationship, the enforcement of any rights the employee had while employed protects the rights of all employees. Continued processing of such cases therefore is deemed to be proper.

The Issue

An arbitrator lacks the jurisdiction to decide a dispute between the parties unless they have given to the arbitrator a particular issue to be resolved. Thus, most hearings commence with the arbitrator's seeking imput from the parties about the issue they wish to resolve. The sophisticated approach is for representatives of both parties to meet in advance in order to agree on the issue and thus avoid wasting time at the hearing and in submitting it to the arbitrator at the commencement of the session.

However, the more common practice is for the parties to try to resolve the issue at the hearing itself. Most arbitrators will not proceed until the parties have agreed on an issue for the arbitrator to decide. Some arbitrators even leave the room, saying that it is a matter for the parties to work out on their own, while other arbitrators may help the parties in seeking to resolve any conflict over identifying the issue.

The problem with the arbitrator's involvement in such an exchange is that the arbitrator has no initial knowledge of the dispute and thus can provide relatively little imput to help resolve the conflict. In an effort to avoid expending excessive time at the arbitration hearing on the framing of the issue, most arbitrators will intervene after a period of unsuccessful discussions and suggest that the issue might be the disposition of the grievance, the disposition of the demand for arbitration, or the grant to the arbitrator of the right to frame an issue.

The rules of the American Arbitration Association suggest that if the parties are unable to agree on the issue, the disposition of the demand for arbitration becomes the issue for the arbitrator to decide. In some cases, the parties seek to defer the agreement on the issue until later in the hearing. The problem with such an approach is that the issue frequently alters during the presentation of the case when the parties become aware of the other side's position, and it becomes even more difficult to reach agreement on an issue thereafter. Initial agreement on an issue prior to the proceeding of the case is preferable, with the parties recognizing that if the issue changes thereafter, they may mutually agree to a change in the wording of the issue.

In disciplinary cases, the framing of the issue is relatively simple. Generally, it is agreed that the issue can be phrased as follows: "Was the discipline imposed upon the grievant for just cause, and if not, what shall be the remedy?"

In interpretation cases, the framing of the issue may be more difficult. An effort should be made to frame the issue as broadly as possible to enable both parties to make whatever arguments that they think are justified in support of their positions. The parties may rankle at the suggestion of confining the issue to what shall be the disposition of the grievance, because the grievance may not have been artfully worded and because the arguments may have changed since the filing of the grievance. The specific wording of the issue is often a contentious problem. It may be avoided by the arbitrator's assuring the parties that he or she will interpret the issue as broadly as is necessary to encompass the positions and arguments of both parties.

Rules of Evidence

Arbitration is geared to be an informal procedure providing both parties with an opportunity for full presentation of their views without the legalities or legal complexities of a court of law. It evolved as a simple process with the union representative and the management's personnel director or other representative being able to process the case up to the arbitration step.

In the early years the arbitrator, who might or might not have been a lawyer, was charged with finding the truth in credibility and factual disputes and in interpreting the parties' agreement in interpretation disputes. Although few of the participants was trained in the law, presumably that was one of the strengths of the system because it permitted the parties to concentrate on the employment relationship rather than on legal complexities. This is not to say that the parties were not conversant with the standards of due process, because such standards were an integral element of the processing of cases, particularly in the area of discipline and discharge.

With the guidance of arbitrators, who were frequently lawyers, the parties were able to develop standards of evidence that were appropriate to the industrial-relations scene. The expansion of the arbitration practice, which has brought with it greater external pressure from reviewing courts, threats of duty-of-fair-representation suits, potential conflicts with external statutory rights, and prospects of cases being appealed to the NLRB and the courts, has introduced an element of legalism that was not present in the earlier practice of arbitration. Thus, it is more common today to see employers and unions represented by attorneys. In addition, the majority of arbitrators appear to be legally trained.

In this context, the rules of evidence tend to become more complex, although arbitrators experienced in the process are anxious to maintain simple procedures consistent with the provision of due process. A person who becomes involved with arbitration presentation therefore is wise to become conversant with the rules of evidence, if only to know when they do or do not apply.[a]

---

a. The reading of any number of books on the matter of evidence in arbitration is important for effective representation. One of these is Marvin Hill, Jr., and Anthony V. Sinicropi, *Evidence in Arbitration* (Washington, D.C.: BNA, 1980).

The Hearing Procedures

The hearing commences with the parties in agreement on the issue. This creates a framework for the arbitrator to focus on during the presentation of the parties' cases thereafter. The next step is for each party to make an opening statement, which shows the arbitrator which items are to be proven during the presentation of the case. Some opening statements tend to be more voluble than others, with the advocate stating in advance what the witnesses will be testifying. The opening statements of both parties, with the union going first in contract cases and the employer going first in discipline cases, not only permit the arbitrator to understand the range of conflict between the parties, but also help the parties to narrow the issue. In addition, they eliminate the need to present evidence on matters that are not in conflict.

At the outset of the hearing, the parties also introduce exhibits that are relevant to their case, usually with the collective bargaining agreement and the grievance papers on appeal being joint exhibits. The parties then introduce either at the outset or in the presentation of their witnesses such exhibits as they deem are appropriate to the proof of the case.

The parties next proceed with the introduction of testimony from witnesses, with the union first in contract interpretation cases and the employer first in disciplinary issues. The witnesses frequently are examined under oath administered by the arbitrator to ascertain their observations and experience on the matter in dispute. Witnesses are subject to direct examination and cross-examination. The arbitrator also may ask questions to clarify matters. The witnesses are examined in a series until the parties have concluded their presentations. There may, at times, be a request by either party to examine the site of the incident or to examine the operation in question, and the parties thereafter may adjourn to a site visit.

At the conclusion of the presentation, the parties make their concluding statements either orally or by agreement to provide the arbitrator with subsequent briefs. In some cases, the parties present both oral arguments and briefs. Although the increasing reliance on lawyers in the arbitration process has encouraged the filing of posthearing briefs, such practice tends to increase the cost of an arbitrator by requiring that there be transcripts so the parties can review the testimony prior to the filing of the briefs. The reliance on briefs stimulates the use of lawyers, who are presumed to be more confident in their preparation.

The briefs entail additional time for their preparation and for the transcripts that may preceed them, thus increasing delay and the cost of potential liability should there be a back pay award. The additional time spent in reading the transcripts and briefs also may increase the cost to the parties of the arbitrator. The more expeditious and more inexpensive procedure is for the parties to argue their closing statements orally at the conclusion of the hearing. That practice is also more reasonable because at that time the parties' advocates are more attuned to the case and thus may be more persuasive to the arbitrator.

From the arbitrator's point of view, an oral summary enables him or her to ask questions, which would not occur if briefs were submitted two or three months later. An oral summary also permits the arbitrator to begin writing the opinion when his or her retention of the case is still fresh.

The Decision-making Process

The arbitrator, having reviewed the issue, the facts, the testimony, the evidence, and perhaps having read all the cited arbitration decisions, is faced with deciding the case as specified in the stipulated issue. The arbitrator must decide issues of credibility of witnesses, evaluating contradictory testimony and consistency of testimony. The arbitrator must examine the contract to determine what the contract governs and controls. This may involve examining the contract language to determine if there has been an inconsistent past practice in its administration, or it may involve examining the contract clause in the light of the parties' negotiating history.

The arbitrator's responsibility is to meld the numerous conflicting elements of the case into a consistent and rational interpretation or application of the contract in order to develop a rational and cohesive ruling that will not only resolve the dispute, but will show the parties how that decision was reached. The arbitrator hopes the decision will provide guidance for avoidance of similar problems in the future. Although the arbitrator's decision-making process is geared to the resolution of a particular dispute, the arbitrator also is concerned with how that dispute will be used as a precedent and may be mindful of the fact that the dispute may be subject to subsequent litigation. The arbitrator must recognize the place of his or her decision in the parties' future relationship.

The Decision

The arbitrator's written opinion is framed in a traditional format of first setting forth his or her authority as granted by the designated agency or by the parties; a statement of the issues that the parties have submitted for resolution; and a statement of facts setting forth his or her interpretation of the facts, the findings of fact that were in conflict between the parties, and the arbitrator's resolution of credibility issues between the parties. Following the statement of facts, which is more or less a chronology of the events as the arbitrator understands them to have taken place, there is a listing of the contentions of the parties, or what the union contends and what the management contends ought to be concluded from the facts.

Thereafter, the arbitrator sets forth his or her opinion of the meaning of the contract language in the light of the facts. That reasoning resolves conflicts in testimony, in understanding of the contract language, in the relationship between the contract and the past practice and negotiating history, and in any prior arbitration award relied on by one of the parties. The arbitrator, through his or her opinion, seeks to bring the parties to agree with his or her resolution of the case, which is found in the subsequent award. It constitutes the answer to the issue and is the binding element that generally is held to be enforceable in the courts. Thereafter, the arbitrator's decision is rendered, and the arbitration matter is closed. So, too, is this book.

Index

About the Author

Arnold Zack is a graduate of Tufts College, Yale Law School, and the Harvard Graduate School of Public Administration. He has been an arbitrator and mediator in the labor relations field for the past thirty years. He has served as arbitrator under many collective bargaining agreements and has issued several thousand awards. In addition he served as the director of the Labor Management Institute of the American Arbitration Association in 1966 to 1968, exploring the adaptability of the private labor management model into the then-new field of public sector collective bargaining. Zack has served as a member of the Board of Governors, a vice president of the National Academy of Arbitrators, and for five years he was chairman of its continuing education program. He has served as a consultant to the International Labor Office training mediators in the Philippines and has also done training in Ethiopia, South Africa, Spain, Malaysia, and lectured in other countries. He is on the faculty of the Harvard Trade Union Program, and has written eight other books on labor relations. He is a recipient of the Whitney North Seymour medal of the American Arbitration (1980) and the Cushing-Gavin Award of the Archdiosese of Boston (1986). He is also recipient of the Mildred Spaulding Award of the Duke's County Agricultural Society for his vegetable and fruit preserves. He is married to Dr. Norma Zack, a physician in Boston, and they have two children.